*The Soviet Union and the Failure
of Collective Security, 1934–1938*

CORNELL STUDIES IN
SECURITY AFFAIRS

edited by Robert J. Art
and Robert Jervis

The Soviet Union and the Failure of Collective Security, 1934–1938

Jiri Hochman

Cornell University Press

ITHACA AND LONDON

First published 1984 by Cornell University Press.
Published in the United Kingdom by
Cornell University Press Ltd., London.

International Standard Book Number 0-8014-1655-8
Library of Congress Catalog Card Number 84-45149
Printed in the United States of America
*Librarians: Library of Congress cataloging information
appears on the last page of the book.*

*The paper in this book is acid-free and meets the guidelines for permanence
and durability of the Committee on Production Guidelines for
Book Longevity of the Council on Library Resources.*

To the memory of
František Kriegel, M.D.

Contents

Preface

This book examines the role played by the Soviet Union in the interwar collective security system following its adherence to that system in September 1934, and in the failure of the alliances it contracted in May 1935. More specifically, it is a study in the Soviet share of responsibility for the overall failure of European powers to resist collectively the expansionist forces, primarily Nazi Germany.

This book is not a chronological account of events and episodes that marked developments in Europe between 1934 and 1938. Rather, it centers on eight issues, chosen on the basis of their relevance to the effective functioning of collective security and of the Franco-Soviet-Czechoslovak alliance system. Examination of each of these issues strives to provide part of the explanation for the failure of these international instruments to meet their purpose insofar as this failure can be traced to the actions and behavior of the Soviet Union.

The behavior and motivations of powers other than the Soviet Union are not systematically analyzed. Comments to that effect rather serve the practical purpose of comparing and contrasting the actions of other governments with those of the USSR. An effort is made, however, to examine the perception of Soviet behavior by other powers, and the reactions evoked by this behavior.

The association of the Soviet Union with the security system is examined in three ways: in the two opening chapters, by way of the circumstances of the Soviet-German "special relationship" in 1933–34, and the actual causes of its termination; through Soviet foreign policy actions in the preceding period which were interpreted by some authors as symptoms of an early Soviet interest in rapprochement with the Western democracies; and by a detailed reconstruction of the processes leading to the Soviet entry into the League of Nations and to the conclusion of the alliances with France and Czechoslo-

[9]

vakia. The first two chapters examine the nature of Soviet interest in the new partnership—a significant criterion of the durability of the new orientation. The five ensuing chapters examine problems of the territorial separation of the USSR from her two allies and from Germany as the presumed opponent; the role of the Comintern; Soviet-German relations between 1934 and 1937; the impact of the Great Purges upon the outside world, upon friends and foes, and the consequences following from this development for the fate of collective security; and finally, the role of the Soviet Union in the crises of 1938.

It is not within the scope of this work to examine to any similar extent and depth Soviet policies in the Far East, especially Soviet relations with China and Japan. Continuing unavailability of primary sources comparable to those that can now be used for the examination of Soviet policy toward France and Germany makes it virtually impossible to assess with reasonable accuracy the Soviet perception of such an important issue as the Japanese threat.

In the entire book, it is not just Soviet foreign policy, and not just Soviet diplomatic activity, that is scrutinized. Under examination is rather the combined effect of Soviet behavior upon the outside world. Soviet diplomacy, as the only agency of the Soviet government licensed to conduct political relations with other states, was of course more visible and also easier to record than other Soviet activities. Consequently its importance as an indicator of Soviet intentions tended to be overestimated, and the reciprocal relationship between external and internal policies of the USSR frequently understated. The relative weight of diplomacy in Soviet politics can well be judged by the fact that before Andrei Gromyko—and in his case only since 1976—the position of the head of the Soviet foreign service had not been regarded as important enough to qualify its occupant for membership in the ruling gremium. That lesser role in internal politics is especially true for Maxim Litvinov, although his spectacular diplomatic performances were at times interpreted as the sole valid expression of Soviet external interests. Soviet diplomatic action should therefore be assigned that import which it realistically could have had under the Leninist-Stalinist conceptual circumstances, and not the weight following from inapplicable standards of normal states. The cream of Soviet diplomatic personnel was almost entirely annihilated during the era when they were practicing a policy of which an essential part was the defense of democracy, and that fact in itself sufficiently illustrates both the consistency of Soviet policy in that era and the value of diplomacy as a criterion for assessing valid directions of the Soviet external outlook.

[10]

This book therefore seeks as balanced a view of Soviet actions and motivations as can be drawn from ideological stands, the Comintern's activities, internal struggles, diplomatic maneuvering, economic and military-strategic interests, and other elements of Soviet behavior which can be recognized or which can be deduced from available sources.

Access to Soviet archives is still obviously largely denied even to Soviet historians, and all the other sources available to us today still remain considerably limited.

A. J. P. Taylor observed some years ago that "there is nothing new to be discovered about Soviet policy." This book has been motivated by the belief that in our knowledge of the past there is always something new to discover and that, in the Soviet case, the main work of historical research of the era after 1928 is most probably still to be done.

I am happy to express my appreciation to Allan K. Wildman of the Department of History, the Ohio State University, for his encouragement and guidance throughout the difficult process of writing this book.

I am also grateful to George F. Kennan for permitting me to quote from, and to print in full in appendix A of this book, his unpublished personal paper drafted in Moscow in 1935; and to Ivan Pfaff of the Heidelberg University for providing me with the full text of the Rumanian note of September 23, 1938 (printed in appendix C), and for his other valuable advice and help.

My wife Suzanne's understanding and support have been substantial, and I remain deeply obliged to her.

JIRI HOCHMAN

Falls Church, Virginia

Acronyms

CPSU	Communist Party of the Soviet Union
CzCP	Czechoslovak Communist Party
ECCI	Executive Committee of the Communist International
GPU	Glavnoye politicheskoe upravlenie, Main Political Administration (Soviet secret police).
KPD	Kommunistische Partei Deutschlands (German Communist Party)
NKVD	Narodnyi kommisariat vnutrenykh del (Ministry of Interior)
PCF	Parti Communiste Français (French Communist Party)
SA	Sturm Abteilung (Nazi Storm Troops)
SPD	Sozialistische Partei Deutschlands (German Social Democratic Party)

The Soviet Union and the Failure of Collective Security, 1934–1938

[1]

The Dissolution of the "Special Relationship"

Between the two world wars, collective security in Europe was anchored in the Paris Treaties and in the League of Nations. Until September 1934 Soviet Russia stood apart from this system, because she had concluded her own peace treaties with Germany and Austria-Hungary in March 1918, did not take part in the Paris Conference, and was not invited to membership in the League of Nations.

The Soviets viewed the Paris settlement as an imperialist enterprise. They especially resented the fact that the conference confirmed the detachment from Russia of territories that had been annexed by the tsars during the previous two centuries, Poland and the Baltic states.[1] They were, however, not strong enough to succeed in their initial drive to regain the lost provinces. Certainly stronger than their neighbors, they were weak compared to the might of the victorious powers, and they were further weakened by internal chaos and widespread resistance. Setbacks in the Baltic and especially the Polish war demonstrated the advisability of a stabilization of their western borders. All these factors persuaded them to try to build a system of expedient bilateral agreements with neighboring states wherever possible or useful. In pursuance of this policy, the Soviets granted de jure recognition to five of the former provinces of the Russian Empire—Estonia, Finland, Georgia, Latvia, and Lithuania—in the form of peace treaties, concluded between February and October 1920. Whether the Soviet government ever intended these acts to be anything other than a *peredyshka* (pause) is, however, a valid question.[2]

The Soviet-Rumanian border was not determined by an agreement between the two countries, because the Soviets refused to recognize the reunification of Moldavia under Rumanian rule. In spite of their official internationalism, they insisted on the validity of the tsarist conquest of eastern Moldavia (Bessarabia) in 1878. This attitude heavily burdened Soviet-Rumanian relations in the interwar period.

Soviet Russia's principal western frontier, with Poland, was drawn in 1921 by the Treaty of Riga, which settled the Soviet-Polish war of 1920. The dividing line satisfied neither side. It did not respect ethnic factors, as the original Curzon Line had done, but was drawn simply where the fighting ceased. This war appears to have further stimulated Russian nationalism as a factor in Soviet foreign policy, a factor certainly not missing in the considerations leading to the Rapallo Treaty with Germany.

This treaty was a by-product of a conference in Genoa, called to reach an all-around settlement between Soviet Russia and the Western powers. Such a settlement, which would have presupposed Soviet recognition of the prerevolutionary Russian public debt, proved impossible. Instead, an identity of interests and similarity of aspirations on the side of Germany and Russia, the two losers of the war, resulted in the treaty signed in Rapallo on April 16, 1922.

Discreetly negotiated for over two years, this treaty, as well as other agreements concluded with Germany in later years, constituted the principal pillar of Soviet foreign policy until the break between the two countries in 1934. It deserves noting that the Rapallo policy was fully endorsed, if not initiated, by Lenin. When the treaty was signed, he was still fully in charge of the Soviet government; his first stroke occurred a month later. The entente with Germany can therefore rightfully be considered a legitimate element of Soviet foreign policy.

Common opposition to the European status quo provided a lasting basis of mutual political support in international affairs. Germany soon reaffirmed her traditional leading position in Russian trade; and in spite of the fact that neither the Rapallo Treaty nor the Treaty of Berlin (1926) was an alliance or was complemented by a military convention, a close cooperation was established at the same time between the armed forces of the two countries. In contrast to the German government, the Soviets were anxious to formalize the military collusion by a direct alliance as early as 1924; the Treaty of Berlin was in fact only a moderate version of an agreement pushed forward by the Russians.[3]

When Germany signed the Locarno Treaty in October 1925, the partnership certainly lost, to some extent, its previous exclusive quality. In Locarno, Germany won a balance in her relations with the East and West, and that was an unwelcome development for Moscow, which preferred the previous *Schicksalgemeinschaft* (Ulrich von Brockdorff-Rantzau's term), the exclusive relationship or "community of fate" of the two outcasts. The Soviets tried their best to dissuade the Germans from signing the treaty.

On the other hand, Locarno was preceded by a significant Soviet-German commercial treaty, designed to emphasize the vitality of Rapallo, and was soon followed by the already mentioned Berlin Treaty of April 24, 1926, "the high-water mark of Soviet-German relations"[4] in the era after World War I, to offset the effects of the Rhine Pact. Part of the agreements concluded in Locarno was German entry into the League of Nations, which the Russians viewed as a hostile and suspicious body. The Treaty of Berlin contained a guarantee that Germany would not take part in any eventual act of force by the league against the USSR.

Practical consequences of Locarno for Soviet-German cooperation appear to have been, on the whole, rather unimportant. The German Foreign Office extended its control over Reichswehr activities in the USSR, but the Wilhelmstrasse was not opposed to secret military collaboration—it was opposed to the Reichswehr's independence in the conduct of foreign affairs.[5] That Moscow managed to retain its "diplomatic ascendancy" over Germany even after Locarno appears to be obvious.[6] The relationship continued to meet both countries' essential foreign-policy interests. For Germany, it meant "maximum possibilities for diplomatic maneuver. . . . Her close relationship with Russia contained the tangible threat which forced Western powers into one concession after another."[7] The most important foreign-policy asset ascribed to the relationship in Moscow was its role in averting a possible anti-Soviet configuration, with Poland, for example. Military and economic advantages drawn from the connection on both sides added weight to these considerations. A memorandum drafted by Ambassador Herbert von Dirksen in October 1929, shortly after his assumption of Brockdorff-Rantzau's office in the Wilhelmstrasse stated that friendly relations between Germany and Russia no longer needed any justification because of "clearly common interests of both countries in East European politics, particularly in regard to Lithuania and Poland."[8]

Military cooperation between Germany and Soviet Russia in this period was the most intriguing aspect of the relationship. It was a many-sided, intimate, and long-lasting cooperative arrangement, in which absence of formal alliance between the two countries was sufficiently replaced by mutuality of interests. To give this cooperation a negotiated framework, more than fifteen secret contracts and agreements were concluded, covering almost all aspects of military coordination as well as joint production of armaments—a noteworthy fact

in view of the complete failure to establish similar cooperation between the Red Army and the French army during the alliance with
France.[9]

In Germany, the policy of Rapallo and its revalidation in 1926 were
sustained by the whole political spectrum; the Berlin Treaty with
Soviet Russia in 1926 was received in fact with more enthusiasm than
the Treaty of Locarno. On the other hand, the Reichswehr enterprise
in the Soviet Union could never count on the support of important
segments of the political structure (the Social Democrats, the Liberals,
the Catholic Center), and occasionally had to be carried out behind
the back of the government in office. The unquestionable unity behind the main lines of German foreign policy after the signing of the
Versailles Treaty did not extend to a unity with respect to the means
to be employed for the promotion of that policy; and military collusion with the Soviets certainly did not belong among those generally
accepted terms. The German General Staff—code-named the Trup-
penamt during the Weimar Republic—had rather to rely upon the
support of selected politicians to secure the necessary cooperation of
the civilian branches of the state for its activities in the USSR.

In contrast, the collusion of the Red Army with the Reichswehr
appears to have enjoyed unreserved support among the entire leadership of the Soviet Communist party. For years it was sustained with
the same élan by Trotsky and Stalin, Voroshilov and Tukhachevsky,
Chicherin and also Litvinov, who took part in all phases of the preparations of Rapallo as well as the Treaty of Berlin, was fully informed
about the military cooperation, and was specifically praised for his
valuable legal advice in the arrangements made for the Soviet-German tank-testing and training facility on the Kama River, near Kazan,
in 1927.[10]

Until 1928, the agenda of Soviet-German military cooperation was
handled by the Revvoensovet, or Military Revolutionary Council, the
forerunner of the Commissariat for War. Other government agencies
had no authority to interfere, because all basic decisions pertaining to
the issue were approved by the Politburo and (according to Ruth
Fischer) first of all by Stalin.[11] Only in 1928, Voroshilov took General
Blomberg, chief of the Reichswehr, into his confidence (something he
would never do in his later contacts with the French military) and told
him that the issues arising from the cooperation with the Reichswehr
would also have to be resolved by the Narkomindel.[12] That, however,
should not be viewed as a sign of the rising importance of the Commissariat for Foreign Affairs; it can be simply explained by the fact
that once the Wilhelmstrasse was handling the business of the

[18]

Reichswehr in Russia, the Narkomindel, as the Soviet administrative counterpart of the German Foreign Office, could no longer be left out of consideration.

Only a few essential facts pertaining to the whole operation can be noted here. Between 1922 and 1927, coproduction of war materials was set up on Soviet territory and especially oriented to aircraft, armored vehicles, and tanks as well as chemical weapons, including at least two types of poisonous gases. Advanced types of German military aircraft (Albatros 1-76, Junkers A-35, Junkers G-24, Junkers W-33, and Dornier-Merkur) were flown to Soviet Russia via Koenigsberg for the purpose of bombing exercises and pilot training. Prototypes of German tanks, produced by Rheinmetal, Daimler, and Gutte Hoffnungshuette, were brought to the USSR and tested and compared with British and French vehicles (Vickers, Garden Lloyds, Peugeot), especially imported for this purpose.[13]

Partial public disclosures in 1926 of these secret activities[14] had little effect on either the policies of allied governments or on the enterprise itself. The International Military Control Commission in Germany, undisturbed by the revelations, ceased to function on January 31, 1927. The termination of allied control made further German industrial activities in Russia unnecessary. Training activities became the main part of the cooperation between the Reichswehr and the Red Army.

It has been estimated that the Reichswehr spent one third of its annual budgetary expenditures in 1926—some 250 million marks—in the Soviet Union.[15] The number of Reichswehr officers sent to Soviet Russia for training continued to increase; in 1928, officers assigned to work with the Red Army numbered at least eight hundred. Munition plants were established under German technical supervision in Leningrad, Perm, Sverdlovsk, and other cities.[16]

Both armies greatly benefited from their secret association. Thanks to the fantastic possibilities offered by the Soviet connection, the Reichswehr was largely able to avoid some of the most sensitive limitations imposed upon Germany by the Versailles Treaty. The Germans were also pursuing illegal military activities in other countries (Holland, Spain, Sweden, Turkey), but on a comparatively limited scale. In the USSR, the Reichswehr found almost no limits to its projects in the production of war materials and for research, testing and training in a variety of fields from submarines to poisonous gases. Discretion was guaranteed: the whole enterprise has been kept in official secrecy in the Soviet Union up until the present.

The advances resulting from these clandestine activities were particularly important in the development of aircraft and tanks, including the training of hundreds of officers in the tactical art of modern aerial warfare and of the employment of tanks and armored vehicles.

The advantages resulting from this cooperation were also considerable for the Red Army. For the first time, Soviet officers became acquainted with the new weaponry that had made its modest debut on the western front in 1917 and 1918, and from the hands of the Germans they received their first instruction in the handling of the new techniques. German assistance, both technical and financial, contributed decisively to the construction of the first centers of Soviet military industry, especially the aircraft industry, production of tanks, and the chemical industry. Friendly relations and broad exchange of personnel, including attendance at war games on both sides, continued until 1933.

The question necessarily arises, How did this harmonious cooperation between the Reichswehr and the Red Army concur with the activities of the Comintern in Germany? Some of these activities, especially in the 1928–32 period, justify doubts as to the assumption that during this time the Comintern was already under full Soviet control. The issue is even more complicated in view of the known fact that not only were the various *Apparaten* of the KPD and of the Comintern entirely intertwined, but in most cases were directly supervised by the GPU.[17] There is no easy answer to the question. The Comintern had been created as an agency for the promotion of the world revolution, and however controlled, it could not be completely subordinated to conform to the changing lines of the foreign policy of the Soviet Russian state. In the long run, the Comintern's activities in Germany were certainly damaging for the Rapallo policy as a whole, but the Comintern was too important a requisite in the overall Soviet enterprise to be closed down, even if such a possibility were ever contemplated after the prevalence of the policy of "socialism in one country" in 1926; and that does not appear to have been the case. Moreover, there is no evidence that the Soviet leadership was aware, before the end of 1932, of the ultimate threat of the Comintern activities in Germany.

At the same time, the fact is that the master plan for Soviet conquest of Germany failed in 1923, and Soviet leadership does not appear to have seriously considered trying it again after that.[18] But the KPD remained the strongest foreign section of the Comintern, the supplier of the main cadre of the international legion of the GPU, and German territory was the main basis of the combined operations of the Comintern and the GPU around the world. Under these circumstances, the Soviet leadership could not hope to escape the consequences of its contradictory policies in Germany.

The negative role of the Comintern in Soviet-German relations became even more apparent after 1928, with the application of the general line adopted by the Sixth Congress. This policy facilitated the rise of the Nazi party, with which even the Communists were sometimes instructed to cooperate in the efforts to bring down the Socialist government of Prussia. Thus, the Comintern, the KPD, and the GPU network in Germany were actively undermining the political framework of the Soviet-German relationship, a dilemma that was obviously not grasped in Moscow in time. Ruth Fischer remembers Stalin's last-minute attempt in December 1932, to arrange a working association between the KPD and the Reichswehr—a rather special variant of the disavowed "united front at the top." By then it was too late to organize a rescue party in any case.[19]

Until 1933, all these activities of the Comintern in Germany had quite limited effects upon the main areas of cooperation between the two states. Political understanding still prevailed, demonstrated by, for example, their common stand on disarmament in Geneva and in attitudes toward Poland. The "special relationship" continued to be significantly buttressed by economic cooperation, in spite of the fact that never before 1940 did the total volume of Soviet-German trade become more than a fragment of the trade exchange between Russia and Germany before 1914.[20] Beginning in 1926, the Soviets were able to obtain in Germany easy export credits guaranteed by the Reich and state governments that led to the spectacular rise in the German share of Soviet imports during the first Five Year Plan: 22.1 percent in 1929, 23.7 percent in 1930, 37.2 percent in 1931, and 46.5 percent in 1932.[21] In 1931, the value of Soviet orders placed in Germany was estimated at 900 million marks, and according to British reports, "the German machine-tool industry had become almost entirely dependent on Soviet orders."[22]

According to Ambassador Dirksen, high on the list of reasons for the Soviet-German friendship was the "common attitude" of both countries toward Poland, which, from their point of view, had been established only at their territorial expense. Dirksen also notes that the Soviets preferred German economic assistance to that of England or France, both of which were considered politically dangerous: The able and energetic Ordzhonikidze, a close friend and countryman of Stalin, was a particular protagonist of this trend toward Germany. The first Five Year Plan brought an influx of more than five thousand German engineers, who worked on projects in all parts of Soviet

Russia, and many were employed directly by Soviet ministries in Moscow."[23]

The role reserved for Germany in the first Five Year Plan may in itself disprove the (much later) Soviet assertion that foreign policy concerns were the primary factor behind the prevalence of V. V. Kuibyshev's crack version of the plan. No prospect of an external threat existed in 1928, and there is no allusion to one in the published Soviet polemics concerning the case. Foreign-policy concerns traceable in N. A. Bukharin's moderate conception seem to follow from his view on financing of the industrialization. Believing in the continuation of NEP and in generally peaceful internal development, Bukharin thought that to obtain credit in the West, on acceptable terms, would not be difficult. Stalin, on the other hand, was determined to terminate the political and economic independence of the peasantry, and once his course was launched, there was virtually no alternative to the German credit.[24] Dirksen's observation about the Soviet preference for German trade, while essentially correct, is better explained in this broader context.

Aside from military collusion, common economic interests were supplying a strong rationale for the special relationship to continue right up to the eve of the Nazi Machtuebernahme. And even after the emergence of the ideological feud as an apparently dominant factor in state-to-state Soviet-German relations, these economic interests provided a constant basis for a possible rapprochement.

On the whole, German-Soviet relations in the post-Locarno period do not really show any significant symptoms of decline or weakening in any of the three major fields of cooperation—political, economic, and military. The special relationship had always been special indeed; Junkers and Bolsheviks made strange bedfellows. Such incongruity cannot serve as a valid criterion of the developmental trends of the Soviet-German relationship in the post-Locarno period, however, because the same heterodoxy also characterized the connection before Locarno.[25] E. H. Carr's opinion that there was a more or less regular downward trend in Soviet-German relations in the post-Locarno period[26] does not allow for the fact that Soviet foreign policy, after 1928, bore a strong isolationist trait, following the setback in Britain (1926) and the defeat in China (1927). The Comintern, "waging a war of extermination on the labor movement and on democracy,"[27] was throwing a long shadow across the whole of Soviet foreign policy. The special relationship with Germany, however, was cautiously nurtured, as Stalin himself made very clear in his widely publicized interview granted to Emil Ludwig in December 1931.[28]

[22]

The possibility that the Nazis might actually capture power in Germany does not seem to have been seriously considered in Moscow before the end of 1932. In the Comintern, the potential of the Nazi movement was so underestimated that even its accession to power was interpreted as a development that would speed up the Communist revolution in Germany. That the Nazis would in fact break down the whole special relationship was not considered in Moscow for another year. Stalin's willingness to continue with the Soviet-German "business as usual" even in the face of the devastating internal German consequences of the Machtuebernahme—that is, the complete annihilation of Communist structures—is very indicative of Soviet foreign policy priorities. Gustav Hilger, a senior German diplomat in Moscow at the time, described Soviet attitudes in the first six months after the Nazi takeover in this way:

> During the first five or six months of Hitler's rule, we noted marked efforts at restraint in the Soviet press. While Hitler was rooting out the entire KPD apparatus which Moscow had spent so much care and money to build up, considerations of Soviet foreign policy retained paramount importance in the minds of Russia's leaders to such an extent that willingness to go on with Germany as before was expressed again and again. Such persons as Krestinsky, Litvinov and Molotov went out of their way to assure us that their government had no desire to reorient its foreign policy.[29]

Hilger's observations are backed up by Ambassador Dirksen:

> On the Soviet side, complete silence prevailed during those first few months. The press refrained from all diatribe and confined itself to reporting mere facts. The anxiety and skepticism which were felt in the inner circles, however, became apparent in all my conversations with leading Soviet politicians. They willingly accepted the thesis that the treatment of German Communists would not affect our relations. But they were extremely skeptical of Hitler's intentions and eagerly awaited the new dictator's first official speech.[30]

According to Walter Krivitsky, "Stalin made no effort after the rise of Hitler to break the secret Berlin-Moscow tie. On the contrary, he tried his best to keep it in force."[31]

In Germany, forces known for their traditional support of the Soviet connection also tried to neutralize the negative impact on Moscow of the Nazi takeover. During the "anti-Marxist" campaign that followed the Reichstag fire (February 27), according to the French ambassador's sources, the Reichswehr Ministry hurried to inform the Soviet diplomats in Berlin discreetly about the existence of the underground corridor from Goering's residence to the Reichstag.[32] And the Wilhelmstrasse apologized promptly for the attacks of SA hoodlums on Soviet institutions in Berlin in March. Hitler's first public speech after the takeover, on March 31, reflected the restraining influence of these forces. It was comparatively moderate, showing willingness for friendly cooperation under conditions of noninterference. This trend was further sustained by Hitler's approval of the extension of Soviet installments on long-term German credits, and by the ratification, on May 8, of the prolongation of the Berlin Treaty of 1926. Carried out under the otherwise infamous Enabling Act and simultaneously extending the Soviet-German Conciliation Treaty of 1929, this step was followed by another reassurance, published in the *Diplomatische Korrespondenz*, organ of the German Foreign Office. It stated that the Rapallo policy had been "endorsed unambiguously and without limitation," and that this act should put an end to "all rumours which were based on the hope that Russo-German relations would deteriorate."[33] The new regime was therefore liquidating the Communist structures in Germany and at the same time making gestures of good will toward Moscow, and had the Nazis shown more consistency, the Soviet leaders appear to have been prepared to give more credit to those gestures.

In mid-May, a group of high-ranking Reichswehr officers, headed by General Blomberg, arrived in Moscow for regular talks with the Soviet High Command. The gala banquet for the visiting German officers was attended by the complete Soviet War Council, led by Kliment Efremovich Voroshilov, and "the visit took place in the old spirit of complete harmony and good will." Nevertheless, Blomberg later complained that he had to listen to bitter reproaches which, characteristically, concerned not the fate of the KPD but Alfred Rosenberg's anti-Russian tirades. State-to-state relations was a more sensitive area than ideological disputes, even though the latter had been brought to bloody extremes.[34]

The Soviet leaders, however favorably impressed by the conciliatory gestures of the German government, were anxious to hear that the earlier professions of the Fuehrer, as embodied in the fourteenth chapter of *Mein Kampf* (dealing with the eastern *Lebensraum*), would not be applied to the foreign policy of the Third Reich. The importance attached in Moscow to this particular issue is obvious both from the Soviet press and from the diplomatic correspondence. Litvinov, for example, went so far in his effort to clear this matter off the Soviet-German agenda that during his visit to Rome in mid-December 1933 he even tried to induce Mussolini "to use his influence with Hitler" to do something about the problem, and particularly "to give up toying with the Rosenberg themes." Mussolini's evasive response was a great disappointment for Litvinov.[35]

The Soviet government was also greatly alarmed by the German rapprochement with Poland, which had been in progress since April 1933. In contrast to the previous practice of consultation and coordination between Berlin and Moscow on all dealings of either side with the Poles (a practice faithfully followed by the Soviets as recently as in connection with the Soviet-Polish nonaggression pact two years earlier), the Germans were now keeping the Russians in the dark, increasing their suspicion.

All these factors combined prompted the Russians' decision, probably in October, to close down some of the jointly operated Soviet-German military installations, specifically the tank-testing station on the Kama River and the air force installation in Lipetsk. This step was doubtless intended more as a means of pressuring the Germans to redefine or reaffirm the policy of cooperation than as an act of final break. Toward the end of November M. N. Tukhachevsky remarked to the German military attaché in Moscow, Colonel Twardowski: "Do not forget, my friend, that it is politics, only your politics, which separates us, not our sentiments—our most friendly sentiments for the Reichswehr.[36]

Maxim Litvinov's speech before the Central Executive Committee on December 29 also kept the door wide open for a reconciliation with Germany. After an extensive restatement of the "extremely valuable mutual advantages" resulting from ten years of close political and economic cooperation (the military cooperation was not mentioned, of course) with Germany, Litvinov declared: "We want to have the best relations with Germany, as with other states. The Soviet Union and Germany will gain nothing but benefit from such relations."[37]

None of the recorded acts of the commissar at that time reveal anything but an effort to forestall a break with Germany, and none of the other leading Soviet personalities who made their attitudes known took a different stand. In a conversation in early January 1934 with the new German ambassador in Moscow, Rudolf Nadolny, for example, Voroshilov expressed sincere interest in furthering the relations of the past years even after the termination of common projects.[38] On January 13 Colonel Twardowski had "a very friendly and frank conversation of two hours" with Marshal A. I. Yegorov, the chief of the General Staff of the Red Army and a known intimate of Joseph Stalin, who "stressed the very friendly feelings of the Red Army for the Reichswehr and the desire to restore the old relationship. Unfortunately, the realization of this wish was being hindered at present by the German policy."[39]

These recorded statements of the commissar for war, the commissar for foreign affairs, and the chief of the general staff—two of whom were personally close to the general secretary—seem to show quite clearly that as late as January 1934, the Soviet leadership still desired an improvement of relations with Germany and a return to the old cooperation. Stalin himself expressed the same attitude in his speech before the Seventeenth Congress of the CPSU on January 26, 1934: "Some German politicans say that the USSR has now taken an orientation toward France and Poland; that from an opponent of the Versailles Treaty it has become a supporter of it, and that this change is to be explained by the establishment of the Fascist regime in Germany. That is not true. . . . The point is that Germany's policy has changed."[40] Divorce, however, was obviously inevitable. E. H. Carr seems to be right to assume that the fatal blow was the German agreement with Poland (signed the same day that Stalin addressed the CPSU Congress in Moscow), which "struck at the perennially sensitive point of the Soviet-German friendship."[41]

This conclusion should be afforded a broader meaning. The process of German-Polish rapprochement started as early as April 1933, and reached the point of a virtual agreement in mid-November. The Soviets were well informed about all stages of the negotiations, which were, after all, regularly covered by the foreign press. Therefore, the actual signing of the agreement was the culmination of a process that had been affecting Soviet attitudes for months. The Soviets' restraint and their repeated attempts to avert the rift are even more noteworthy considering this circumstance, and show the value acribed to the relationship with Germany.

Three main reasons for the final breakup emerge: First, the Nazis' doctrine contained inflammatory elements that were clearly directed not against the Soviet system, but against Russia as a state (e.g., the demand for the colonization of "eastern territories"). Second, the Soviets overestimated the factual weight of these postulates in the foreign policy of Nazi Germany (in later years, Soviet assessment of German intentions and their priorities became much more realistic). Third, Hitler's policy of rapprochement with Poland was interpreted in Moscow simply as a conspiracy against the USSR, although in reality it was aimed at the French security system in the area.

The principal conclusion to be drawn from the above evidence is that the nature of the new German regime was not in itself viewed as sufficiently important in Moscow to cause an immediate separation, and the Nazi anti-Communist ideology per se cannot therefore be listed as a direct automatic cause of the divorce. The Soviet behavior reveals no conscious resolution to terminate the relationship. The technical decision, in October 1933, to discontinue German participa tion in the joint operation of the installations in Lipetsk and Kazan can be interpreted as a warning rather than a final break. On the whole, the Soviet reaction to the development appears to have been generally passive, showing principally annoyance and regret in face of the vanishing chances to save the old relationship, but no readiness to draw conclusions until at least eight months later.

Whether or not the Soviet government, as Carr asserted, had since 1931 been looking for other friends no matter what the state of Soviet-German relations,[42] appears in this context rather unimportant as long as this activity was strictly subordinated to the primary concern to preserve the special relationship with Germany. That such was the case was sufficiently demonstrated during the negotiations of the Soviet nonaggression pact with Poland, the contents of which, point by point, the Narkomindel made subject to the approval of the Wilhelmstrasse.[43]

THE "ALTERNATIVE POLICIES"

It is nevertheless important to note and to examine other, parallel activities of Soviet foreign policy in the period between Locarno and the Nazi accession. The view that Moscow was moving away from its German orientation years before its break with Berlin has been rather common in Western works on the period, and it has also been given increasing emphasis in postwar Soviet interpretation of the era. The question therefore is whether the roots of the Soviet turn toward France and collective security in 1934 can be found before the Nazi rise to power and Hitler's disavowal of interest in the special relationship with the Soviet Union.

A great deal of Soviet foreign policy activity in the post-Locarno era was devoted simply to the normalization of the international position of the Soviet Union. Efforts to win broad formal recognition had so far brought a rather limited success,[44] but Soviet diplomacy negotiated various bilateral agreements with a number of foreign states, including some countries that had not yet formally recognized the USSR. These agreements covered a variety of areas, from fishing rights and border disputes to protection of trademarks, and on the whole indicated growing Soviet interest in normal state-to-state international intercourse.

Consular treaties and trade and credit agreements were in most cases concluded with states that had regularized their political relations with the Soviet Union one way or another. In consequence, almost 50 percent of Soviet exports in 1927–28 went to Germany, Great Britain, and Italy, which had granted the USSR their formal recognition. The same countries provided for almost 32 percent of all Soviet imports in the same period, and they also supplied the hard currency needed for substantial Soviet purchases in the United States (almost 20 percent of all Soviet imports in 1927–28).[45]

Between 1925 and 1927, the Soviet government also concluded treaties of neutrality and nonaggression with Afghanistan, Persia, Latvia, and Lithuania. These treaties were mostly more elaborate versions of postwar agreements and have to be placed in a different category than similar treaties negotiated in 1932, which will be discussed later.

A noteworthy activity of Soviet foreign policy in this period was the adherence to a number of international conventions and protocols, mostly of technical nature. All these activities, however, bore no consequences for the main Soviet foreign policy orientation in the period; that is, on the special relationship with Germany. Nor could they be interpreted as preparatory steps in an alternative direction. They were rather pursued on the assumption that they would further promote foreign recognition of the Soviet regime and improve the advantages that could be drawn from broadly based foreign trade. Other interests behind these efforts must also be recognized: each Soviet embassy, consulate, or mission abroad automatically became a base for the activities of the GPU, the military intelligence, and, of course, the Comintern. On the whole, however, no tendency toward weakening of the Rapallo policy is traceable in this field.

This conclusion is illustrated by the fact that Soviet interest in international contacts did not apply to the League of Nations. In 1925, Chicherin postulated in the name of the Soviet government that the league "implied the possibility of measures of constraint . . . against a particular state,"[46] and in the following years—in fact until the end of 1933—the Soviet attitude toward the League of Nations remained negative, if not hostile.

Soviet reservations regarding the league's potential of international constraint reflected the suspicion that the league might organize another intervention against the USSR. Such a fear was entirely unfounded, but the Comitern and the GPU were involved in a number of external activities that left Moscow's conscience not quite at peace.

For example, Richard Krebs remembers how—as late as August 1933—the Comintern organized a "training" general strike on the Aisne-Oise river system and on the adjacent canals in France, which included the building of barricades from river boats and the use of explosives. The aim of this exercize was to paralyze completely the transportation on French internal waterways in the strategically important territory between Paris and Le Havre. This action, like similar acts in earlier years, was supervised by the GPU, and international complications could not, of course, be ruled out.[47]

The Soviets also believed that the league was "the organizational center of imperialist pacifism, with its predictions of peace, prohibition of war, and demands for disarmament."[48] Denouncements of pacifism were standard fare in Soviet media and public speeches at the time. Stalin himself set the tone of this campaign in a speech before the Leningrad party organization on July 23, 1928. "Imperialist pacifism," he said,

> is an instrument for the preparation of war and for disguising this preparation by hypocritical talk of peace. Without this pacifism and its instrument, the League of Nations, preparations for war in the conditions of today would be impossible. There are naive people who think that since there is imperialist pacifism, there will be no war. That is quite untrue. On the contrary, whoever wishes to get at the truth must reverse this proposition and say: since imperialist pacifism and the League of Nations are flourishing, new imperialist war and intervention are certain.[49]

This may not be an accurate example of thorough Marxist analysis, but it leaves no doubt that the Soviet opposition to the League of Nations and to the security system built around it was unreserved and complete. It was also substantiated by the active participation of the Soviet Union in the secret rearmament of Germany, obviously with the assumption that Germany would attempt, by force of arms, to rectify the results of the last war.

The Soviet government persisted in its opposition to the league throughout the years of the tacit alliance with Germany. Only at a very advanced stage of the agony of the special relationship, on December 28, 1933, did V. M. Molotov, then chairman of the Council of People's Commissars, initiate preliminary cautious corrections in the standard Soviet view of the League of Nations.[50]

However opposed to the League of Nations and its "imperialist pacifism," the Soviet government was also bound to promote international peace. Its foreign policy was in essence only an extension of

Lenin's Decree of Peace, issued in October 1917. It was impossible simply to apply Stalin's thesis to day-to-day diplomatic practice. In 1925 and again in 1926, for example, it would have been politically damaging to decline the formal invitation to participate in the works of the Preparatory Commission on Disarmament, which was, after all, cosponsored by Germany as a new member of the League of Nations. A Soviet delegation, consisting of Litvinov, A. V. Lunacharsky, and Stein, then Soviet ambassador to Rome, arrived at Geneva in November 1927. The Soviet delegates did not waste much time acquainting themselves with the state of the talks, which had already moved through three sessions, and immediately made a proposal for the complete disbanding of all armed forces, the closing down of all armament factories, and the revoking of all conscription.

The commission, which had been unable to agree on much more modest projects in the field of international security, was astonished, especially when the only delegation that offered its support for the Soviet plan was the Germans. (At least one of the German delegates must have been greatly amused by the profession of Soviet antimilitarism—the chief of the Reichswehr, General Werner von Blomberg.)

Joseph Paul-Boncour, head of the French delegation, described the behavior of Soviet delegates at the disarmament talks in this way: "Until 1933, when the arrival of Hitler pushed the USSR toward the Western democracies and toward the League of Nations, the attitude of the Soviet delegation . . . was negative, reminiscent of an auctioneer. It was designed more for the purpose of propaganda than for our discussions, during which they exercised no real influence."[51] More important than their actual influence is the fact that in their maximalistic approach, Soviets were largely supportive of the German thesis that complete disarmament was the only acceptable alternative to "equality of armaments." When the Germans decided to leave the Disarmament Conference in October 1933, the Soviet delegation still abstained from voting for the collective reply of the conference to the government of the Reich.

Another enterprise of "imperialist pacifism" in which the Soviet Union did take part, was the Briand-Kellogg Pact, put forward by the French foreign minister, Aristide Briand, and the American secretary of state, Frank B. Kellogg, in June 1928. Initially, this project was furiously criticized by the Soviets along the lines drawn by Stalin in his Leningrad speech in July.[52] The chancelleries of France, the United States, and England reacted to Soviet accusations that the project was an instrument of encirclement of the USSR by inviting

Moscow to join the pact. This move left the Soviet government with little option but to validate its peace-loving general declarations by signing the pact, in spite of its recent characterization of the project as an anti-Soviet scheme. The question whether this Soviet attitude should be interpreted as an early sign of an alternative Soviet orientation seems unnecessary, considering the circumstances. Germany, it should be noted, had also signed the pact.

More interesting in this context is the aftermath of Soviet adherence to the Briand-Kellogg Pact, the Litvinov Protocol. (In Soviet postwar works it is called "the Moscow Protocol," because of the official disfavor of the former commissar at that time.) What is frequently thought a noteworthy Soviet initiative toward a multilateral agreement (the Soviets had consistently preferred bilateral contracts), followed, according to two historians of the interwar Polish foreign policy, from an initial proposition addressed only to Poland. The Poles, however, stuck to their usual policy, which insisted that all deals with the Soviets be part of multinational arrangements, and demanded the participation of other states in the area, particularly Rumania, with which Poland was allied.[53]

The Litvinov Protocol, which sought a pledge to respect the Briand-Kellogg Pact in case it failed to win sufficient support, soon proved superfluous, because the pact was quickly ratified by forty-four countries and entered into force in July 1929. As an attempt to undo the impression created abroad by the initial Soviet campaign against the pact, however, the protocol was quite successful.

The rise of Stalinism in the Soviet Union and the wild era of the Comintern after 1928—not to mention the parallel highlights of Soviet internal development—coincide with the rise of Maxim Litvinov in the ranks of Soviet diplomacy. Any search for early signs of change of Soviet mood in relation to collective security is very closely tied to this man. His personality and style, as well as the policies for which he became best known after 1934, are not easy to associate with the extremism of the era in which he assumed the office of commissar for foreign affairs (June 1930). Nevertheless, according to his own official statement, he "had actually led the Commissariat in the previous two years" during Chicherin's illness.[54]

Litvinov's prominent role in the conduct of Soviet foreign policy even before 1928 has already been mentioned. That he was a Bolshevik deputizing for a non-Bolshevik in itself indicates his special power. His actual share in the formulation and conduct of Soviet foreign policy, however, is subject to differing opinions. Louis Fischer, for example, believed that "Soviet foreign policy between

1929 and 1939 followed the pattern of Litvinov's mind more that of his chief's."[55] H. L. Roberts does not believe that Litvinov could, at any point, pursue any independent course.[56] According to Max Beloff, Litvinov "seems to have had a fairly free hand in these years in the day-to-day conduct of Soviet foreign policy."[57]

Available Soviet sources, including Ambassador Maiski's memoirs,[58] do not throw much light on the question. (I. M. Maiski, Litvinov's intimate from the time of their exile in England before World War I, was his only friend to later survive the purges.) Litvinov's own diary, in which the whole part covering the years 1933–35 is missing, can be used only with reservations.[59] Arthur U. Pope's work on Litvinov, based on his many conversations with the former commissar during Litvinov's term as ambassador to Washington, was published in 1943 and largely lacks critical insight. Some observations, nevertheless, deserve noting. For example, characterizing Litvinov's positions in the 1928–32 period, Pope observes: "Through all this, Litvinov was unwaveringly loyal to Stalin. Both were old Bolsheviki but neither was doctrinaire, and their common practicability led both to ready adjustments in terms of actual fact, and to medial solutions."[60]

According to Pope, the two men differed in that Stalin was a strong isolationist; Litvinov was not. Both rejected the concept of world revolution as absurd, and Litvinov (at a later point) won Stalin over to his thesis to secure the USSR by way of collective security.[61]

German ambassador in Moscow Dirksen, while admitting that Litvinov followed faithfully the Rapallo line until 1933, nevertheless suspected the commissar of pro-Western sympathies, because of Litvinov's long years in exile in England and because his wife was British.[62] Numberless diplomatic reports that are now accessible fail to substantiate Litvinov's alleged pro-British sympathies. Mrs. Litvinov's nationality is of course an attractive argument in the cherchez-la-femme line, but it cannot in itself justify political conclusions. Nor do these sources indicate any tendency, especially before 1933, on the part of Litvinov to be the initiator of the new political orientation. His diary shows Litvinov in unreserved agreement with Stalin and with the Rapallo line. In any case, an alternative course to the Rapallo policy had to have primary bearing upon France, not Britain. Signs of Litvinov's affection for the motherland of continental revolutionary traditions are also missing. Occasional expressions of respect for Edouard Herriot could hardly suffice to redress the role the USSR was playing in the rearmament of Germany, and Litvinov is not on record as an opponent of this policy.

[32]

Theodor von Laue expressed the opinion that Litvinov's "bitter hostility toward the League of Nations" had been, as early as 1927, just a tactical game played in agreement with Stalin, who "had already determined upon a policy of cautious rapprochement with the Western powers."[63] It is an interesting speculation, but available sources fail to supply evidence for it, and this alleged attitude cannot be traced to any factual Soviet diplomatic action.

Litvinov himself, in a conversation with foreign correspondents in Moscow after his appointment to the office of people's commissar for foreign affairs on June 25, 1930, emphatically stated that his nomination meant no change in policy. He did not fail to criticize the Versailles Treaty for "placing too heavy a burden on some countries for the benefit of others," and he said that "in general, we are going to continue in our old, well tried foreign policy."[64]

A close examination of his activities in the period does not contradict this statement. Litvinov was tied to the policy of Rapallo like any other member of the Soviet leadership and took no known steps— namely, none before 1933—that would indicate his preference for another orientation, toward France and the League of Nations.

It will still be shown that even in the years following the redirection of Soviet foreign policy in 1934 and 1935, Litvinov's consistency in the pursuit of the new course is subject to doubts. The fact that the oratorical hero of Geneva during the struggles for collective security had also been in charge of Soviet foreign policy before 1933, and to a significant extent even before 1928, should therefore not be underemphasized.

Soviet attitudes toward France in the era before the break with Germany are of course very pertinent. Until at least September 1931, that is, until the Japanese invasion of Manchuria, those attitudes were clearly hostile. Stalin's lapidary characterization of France in his report to the Sixteenth Party Congress in 1930 may serve as a proper example: "Present-day bourgeois France, the birthplace of the philanthropic 'pan-Europe' scheme, the 'cradle' of the Kellogg Pact, the most aggressive and militarist of all aggressive and militarist countries in the world."[65] Almost a year later, in April 1931, the Soviet view of France showed little improvement: "The French bourgeoisie—that chief organizer of an anti-Soviet war—has already created a number of political and military alliances for the purpose of encircling the USSR (Poland, Rumania, Finland, the states of Little Entente)."[66]

Franco-Soviet relations were generally in a troubled condition when both countries opened their negotiations on this pact in May 1931. One of the most difficult problems between France and the

USSR was the Russian debt dating from before the Bolshevik Revolution. Hundreds of thousands of French families had invested their savings in "Russian papers," and they felt robbed by the renunciation of foreign debts by the Soviets. Public opinion in France was also more sensitive than that in Germany to the never-ending news from Soviet Russia about violence and repressions. The numerous Russian émigré colony in Paris, politically very active, constituted another disturbing element. Franco-Soviet relations were further complicated by the activities of the French Communist party and the Comintern, which even before the Nazi victory in Germany had established in Paris an important operational basis.

According to Soviet sources, the USSR had shown its interest in a nonaggression pact with France in 1926 and 1927, and the last time in February 1928; between 1929 and 1931, however, "Soviet diplomacy did not officially raise the question of a non-aggression pact [with France]."[67] It was the French government (Prime Minister Pierre Laval, Foreign Minister Briand) who initiated the talks in April 1931. The Soviets, whose interest in a secure European rear was stimulated by rising tensions with Japan, responded very quickly, presenting a specific draft in May. During the ensuing negotiations, the main problem was how to harmonize the Franco-Soviet nonaggression pact with French treaty obligations toward Poland and Rumania. The French insisted on the conclusion of similar Soviet agreements with both French allies in Eastern Europe before the Franco-Soviet pact would enter into force. With that assumption, the pact was initiated in August 1931.

The Soviets had already proposed to conclude a nonaggression pact with Poland in 1928, aside from the common pledge to respect the Briand-Kellogg Pact (the Litvinov Protocol). In both cases, Warsaw imposed the same condition, that is, the conclusion of a similar pact between the USSR and Rumania, as well as with the Baltic states and Finland. Moscow then had, in fact, valid nonaggression pacts with two of the five countries—with Lithuania (contracted in 1926) and Latvia (1927). Until 1931 the Soviets took no further steps to meet the Polish counterproposal, and no further Soviet-Polish negotiations on the subject took place.

In October 1931 the Japanese march on Mukden and Soviet interest in the nonaggression pact with France prompted Moscow to renew its proposal to the Poles. Warsaw, although more interested than three years earlier, repeated the previous condition. This time, the Soviets acted swiftly. Between January and May 1932, they negotiated and signed nonaggression pacts with Estonia, Finland, and Latvia; the old pact with Lithuania had been extended earlier (May 1931). Finland and the Baltic states were in fact no problem. The problem was Rumania.

Bucharest had signed the Litvinov Protocol in 1928 with the reservation that it also covered the case of Bessarabia, but the Soviets never granted the point clearly; and during their talks with the Rumanians in 1931 they again refused to give any solid guarantees. The prospect of a Soviet-Rumanian nonaggression pact was therefore very bleak, especially without further pressure on Moscow by Poland and France. The Poles, however, showed no consistency. Satisfied with the conclusion of Soviet pacts with Finland and the Baltic states, and obviously worried by their own increasing tensions with Germany, they signed the nonaggression pact with the USSR in January 1932.[68]

The more interesting side of these Soviet dealings with France and Poland is, of course, the attitude of Germany and the possible effects of both nonaggression pacts on Soviet-German relations. The pact with Poland was, in this respect, more important and more sensitive. The Soviets therefore took great care to secure the consent of Berlin to the whole affair. Litvinov regularly discussed various aspects of the Soviet-Polish negotiations with German Ambassador Dirksen in Moscow, and he also visited Foreign Minister Konstantin von Neurath in Berlin, "giving his assurance of the unchanged loyalty of the [Soviet] Union toward Germany." The pact indeed met both main German demands: it did not guarantee Polish borders, and it reserved for Moscow freedom of action in case of Polish aggression against "a third party," that is, against Germany.[69] The only situation imaginable in which Poland might act militarily against Germany was of course in coordination with France, and in such an eventuality, Moscow reserved for itself a free hand to act against—Poland.

Especially when the agreement between Paris and Moscow was negotiated, between May and August 1931, German sources show no perturbation or displeasure with the Soviet nonaggression pact with France. The Wilhelmstrasse does not appear to have seen it as a possible device of a serious Franco-Soviet rapprochement that could endanger the special relationship between Soviet Russia and Germany. No known source indicates that the Soviets viewed the agreement otherwise. Without the Nazi takeover in Germany, which by pure chance occurred a few days before the Franco-Soviet pact entered into force, it is difficult to imagine that the agreement might ever have played such a role.

To discuss Soviet behavior after the arrival of the Nazis to power in

Germany in this particular context would be largely irrelevant. The course of action taken after January 30, 1933—which included, for example, the presentation of the Draft of the Definition of Aggression[70]—followed from a different situation, characterized by a steady decrease of options, and belongs to a different historical category.

During the years preceding the Nazi accession to power, however, it can safely be concluded that the Soviet Union followed neither a course of gradual withdrawal from the policy of preferential friendship with Germany nor a course of gradual or even purposeful rapprochement with the West. No intention to change clubs can legitimately be detected in the documented actions of the Soviet government. Lack of proportional groundwork that would facilitate the upcoming realignment is in fact a rather striking characteristic of Soviet policy in the period. Until the last moment, commitment to the German connection appears to have been complete. The Comintern continued to adhere to its extremist line, practiced since 1928, all through 1933 and shows no sign of coming to its senses before spring 1934. Soviet internal policies—especially the forceful collectivization, which amounted to another civil war—made the upcoming rapprochement with the Western democracies even more difficult.

Whether all those Soviet attitudes and activities provided a suitable ground for a principled adoption of a reversed policy is therefore very questionable.

[2]

The French Connection

The gradual deterioration of Soviet-German relations in 1933 was observed in France with understandable satisfaction. The newly appointed French ambassador in Moscow, Hervé Alphand, was "frankly delighted" by the state of Soviet-German relations in August 1933,[1] and the same state of mind can be read in the notes circulated by the political directorate of the Quai d'Orsay in the summer of 1933.[2] For the French, the Soviet-German entente had for years been a highly negative foreign policy factor with an obviously dangerous strategic potential. Moreover, the French government and the French General Staff had recently been confronted with rather comprehensive evidence of collusion between the Reichswehr and the Red Army,[3] and the possibility that this collusion might also be terminated as a result of the ideological feud between Berlin and Moscow brought unexpected relief.

At the same time, however, the French do not appear to have been prepared to exploit the Soviet-German divorce beyond a rather modest limit of securing a greater share of Soviet foreign trade.[4] According to Alexis Saint-Léger, the main thrust of the French diplomatic effort to solve the problem of French security—the center of which was Germany—was then still oriented toward Geneva and the League of Nations.[5] General Gamelin also asserts that the French "were still living in euphoria, placing [their] hopes in the League of Nations. . . . The mystique of the League," he adds, "in spite of the fact that it had somewhat lost the initial enthusiasm and faith, remained the essential element of our foreign policy as well as of our domestic policy."[6] This was understandable, considering the fact that after the war, France had failed to obtain effective guarantees for her future security from either Britain or America. In the west, France had only one ally, Belgium; new "rear alliances" east and south of Germany, with Poland and Czechoslovakia, were no substitute for the prewar alliance with Russia. After 1925, the British guarantee embodied in the Locarno Treaty became the only significant external connection France could rely upon, and to work in close cooperation with England in Geneva was consequently fundamental to French foreign policy.

In 1933, however—and even more in 1934 and 1935, when German rearmament became a fait accompli—these guarantees were insufficient to permit French politicians and military men to sleep easily. Even were England to honor her commitment, whether she could cope with the revived German war machine was dubious. The fact that German rearmament was accompanied by the deterioration of Soviet-German relations was therefore bound to cheer French policymakers, whose remembrance of the prewar alliance with Russia and of Russia's substantial contribution to France's survival in the First World War was still fresh, notwithstanding the "affair" of 1917. Since 1922, however, Soviet Russia had been effectively allied with Germany, and we have already noted the troublesome state of Soviet-French relations and the entirely hostile Soviet view of France as late as mid-1931. The Franco-Soviet Non-Aggression Pact, in spite of the fact that it happened to enter into force a few days after the Nazi takeover in Germany, represented only a very modest and noncommital stage of rapprochement.[7] How far that would go, however, was quite uncertain in the summer of 1933.

In July 1933, during a short stopover in Paris, Litvinov made a speech at a reception at the Soviet Embassy that bore a strikingly amiable tone toward France. He notably observed that "neither politically nor economically do our interests conflict with those of France in any part of the world, and therefore in our view there is no obstacle to further political and economic rapprochement."[8] That was an overstatement, considering, for example, the activities of the Asian Bureau, and the West European Bureau of the Comintern (which was just moving a substantial part of its agenda from Berlin to Paris). However noteworthy it may appear in the context of the future development of Franco-Soviet relations, Litvinov's statement is placed in focus by his itinerary: from Paris he headed for Berlin to meet the German foreign minister Baron Neurath, at a very delicate point of Soviet-German relations. Litvinov's statement in Paris could not therefore lack the primary purpose of making a particular impression in Berlin, and the sudden invitations to Edouard Herriot and Pierre Cot to visit Moscow are also best explained in the same framework.[9]

Both these visits took place in September: the visit of Cot, a cabinet minister in Edouard Daladier's government (January–October 1933), carried more official weight than the private visit by Herriot shortly before.[10] Two widely quoted French journalistic accounts assert that during their stay in Moscow, both Cot and Herriot were directly offered a military alliance with Russia,[11] but French documents now available do not substantiate such assertions. Any such Soviet proposals could not have been omitted from Pierre Cot's detailed report for Joseph Paul-Boncour, then minister of foreign affairs. Cot's report, however, contains no information of this kind; nor is there any allusion to such a noteworthy initiative in Ambassador Alphand's reports or in relevant Soviet sources.[12]

French sources record only two specific Soviet propositions of a political nature: first, to conclude "a secret verbal agreement, under the terms of which the two governments would inform each other about their respective views pertaining to general questions of interest for both sides, and about the treaties they intend to sign with third parties." The Soviets, when making this proposition, themselves emphasized that they already had a similar (written) agreement with Germany. Second, the Soviets proposed to the French to accede to the Convention of the Definition of Aggression.[13]

Cot's trip had been approved not only by Paul-Boncour, but also by General Maxime Weygand, then chief of the French General Staff.[14] Cot's task appears to have been to probe the Soviet mood; he made no propositions himself. Paul-Boncour's ideas, nevertheless, were already moving in a fixed direction.

In his report for Paul-Boncour, which is the most complete document on the matter, Cot made four recommendations:

(1) To negotiate a technical agreement with the Russians that would open the door to the sending of French transportation experts to Soviet Russia, a welcome arrangement "due to the unemployment in France."

(2) To exchange military missions.

(3) To examine the possibility of an industrial assistance in case of war.

(4) To study the question of a pact of mutual assistance.[15]

Cot's thoughts may well be assumed from the conclusion of his report: "In a few years, in the course of a conflict which would last more than a year, the industrial power of France would be equal to 1, that of Germany to 2, that of Russia to 4 or 5. Under these conditions, a collusion between Germany and Russia would result in the destruction of France."[16]

According to Alphand's report, Litvinov "repeated on various occasions" that Germany would start a war within two years by attacking Poland, the Baltic states, the Ukraine, and eventually Alsace-Lorraine.[17] The fact that Moscow felt imminently threatened on two fronts was witnessed by William Bullitt, who reported from Moscow that according to Litvinov, "the Soviet Union considered an attack by Japan in spring [1934] so probable that it must secure its western frontier in every way."[18] Fear of the Four-Power Pact added another aspect to Soviet behavior at that time. The French Embassy in Moscow repeatedly reported Soviet alarm at the prospect of the pact between the four West European powers. At one point, Alphand even urged Paris to calm the Russians down with regard to the possibility of a Franco-German collusion.[19]

The general international framework appears to have been suitably set to prompt the Soviets to seek improvement of their relations with France (as well as with the United States). At the same time, Soviet dealings with France were still clearly subordinated to the possibility that the German connection might be preserved—hence the proposition to keep the eventual agreement secret and verbal. In October, the Soviet ambassador in Paris, V. S. Dovgalevsky, strongly insisted in his conversations with Paul-Boncour and Léger on complete secrecy of the talks as an express Soviet condition: "Nothing must be revealed. . . . Secrecy is of great importance to us."[20] Publicity afforded to Herriot's visit in the USSR and to Litvinov's stopover in Paris, can safely be conceived as warning signals to Berlin. At the same time, Moscow was anxious not to impair the remaining possibilities for the preservation of the friendship with Germany by indications of any real involvement with France. The possibility of an alliance between France and the Soviet Union was obviously raised for the first time, on an official level, by Paul-Boncour in a conversation with the Soviet ambassador in Paris on October 19, 1933.[21] Léger's version, according to which the whole enterprise resulted from a Soviet initiative, is contradicted by French documents.[22]

Paul-Boncour remembers that after the Nazi takeover in Germany, he immediately thought of the necessity "to fortify French alliances, and in that context, he did not think it was less necessary, or possible, to conclude another alliance with Russia, in order not to make Poland and Rumania feel threatened from behind."[23] In early summer 1933, after his return from Geneva, Paul-Boncour worked on this problem with Léger and with Bargeton, director of political affairs in the French Ministry of Foreign Affairs. During their consultations it appeared that a new agreement with Russia could not take any other form than that of a pact of mutual assistance, similar to that which linked us to Poland and, if possible, coordinated with and also signed by the latter. It was also obvious to all participants that to retain and to protect other French alliances, it would be necessary to bring the Soviet Union into the League of Nations which . . . the Russians had so much calumniated in the earlier period.[24]

This plan, according to Paul-Boncour (and confirmed by Soviet sources), was discussed with Dovgalevsky on October 19 and then with Litvinov, who stopped in Paris again on his way to Washington, on October 31. Litvinov asked for time to consult Moscow. A few days later, Ambassador Dovgalevsky brought the Soviet reply. Moscow agreed to talk on a tentative basis, but it again insisted on complete secrecy.[25]

Conversations with Dovgalevsky continued in November and December, and according to Yu. V. Borisov, the Soviet historian of Franco-Soviet interwar relations, Paul-Boncour insisted on Soviet entry into the League of Nations.[26] French sources show that the necessity of Soviet entry into the league emerged during an examination of the project by leading officials of the Quai d'Orsay, who concluded that without Soviet membership in the organization, an alliance with Moscow would cost France the guarantee embodied in the Locarno Treaty.[27]

Already at this early stage of the negotiations, the absence of a Soviet border with Germany was also considered by the French. "The geographical position of Poland would strongly implicate the latter country in a conflict between Germany and Russia." An alliance between Poland and Russia was therefore viewed as indispensable. On September 15, Ambassador Alphand in Moscow was instructed to inform Litvinov about the position of the French government with respect to the ways and means of an agreement between Paris and Moscow.[28] Soviet sources assert that the issue was then discussed by the Central Committee of the Communist party, which approved a document prepared by the Commissariat for Foreign Affairs.[29]

The Soviet reply, which Dovgalevsky brought to Paul-Boncour on December 28 and to Léger on January 4, 1934, was obviously based on this decision. In response to the French demand that the USSR should adhere to the League of Nations, the Soviets imposed several conditions, of which the most difficult was the recognition of the USSR by all member-states of the league. The French judged the Soviet conditions as "surmountable"; in any event they were later dropped. The Soviets also proposed to extend the original French plan of a French-Polish-Soviet combination into a regional agreement that would include the USSR, the Baltic states and Finland, and Poland and Czechoslovakia, as well as France and Belgium. "In this way," Borisov declares categorically, "originated the idea of the Eastern Pact—a Soviet, and not a French idea, as it is believed by bourgeois historiography."[30]

This claim is confirmed in another document of the Quai d'Orsay, dated January 4, 1934. Moreover, this document gives a much more detailed account of the Soviet project than the available Soviet sources, Some aspects deserve to be noted.

First of all, the obligation of states entering the grouping would not be limited to Europe, contrary to Paul-Boncour's specification in the previous discussions. Dovgalevsky personally argued against "French neutrality in the Far East." Declaring himself to express official views of the Soviet government, "the Ambassador positively stated that it was better to account for the real interests which Russia sought in this project."[31]

Dovgalevsky further requested that the French and Soviet governments "direct the national press" of both countries to write favorably about each other during the duration of the pact. That, of course, would sooner or later require the imposition of censorship in France and other countries entering the agreement.[32]

It can therefore be concluded at this point that the Soviets preferred a broader system along their western borders to Paul-Boncour's rather explicitly anti-German front of France, Poland, and Russia. The Soviets also wanted the pact to apply to the Far East as well as to Europe, that is, against Japan as well as against Germany; they were willing to join the League of Nations as the price of such an arrangement, but they demanded certain exceptions for their membership status, such as exclusion from the league's arbitrage system. Soviet stipulations were largely unacceptable to the French, and after January 4, 1934, no further conversations are reported. According to Borisov, until April 1934, the Quai d'Orsay was showing "no symptoms of life."[33] Nevertheless, a Franco-Soviet trade agreement was signed on January 11 that showed significant French concessions, such as the granting of diplomatic status to the Soviet Trade Mission in Paris and removal of import restrictions that had been in effect in France since April 1933. Political negotiations, however, appear to have been entirely stalled during the last weeks of Paul-Boncour's term in the office of foreign minister.

In the government crisis that followed the Stavisky affair, Paul-

Boncour was replaced by Louis Barthou. The very first day in office, Léger remembers, the new minister called him in and said: "You know that the Right expects me to relieve them of the Russian offers of collaboration. So tell me all about the transactions with the Soviets."[34]

According to Geneviève Tabouis, Léger then informed Barthou about "the Soviet offer of a direct bilateral alliance," which in his view had to be taken advantage of "if we did not want to throw the Soviets into the arms of the Germans." Then he allegedly proposed to mold the Soviet plan into an acceptable shape and to include certain conditions, such as the limitation of the pact to Europe and coordination of the pact with other French alliances. He also recommended that the agreement be built upon the principle of "collectivity," which would make possible even the adherence of Germany. Here Barthou is said to have called the project "the Eastern Locarno."[35] The label, of course, is not very important; disregarding certain obvious inaccuracies, this was the essence of the plan that Barthou later proposed to Litvinov.

On April 20, 1934, Dovgalevsky received Barthou's invitation to renew the talks on the basis of the proposals made by Paul-Boncour.[36] This plan was then discussed at the first meeting between Barthou and Litvinov in Geneva on May 18, 1934. The French proposed a regional Eastern Pact between the USSR, Germany, Poland, and Czechoslovakia. This pact would be guaranteed by France by way of a Franco-Soviet alliance.[37]

New factors were now affecting Soviet considerations. The Soviet-German divorce became final in February, and the new German military budget, recently published, demonstrated that "the Reich was beginning to rearm without further ado."[38] In Germany, an anti-Soviet campaign was in full swing. In his conversation with Barthou, Litvinov no longer insisted on secrecy. The French record of the meeting shows that the accepted basis for further discussion was the French draft, of which Litvinov complained only that he had not had enough time to study it. Soviet sources throw some doubt on this assertion: Barthou's plan had been presented to the Soviets on April 28, and Dovgalevsky informed Léger on May 5 that the project was "acceptable in principle" to the Soviet side. Dovgalevsky could hardly make such a statement without instructions from Litvinov.[39]

The conversation on May 18 nevertheless consisted mostly of Litvinov's questions and Barthou's answers. Without so stating directly, Litvinov seems to have been reconciled to the necessity of Soviet entry into the League of Nations. He asked Barthou whether he was planning to invite Germany to take part in the pact. "Do you think she will accept?" he asked. "Do you think she will return to Geneva? And if she will not accept, are we going to make the pact without Germany?" Barthou replied: "If Germany declines, we will be justified in concluding the pact without her. But we do not have to show any haste. We must not do anything that would look like an act directed against her. If she joins the security system, all the better. If not, she will put herself in the wrong."[40]

Litvinov also raised the question of the attitude of Poland. Barthou, who had visited Warsaw in April, sounded optimistic. Litvinov was skeptical. Alluding to intelligence reports, he suggested the possibility of a secret deal between Poland and Germany, presumably against Soviet Russia. Barthou tried to assure him that there was no secret agreement between the two countries beyond the nonaggression pact of January 1934. Barthou's expectation, that Poland would join the pact sponsored by France, seems to have been entirely sincere.

In conclusion, it was decided to entrust Léger and Dovgalevsky with further negotiations. No changes in Barthou's plan, however, appear to have followed from their conference. The French government approved the project a few weeks later and on July 12 won British agreement to it at Barthou's conference with Viscount Simon, the foreign secretary, in London. The British also agreed to support Soviet entry into the League of Nations. Soviet sources note no corresponding action taken by the Soviet government, or by the Politburo, on the project. The next step in the realization of the project was to ensure the agreement of Germany, Poland, and Czechoslovakia.

The question whether or not Barthou tried hard enough to sell the plan to Germany is outside the scope of this study. The fact is that Germany received the text of the project from London and not from the actual sponsors of the plan, that is, from the French or from the Soviets.[41] That, however, seems to have been a procedure agreed upon between Barthou and Simon during their talks in London. Following the same agreement, the British Foreign Office also formally informed the government of Italy and Poland about the project. Whether that was, from Barthou's point of view, a "studied discourtesy," is therefore open to doubt.[42] Ambassador Bullitt's assertion that Moscow was assured, as early as mid-July 1934, that France and Czechoslovakia would conclude alliances with the USSR no matter what happened to the Eastern Pact sounds highly improbable, at least regarding its timing, and is not confirmed by any other available sources.[43]

Litvinov's handling of the issue of German participation certainly does not show any "studied discourtesy." The commissar does not appear to have been an ardent proponent of the whole idea of an Eastern Locarno; and in relation to Germany, his behavior was entirely positive. On his way from Geneva to Moscow, he had the Soviet Embassy in Berlin arrange a meeting with Neurath, the German foreign minister. The meeting took place July 13, before the final text of the project was worked out. Nevertheless, Litvinov informed Neurath about the plan, "without going into details," before talking about any other issues.[44]

Neurath suggested that there were reports that the new pact was not Litvinov's idea, but a French enterprise. Litvinov, showing neither any clear identification with the plan nor any solidarity with Barthou, made no attempt to deny that the plan was indeed a French project. According to Neurath's record of the conversation, the commissar rather

> tried to get around it by saying that this proposal had been discussed at Geneva. . . . At various points in the conversation, Litvinov kept reiterating that the idea that he took a hostile attitude toward Germany for ideological reasons was entirely erroneous, and that he saw no reason why relations between our two countries should need to undergo further deterioration.[45]

On July 20, 1934, Soviet ambassador Y. Z. Suritz, on instructions from Moscow, made an urgent call on Secretary of State Buelow. Suritz explained that his government had only recently received the French draft of the projected Eastern Pact, which "they had not studied jointly with the French government," and had therefore not communicated the draft to other governments in its own name. Suritz was instructed to inform the German government that the Soviet Union agreed to the extension of the guarantees contained in the draft, to include Germany.[46]

On close analysis, both Litvinov's behavior during his conversation with Neurath and Surtiz's remarks in his conversation with Buelow constitute repeated attempts to show the Soviets at a measured distance from the project which they were supposed to promote. And diplomatic correspondence reveals no other Soviet effort in this direction, particularly not in Warsaw. Here, eventually, Soviet initiatives were even more in place than in Berlin. Whereas the French did their utmost to secure Polish consent to the plan, the Soviets appear to have been entirely inactive.[47]

The French chargé d'affaires in Moscow, J. Payart, analyzed Polish reluctance to participate in the Eastern Pact in a report dated August 20, 1934. He pointed out that "in a system of common guarantees, Poland would occupy a central geographical position. Her own historical experiences prove that assistance of foreign troops is not without danger." The risks that a passage of foreign troops would pose to their independence had been illustrated, in Payart's account, in 1757, when the crossing of Russian troops marching against Frederick II, agreed upon with Warsaw, resulted in the first division of Poland. Soviet constitution, argued the Poles, was open to annexations of new "Soviet republics," for which the convenient method was the formation of a "revolutionary government." Payart concluded: "In the Polish mind, fear of the ideological Soviet imperialism has therefore, with some justification, a two-fold dimension compared to the fear of the Russian territorial imperialism."[48]

The Soviet government made no known effort to dispel these apprehensions, and French assurances were not found persuasive enough in Warsaw. Poland also refused to take part in any guarantees applied to Czechoslovakia, and finally declined to enter the system without Germany. Berlin declared its opposition to the Eastern Pact on September 8. Of all the projected members of the grouping, besides France and the USSR, only Czechoslovakia accepted; and her accession contributed nothing to the solution of the geographical problem of direct territorial connection between the security system and the Soviet Union.

The noncommital Soviet behavior during the months of Barthou's attempt to organize the Eastern Pact was aptly explained by the Italian ambassador in Moscow, Bernado Attolico, who then enjoyed special treatment from the Soviet leadership previously reserved for German envoys. "No one here [in Moscow] feels very happy at the thought of the Soviet Union in this way being compulsorily drawn into European affairs," he said. But in face of the "evil intentions of Germany" the Soviet leaders saw no other option but to swallow the bitter pill, join the League of Nations, and make an alliance with France, "unless German policy succeeded in meeting the Russian *pact mania* in a form acceptable to them."[49]

A German political report from Moscow, characterized as "a careful comparison of statements by leading Soviet politicians about the Eastern Pact" as collected by Moscow diplomats "surprisingly unanimous in their assessment of the situation," observed:

> The general conviction prevails here that the Soviet government only desires an alliance with France if it is unable to obtain any real security for their western border. Little credence is therefore attached to the news put about from the French sources that the Soviet Union is pressing for an alliance. . . . The extremely realistic Politburo certainly does not wish to entrust themselves at all unconditionally to France's political leadership. . . . Litvinov . . . told others that should an Eastern Pact fail to come about, Germany should be included as a third party in a Franco-Soviet alliance.[50]

These observations seem to characterize the state of Soviet considerations in late summer 1934 very realistically. The net result of the whole diplomatic campaign was Soviet entry into the League of Nations in mid-September, to which the Soviet government had agreed toward the end of July, reducing its previous list of conditions to two: first, that the USSR would be invited, and second, that it would get a seat on the Council.[51] Beyond this step, however, Paul-Boncour and Barthou's plan of attaching Soviet Russia to the French security system did not move ahead. The termination of the Soviet-German cooperation, namely in the political and military field, was certainly an important development, but it was the result of neither French diplomacy nor a purposeful Soviet policy. Moreover, it did not significantly affect the economic cooperation between Germany and the Soviet Union, and the possibility of a new Soviet-German rapprochement, in line with their continuing economic links, was far from being ruled out.[52] That was the situation at the moment of Barthou's death on October 8, 1934. The principal concern of his successor, Laval, appears therefore rather understandable: "For the moment, it was necessary to prevent a German-Soviet collusion."[53]

Seen without the nimbus that he attached to himself six years later, Laval seems to have differed from Barthou more in style than in outlook. Lacking his predecessor's brilliant intellectual qualities, Laval could hardly make a favorable impression on foreign statesmen like Anthony Eden or Eduard Beneš, both distressed over the change at the Quai d'Orsay. On the other hand, when assuming office Laval was faced with a situation characterized by the Polish refusal to take part in the Eastern Pact without Germany,[54] whereas Barthou had obviously operated on the optimistic assumption that Poland would,

[47]

in the end, line up with France. The crucial geographical position of Poland for the whole project of recruiting Soviet Russia for the cause of collective security was certainly clear to both men, but we simply cannot know what Barthou's course of action under the new circumstances would have been.

Laval's immediate efforts to strengthen French ties with Italy show a very consistent continuity with Barthou's conception. General M. G. Gamelin, who was a member of the French delegation to Geneva in May 1934, recorded Barthou's political plan, of which point 4 called for "bringing round to us Italy, and making the Soviet Union enter the concert of Europe on our side."[55]

Nevertheless, the Marseilles *attentat,* in which Barthou lost his life together with King Alexander of Yugoslavia, was interpreted by many as affecting an important qualitative change in French foreign policy. This reaction may simply have followed from the unfavorable way in which Laval compared with his predecessor. Moreover, the death of King Alexander was believed to have considerably weakened French influence in the Balkans. Eden later compared the shots fired in Marseilles to those in Sarajevo—an obvious overstatement.[56] Beneš believed that Barthou's death "represented a blow for the policy of rapprochement [with Russia],"[57] and in agreement with Nicolae Titulescu, the Rumanian foreign minister, set in motion the diplomacy of the Little Entente as leverage to speed up the negotiations with the Soviets. Titulescu bluntly informed Laval that "Rumania would lean on France only in case of the conclusion of the Franco-Soviet agreement. If, in consequence of its non-realization, the Soviet Union would go with Germany, Rumania would follow suit. Yugoslavia would do the same. The Little and Balkan ententes cannot exist without the Franco-Soviet pact."[58]

Until May 1935 diplomatic pressures from this side represented a noteworthy factor in the development leading to the conclusion of the Franco-Soviet alliance. The prospect that not only Rumania and Yugoslavia but also Czechoslovakia might, in the end, follow the example of Poland and strive for some kind of accommodation with Germany could not, of course, be ignored either in Paris or in Moscow. Another, rather permanent factor was the apprehension both in France and in Soviet Russia that the other side might make a deal with Germany. Moscow was still haunted by the ghost of the Four-Power-Pact, which according to Beneš provided the main stimulus urging the Russians to join the League of Nations.[59] Moscow's reluctant consent to the softening of the line of the French Communist party toward the SFIO (probably in May–June 1934) appears to be another expression of the same concern.[60]

THE CHANGING SOVIET INTERESTS

Immediately after Barthou's assassination, the Soviet leadership began to voice doubts about the value of the French connection "due to the loss of French influence in the Balkans, resulting from King Alexander's death."[61] In the face of continuing German rearmament and noisy anti-Sovietism, the Soviet government concluded, probably at the beginning of November, that the security afforded by membership in the League of Nations was inadequate. According to Borisov, it was therefore decided to "conclude the Eastern Pact without Germany and Poland, on the condition of the consent of France and Czechoslovakia, or at least France."[62] And in order to secure themselves against the possibility of a French deal with Germany outside the framework of the Eastern Pact, the Soviets proposed, on November 22, to sign a Franco-Soviet protocol confirming previous agreements with Barthou, pledging both sides to continue preparations for the project, and forbidding separate negotiations with other powers.[63] This proposal is important in that it constitutes a Soviet confirmation that the project of the Eastern Pact had indeed been an agreement between Barthou and Litvinov, something that the commissar did not concede in his conversation with Neurath four months earlier.

Laval preferred to make the same pledge in the form of a statement in the French Chamber of Deputies, but Litvinov insisted on his proposal. According to a Czech historian, R. Kvaček, the commissar sufficiently impressed Laval with the alternative of a German-Polish-Soviet agreement without France and Czechoslovakia.[64] Beneš and Titulescu applied additional pressure on Laval, who finally signed the protocol on December 5. Czechoslovakia acceded to it a few days later.[65]

Concurrently with the political talks between Paris and Moscow, Franco-Soviet economic relations were the subject of negotiations conducted in Moscow by the French minister of commerce, Paul Marchandeau. The French, however, were not ready to offer credit conditions similar to those which the Soviets were still enjoying in Germany, and the actual result, the trade agreement signed in December, was rather limited, especially because of the French refusal of government guarantees of private French loans. Trade between the two countries failed to develop to an extent that would have provided a supportive base for political rapprochement.[66]

In January and February 1935, Laval and Simon made a new attempt to reach an agreement with Germany that would bring her back into the League of Nations and establish a legalized framework for a revision of the Versailles Treaty. Germany would, on that basis, pledge to keep her rearmament within certain limits. Part of this project was to change the character of the Eastern Pact from an alliance system into a collective nonaggression and consultative treaty, which seemed more acceptable to Germany and Poland. A Franco-Soviet guarantee pact would complement this system, according to a proposition made by Léger to the new Soviet ambassador, V. P. Potemkin, on February 27, 1935.[67]

The Soviets strongly opposed this new plan, which might bring Poland in the grouping again, referring to the protocol of December 5 which had bound both sides to the initial variant. Unilateral German actions in March 1935 made the Anglo-French attempts irrelevant, anyway: Goering's announcement of the militarization of the German Air Force (March 9) and Hitler's announcement of the reintroduction of conscription (March 16) made a mockery of the offer to provide international legalization for German rearmament.

When Anthony Eden visited Moscow toward the end of March (the first official British visit at this level to the Soviet Union since 1917), he had several conversations with Litvinov. On one of these occasions, Litvinov made a statement on Soviet-German relations. For many years, he said, these relations had been excellent, both with the government and with the Reichswehr. Rapallo, the commissar emphasized, had had no secret clauses. The situation changed after the Nazi takeover. "The original German plan," declared Litvinov, "was to attack France and then to attack in the East. Since then German plans have changed. The plan now apparently is to leave France alone, but to attack in the East only."[68]

This statement is a valuable clue to the changing Soviet attitude toward collective security, as well as toward the idea of a Franco-Soviet alliance. It can hardly be interpreted as an attempt to impress Eden; in that case, as he did on other occasions, Litinov would rather have emphasized German schemes against the West. Litvinov's statement (which may well have been a rare slip of the tongue), shows that Soviet attitude toward collective security depended upon the expected direction of German expansion. As long as it had been directed against France, the attitude was indifferent or even hostile. It was becoming more positive only when German aggressiveness threatened to turn to the East.

As an expression of this changing mood, on March 29, Potemkin presented to Laval a formal Soviet proposal to conclude a direct alliance between France, the USSR, and Czechoslovakia. A few days later, dissatisfied with the speed with which Paris handled the offer, Potemkin threatened Laval that if the French government did not feel bound by the protocol of December 5, 1934, he would signal his government to reestablish its "freedom of action."[69] Hardly by chance, *Pravda* published an article by Marshal Tukhachevsky on March 31 that characterized the French army as "incapable of active opposition to Germany."[70]

Herriot notes in his memoirs that the Soviet-German credit agreement, which was signed April 9, was another reason for French alarm, because it could have "inaugurated a return to the tradition of Rapallo."[71] The French cabinet adopted the decision to conclude a bilateral treaty with the USSR on that same day. Laval asked Potemkin to inform Moscow that France would sign the alliance pact on May 1 at the latest.[72]

Mounting pressures of the Little Entente, and especially of Beneš and Titulescu, also deserve noting. According to Czech diplomatic sources, both men were embroiled in the whole affair to the point where the French official communiqué of April 9, which announced the intention of France to conclude a treaty of alliance with the USSR, was drafted in the Quai d'Orsay by the two ministers of foreign affairs.[73]

In the end, therefore, Soviet diplomacy was pressing for the agreement that it had still been cold-shouldering several months before. Czechoslovakia and Rumania, caught in the development because of their geographical position in Europe, provided significant support. The question now was how these shifting interests would be fixed in a mutually acceptable and satisfactory document.

THE FINAL PHASE

Negotiations on the text of the treaty started with little delay in Geneva, where on April 15 Litvinov dropped the initial Soviet proposal of a trilateral pact and agreed instead to the signing of two separate bilateral pacts, one with France, one with Czechoslovakia.[74] The exiled Czech historian Ivan Pfaff views this step as in direct contradiction to previous Soviet commitment to Czechoslovakia:

"[Litvinov] markedly broke all promises which he had repeatedly given to Beneš. In this way, the Soviets themselves for the first time made way for such a mechanism of the treaties which allowed for the avoidance of the fulfillment of their treaty obligation toward Czechoslovakia."[75] The draft of the Franco-Soviet pact was negotiated in Paris in the last days of April, and signed by Laval and Potemkin on May 2. A parallel Soviet-Czechoslovak pact was signed in Prague on May 16.

The applicability of the two pacts was intertwined in paragraph 2 of the Protocol on the Signing of the Soviet-Czechoslovak Treaty or, as it is usually alluded to, "the Supplement." This paragraph rendered the obligation of mutual assistance between the USSR and Czechoslovakia effective "only in so far as, under the conditions provided for in the present treaty, aid will be accorded by France to the party who is victim of the attack."[76] The linkage of the two pacts was sadly demonstrated at the only instance when their validity was put to practical test—during the Czechoslovak crisis in September 1938. It is therefore important to examine the background of this unusual arrangement.

The framework of both pacts was even more complicated because it also implied the relevant articles of the Covenant, the Locarno Treaty, French pacts with Poland and Rumania, and, to a lesser extent, the treaties of the Little Entente. The fundamental weakness of all these alliances was their geographical asymmetry. Whereas two of the allies had common borders with the presumed enemy, one (Soviet Russia) was separated from Germany by Poland, which was showing no intention to open her territory for the movements of the Red Army.

The crucial point of both treaties, as far as their mechanism was concerned, was the implication of Article 16 of the Covenant, which made "immediate" mutual assistance dependent upon a unanimous recommendation of the Council of the League of Nations.[77] Both sides accepted this formula for reasons of their own, and Czechoslovakia was obliged to follow suit in her treaty with the Soviets.

To suppose that Moscow resisted this aspect of the treaties would be incorrect. In its first edition, edited by Potemkin himself, the Soviet *History of Diplomacy* declares clearly that "Soviet diplomacy had no intention to juxtapose the Franco-Soviet treaty against the Covenant . . . [and] succeeded in bringing the French to accept the corresponding formulation of the Treaty."[78] In the absence of other evidence to the contrary, the version approved—if not authored—by Potemkin deserves credit. The "corresponding formulation of the Treaty" was, accordingly, proposed by the Soviets, who "succeeded in bringing the French" to that end. As will be shown, the Soviets started to disclaim this version, politically distasteful in view of Munich, only thirty years later.

In line with the French demand, on the other hand, both pacts were limited to Europe, but Czechoslovakia, a major armament exporter, pledged not to supply Japan with war matériel (Article 4 of the Soviet-Czechoslovak Treaty).[79] What deserves special attention is the already mentioned supplement to the last-named pact, even though the role it played at the time of Munich was much less important than is usually believed.

This supplement had dual meaning. On the one hand, it indirectly connected both pacts, although it could not give them the effective character of a trilateral agreement. On the other hand, it made Soviet assistance to Czechoslovakia (and vice versa) dependent on the simultaneous action of France. Again, the authoritative Soviet source claimed full credit for the supplement, calling it "a wise reservation of Soviet diplomacy."[80] The fact that the text was drafted by Beneš is not important; he was simply the best craftsman on the negotiating teams. He had neither the power nor the influence to impose it upon the Soviets, as they started to assert thirty years later.[81]

When accepting the supplement, according to contemporary archival sources, Beneš had several considerations in mind. He did not want to be drawn into a Soviet conflict with Poland;[82] he was looking for a way to avoid the possibility that Moscow might employ the treaty on its own initiative, an apprehension shared by all neighbors of Russia; and finally, he conceived of both pacts as a nucleus of a "broader security system," as he himself explained in a circular letter to the Czechoslovak embassies.[83] But he was primarily complying with Soviet desires. Czechoslovak archival sources confirm that the Soviets themselves proposed the inclusion of the supplement into the treaty at an early stage of Soviet-Czechoslovak negotiations, on March 29, 1935. They further strove for some other specific limitations of the treaty; for example, in case of a Czechoslovak intervention against the Anschluss with Austria, where they did not want to be involved. Former Czechoslovak ambassador to Moscow, Zdeněk Fierlinger, observed in his memoirs that the form of the treaty did agree with the interests of the USSR, which "would not be, at that time, in a position to bind themselves unilaterally [to help Czechoslovakia] without the participation of the other Power."[84] On the whole, the evidence is sufficiently strong to establish Soviet responsibility for the supplement. Later claims to the contrary obviously follow from politics, and not from historical truth.

[53]

The Franco-Soviet treaty of 1935 differed substantially from the pre–World War I alliance between the two countries. This difference largely followed from the fact that before 1914, both countries had common borders with Germany, and in the absence of an international agency similar to the League of Nations, the mechanism of the alliance was direct and automatic.[85]

Neither of the two alliances which Moscow contracted in 1935 was complemented by a military convention. The failure by both France and Czechoslovakia to conclude a military convention with Soviet Russia can be explained by a number of factors, some of which are discussed in detail in the proper context. In 1935 as well as in later years, however, the principal factor limiting the possibility of military coordination was the absence of a common border between the Soviet Union and Germany, or at least with the nearest ally, Czechoslovakia. Any intervention by the Soviet armed forces against Germany in case of conflict was therefore preconditioned by the consent of Poland or at least Rumania to the transfer of Red Army troops over their territories. Poland, for obvious reasons of geography and infrastructure, could of course matter more. No negotiated solution to this problem was found, and the Soviet government in fact did nothing to overcome this obstacle. This may well have been Barthou's main reason for insisting on the participation of Poland, and it also appears to have been the substance of Léger's reluctance to negotiate an alliance without first solving the problem of its essential practicability.[86]

It can therefore be concluded that when the Soviet leadership finally decided to contract the alliance with France—and that did not clearly occur before November 1934—the existence of the territorial barrier made the decision easier for Moscow than for her allies. The treaty met the main Soviet goals and concerns at that time: it secured the western flank at a moment of Japanese threat in the Far East; it blocked a French-German rapprochement and the Four-Power Pact (both highly improbable, but for the Soviets apparently feared possibilities); it averted the eventuality of a German-led combination in Central Europe, which in 1935 could not be entirely ruled out. The decision to join the Versailles camp, however, followed primarily from German implacability: the whole process of rapprochement with the West starts as an offshoot of the rupture with Germany.

Soviet perceptions can not of course be evidenced by quotations from stenographic records of the meetings of the Politburo and the like. Other available sources, however—including known Soviet official standpoints, interpretations, and also the tightly controlled press—seem to support a contemporary observation of Viscount Chilston, the British ambassador in Moscow, who characterized the Soviet decision to contract the French alliance as "to be designed to neutralize [Soviet] western front while engaged in the east." As for the reciprocal nature of the alliance, however, the British ambassador believed that the Soviet government "had no idea, really, of the Red Army ever marching, or the Red Air Force ever flying against Germany for the sake of France."[87] Soviet considerations, as already noted, were rather openly presented by Litvinov in his conversation with Eden toward the end of March 1935. It followed from the commissar's explanation that as long as Germany had planned an aggressive war against France, the Soviet government was not particularly concerned about it (in fact they even were helping to train Reichswehr officers for the job, and made it possible to develop the proper hardware on Soviet territory). Then, however, the situation changed, because the new chancellor apparently preferred a *Drang nach Osten* to the initial plan. That was what prompted the Soviet interest in a rapprochement with France.

George F. Kennan, then in Moscow, viewed the Soviet willingness to enter into pacts and to accept membership in the League of Nations as "the reflection of a desire . . . to assume that [the next] war would be fought by others and among others, that is, against each other, and above all to prevent any sort of peaceful settlement among Western powers."[88] The fact is that the assumptions that prompted Soviet interest in the French alliance soon proved to be unfounded. The edge of German expansion turned to Central Europe instead of the USSR, and with the Japanese invasion of China, the threat in the Far East became manageable. The need to show moderation in domestic affairs, practiced with some success in 1934 and 1935 as a show of qualification for membership in the democratic club, proved unnecessary; the Great Purges were launched, and efforts to reach an agreement with Germany were intensified. The Soviet foreign policy course adopted in 1934–35, still hanging over for the next four years, became largely meaningless, because it reflected a lack of options.

Thus the value of Soviet accession to the Versailles camp was determined by a set of interests and goals that offered only a temporary, conditional, and limited interest in that orientation. The next course of events was soon to prove it.

[3]

On the Access to Battlefields:
The Passage Problem

The alliances of May 1935, as already noted, were characterized by two significant weaknesses: the complicated mechanism of both pacts, and their geographical asymmetry.

The mechanism of the treaties did not in fact represent an insurmountable problem. Had all three countries been sufficiently interested in coming to each other's aid in the event of war, they would have found ways to meet the legal preconditions embodied in the treaties. But the geographical separation of the USSR from the presumed aggressor (Germany) by the territory of other states (Poland and Lithuania) could not be overcome by an interallied decision. The same applied to the territorial barrier separating the Soviet Union and Czechoslovakia, which involved Rumania in addition to Poland. The only legal solution to this problem could have been firm and clear agreements with the affected states on the conditions under which Soviet troops would be allowed to enter their territory. Such agreements, negotiated and signed by the Soviet government, would have had to give certain guarantees concerning, for example, noninterference in internal affairs and complete withdrawal of troops after the cessation of hostilities.

The main question raised by these flaws is therefore that of the Soviet attitude toward this problem, which constituted an apparently insurmountable handicap to an alliance that the Soviets had, after all, been striving to contract between December 1934 and May 1935 with a vigor strikingly absent in the previous negotiations for the Eastern Pact. It has already been noted that the scarcely veiled Soviet threat to return to the policy of Rapallo prompted Laval to sign the alliance disregarding its obvious structural defect.

In contrast to their allies, who assumed only a regularly negotiated framework for the passage of the Red Army through Poland (or Rumania), the Soviets initially viewed such an arrangement as an entirely unnecessary formality. The question came up, for example, during the visit of Czech foreign minister Beneš (later president of Czechoslovakia) to Moscow in May–June 1935. According to the Czech record of these conversations, Commissar for War Voroshilov stated that in case of Hitler's aggression against Czechoslovakia, the Red Army would march against Germany. The fall of Czechoslovakia, he added, would be followed by German advance against Rumania, the implication being that this would be definitely unacceptable from Moscow's point of view.

Beneš asked the commissar how he envisaged such an action in geographical terms: Did it mean the Soviet Army would march through the territory of others?

According to Beneš, Voroshilov replied, "Certainly. That is quite obvious, no matter whether there is an agreement or not." Beneš noted that the commissar spoke energetically and directly. The next day, Beneš asked Litvinov whether the Soviet government shared Voroshilov's opinion, and Litvinov "confirmed it categorically."[1]

The same frame of mind is reported by the British military attaché in Moscow in April 1936 who recorded the following conversation during an official lunch given for him by high-ranking Soviet commanders at the Frunze Academy:

> The question arose of the Franco-Soviet Pact, and the Corps Commissar stated that if Herr Hitler had not contented himself with occupying Rhineland, but had infringed French territory, the USSR would have come to the aid of France at once. I immediately asked him how it was proposed to do so, bearing in mind the territory intervening between the USSR and Germany. They all laughed and the Chief of Staff remarked: "You want to know what the General Staff's plans are." I said: "No, but I do see a difficulty," whereupon Corps Commissar Shchadenko amidst the laughter of all of them replied that Germany had found no difficulty in a similar situation in 1914 when she attacked France.[2]

This Soviet attitude was later subject to substantial changes, as will be shown. Nevertheless, Soviet lack of interest in negotiated arrangements for Red Army movements across the territory of Poland and, eventually, Lithuania and Rumania is obvious even at this early period which followed the signing of both treaties (May 1935) and their entry into force (February 1936). And given the historically justified distrust and suspicion both in Warsaw and Bucharest (not to mention

Kaunas) vis-á-vis their powerful eastern neighbor, this was an attitude least suited to facilitate a negotiated solution. Only a meaningful, persuasive Soviet initiative, following from the momentum of the Franco-Soviet Pact and coinciding with the period of relatively peaceful internal development in the USSR, might have brought positive results. But on the contrary, the Soviets passed the whole responsibility for the state of Soviet-Polish and Soviet-Rumanian relations, including the passage problem, on to France.

Of the countries whose consent to Red Army movements on their territories was the objective precondition for Soviet validation of the treaties of May 1935, Poland was the most important both in terms of geography and infrastructure. In the mid-1930s, Soviet-Polish relations were, on the surface at least, relatively relaxed. Both countries were bound by their nonaggression pact of 1932 which was, during Colonel Josef Beck's visit to Moscow in February 1934, extended until 1945, reducing to some extent Soviet fears of a German-Polish collusion.

Improvement of Polish relations with the USSR had in fact been a noteworthy tendency of Polish foreign policy since Józef Pilsudski's coup in 1926, and the nomination, in Patek, of an ambassador to Moscow who had before 1914 defended Russian revolutionaries in tsarist courts was a distinctive step in that direction. The fact that Warsaw decided to sign the nonaggression treaty with the USSR in January 1932 without waiting for an analogous Soviet pact with Rumania is attributable to the same concern. The Poles, of course, were fully aware of the anti-Polish aspects of the Soviet-German friendship practiced along the lines of the Rapallo policy, and tried to neutralize the threatening consequences of that combination both in Moscow and in Berlin. Efforts to retain their uncomfortable balance between both powerful neighbors was the principal factor of their maneuvering around the project of the Eastern Pact in 1934, to which they finally refused to adhere. Their decision ruined Barthou's obvious aim to put the "rear alliances" into a coherent shape by bringing Poland, Czechoslovakia, and the Soviet Union into one combination.

As Polish historian Roman Debicki explains the decision of Warsaw to stay out of the project after Germany's refusal became clear, without Germany being part of the grouping, "the introduction of preponderant Soviet influence into the East Central and Baltic areas of Europe" would become unavoidable, because "Russia's geographic position and power would make her dominant in deciding security problems in that area." He concludes:

If Poland joined, she would destroy the equilibrium established by her non-aggression arrangements [with Germany and the USSR], depriving herself of her relative freedom of action. The participation of Lithuania and Czechoslovakia, whose territories Poland had no special reason to guarantee, and the non-participation of Rumania, Poland's only ally in Eastern Europe, created additional difficulties.[3]

It would be irrelevant to judge which of these postulates were wise and which were not. No decision was easy. In the end, Warsaw ascribed more value to her nonaggression pacts with Germany and Soviet Russia than to her alliance with France and the possible extension of this alliance to Russia, the least trustworthy, in Polish eyes, of all countries involved. The fact is that, with the exception of Czechoslovakia, all Poland's neighbors had revisionist claims to some parts of her territory, and the nonaggression pacts with Germany and the USSR offered no more security than the refuted plan of the Eastern Pact. And in the absence of the guarantees that Barthou's project would provide, the concept of *Doch ist Polen nicht verloren* was, in the end, easier to be carried through.

The fact that Moscow took no initiative to ease Polish apprehensions in 1935 and the first half of 1936, and offered no clear guarantees that would facilitate some solution of the passage problem, is obviously one of the most important root causes of the final failure not just of the alliances of 1935, but of the whole collective security system. The maximum concession that the Poles appear to have been willing to make, under French pressure, in March 1936 (after the reoccupation of Rhineland), was their tentative consent to the eventual flights over Polish territory by Soviet airplanes in actions against Germany in case of war.[4] Laval, on behalf of the French government, appreciated this fact when stating that "Marshal Pilsudski and Colonel Beck remained persuaded that once the Soviet armies enter Poland, they will never leave again like the soldiers of Catharine II at the end of the 18th century."[5]

Marshal Rydz-Smigly conveyed the same opinion to the chief of the French General Staff: "Once the Bolsheviks penetrate the territory of Lithuania or Poland, they will never get out."[6] Neither the French nor the Czechs were able to dispel these fears, widespread in all countries bordering on Russia. Even friendly Soviet gestures in this period made statesmen and politicians in the area shiver. It may well be illustrated by the opinion of the Estonian minister of foreign affairs, Tofer, recorded in British diplomatic correspondence: "M. Tofer is especially perturbed by the friendly attitude which the Soviets are now showing his country and which, he fears, can bode no good. He is afraid that they will demand treaties of mutual military assistance from both Latvia and Estonia. . . . The danger of such a pact is obvious. In M. Tofer's words, 'Once they get into your country, they never get out.' ''[7]

These apprehensions, which in 1935 and 1936 might not have seemed quite justified, were tragically vindicated by the later experiences of all Russia's smaller neighbors. And the fact is that for a combination of reasons—to which Soviets' inactivity, especially in relation to Poland contributed—in the period most favorable for possible solution (1935 and the first half of 1936), no settlement of the passage problem between Moscow and Warsaw was either negotiated or found.

THE CASE OF RUMANIA

As a ground for massive Soviet military movements westward to engage Germany in case of a Franco-German war, Rumania was, for purely geographical reasons, of rather limited importance. Her territory could however serve as a substitute route for Soviet troops sent to join the Czechoslovak army in attacking Germany from the south in case of German aggression against France. In 1935 and 1936, such a possibility did not look improbable. The Rumanian passage was also important in case Germany attacked Czechoslovakia. Through Rumania, the Red Army could have come to strengthen the defenses of Czechoslovakia. This latter possibility became more apparent in 1937, with the rise of separatist tendencies among the Bohemian Germans and the obvious Nazi involvement in this affair. Consequently, Soviet access to the Czechoslovak border via Rumania grew in importance as time went on.

As regards the general capacity of this route, it is best to avoid various conflicting secondary opinions and to accept as more realistic the assessment of the General Staff of the Rumanian army, which was years later essentially confirmed by the chief of the General Staff of the Czechoslovak army during the prewar years, General Ludvík Krejčí.[8] The length of the railway which ran across the Rumanian territory between the Soviet and Czechoslovak border, from Chotin to Negresti, was 473 kilometers (circa 295 miles). Most of this railway was a one-track railroad of mediocre quality, but some improvement was made in 1937 and 1938, financed by Czechoslovakia.[9] A train, going a safe speed of 25 kilometers per hour, would cover this route in nineteen hours, which would permit the transfer of quite substantial forces into eastern Czechoslovakia (Ruthenia). In the latter country, a modern railway system would have provided means for further transportation westward. If an air corridor were also opened, and both routes were then available to the Soviets, a force of 250,000–350,000 men with equipment could be moved through in twelve days.[10] This, of course, would have decisively reduced German supremacy over the Czechoslovak army and, if nothing else, facilitate the stabilization of the planned defensive line in Moravia. One of the most important results of this variant would of course be the neutralization of Poland and Hungary. Czechoslovak borders against both these countries would be secured.

The availability of this route, as it appeared at the time when the treaties between France, Soviet Russia, and Czechoslovakia were contracted, depended upon a satisfactory regulation of Soviet-Rumanian relations. The chief obstacle to such a normalization was a dispute over the eastern part of historical Moldavia between the Prut and Dniester rivers, called Bessarabia (probably after a Wallachian princely family of Bassarabs, who had ruled this land before it was conquered by the Ottoman Turks in the early sixteenth century). Before the first Russian annexation of Bessarabia in 1812, the country had been part of Moldavia, a semiautonomous principality under the sovereignty of the Porte. Returned to Moldavia after the Crimean War, Bessarabia was reannexed by Russia in 1878, and the new conquest was confirmed by an agreement of the great powers at the Congress of Berlin. Newly formed Rumania, which vainly resisted the loss of one-half of one of its two historical lands, was compensated by the Dobrudja at the expense of the Ottomans or, respectively, Bulgaria.

In 1918, Rumania took advantage of the situation created by the Bolshevik revolution and by the temporary secession of the Ukraine from Russia, and established its authority over Bessarabia, where the Moldavians (Rumanians) still comprised the strongest ethnic element—48 percent according to Russian statistics and 78 percent according to Rumanian sources. Neither source, however, put the proportion of the Slavic population of Bessarabia at that time above 28 percent.[11]

The loss of Bessarabia annoyed equally the White Russian émigrés and the Bolsheviks; the latter showed in fact less willingness to accept it than any other territorial reduction of the old empire. The three Baltic provinces were initially, in December 1918, recognized by Moscow at least as independent Soviet republics; the Russo-Polish territorial problems were formally settled by the Treaty of Riga; the

[61]

independence of Finland was recognized. Bessarabia, on the other hand, was never disclaimed by Moscow—in spite of the fact that at the moment of its takeover by Rumania, Bessarabia was independent by an act of its population, and not a part of Soviet Russia. Soviet doctrine of national self-determination simply did not apply to this clearly non-Russian and non-Slavic land. Soviet claims to Bessarabia brought Rumania into the defensive alliance with Poland in 1921 and remained the stumbling block to reasonable improvement of the relations between both countries even after the normalization of their diplomatic relations in 1934.

Moreover, Soviet behavior toward Rumania during the interwar period was characterized by a strange arrogance that was not, on the surface at least, directed toward other governments then administering "lost provinces" of the Russian Empire. A contemporary Rumanian historian, I. M. Oprea, lists numerous early attempts by Bucharest to regularize relations with Soviet Russia: propositions made by Alexandru Vaida in Copenhagen in 1920, by representatives of Averescu's government in Warsaw in 1921, by Diamandi in Genoa in 1922, by I. G. Duca in Geneva in 1923, and so forth.[12] Without exception, all Rumanian approaches were rebuffed.

To make their intentions very clear, in 1924 the Soviets established a miniature "Autonomous Soviet Socialist Republic of Moldavia" along the eastern banks of the Dniester, which "provided a nucleus of which Bessarabia could be regarded as an irredenta."[13] Louis Fischer, who extensively interviewed several Soviet officials on the problem—including Kh. G. Rakovsky, then (1928) in banishment in Saratov—claims that only Trotsky and Litvinov were able to reconcile themselves to the eventual loss of Bessarabia as the price for a settlement with Rumania. Stalin, Voroshilov, G. V. Chicherin, M. V. Frunze, and Rakovsky himself were strongly opposed. It was Stalin's opinion that prevailed, of course, and in line with the pro-German view of the post-Versailles world, Bessarabia was soon called in Moscow "the Alsace on the Dniester."[14] And so was the issue treated by official Soviet foreign policy. The Soviet government lodged a strong protest against the conclusion of the Franco-Rumanian alliance of June 1926, declaring that the treaty sanctioned "the present territorial status quo [that] allows it [Rumania] to continue the illegal and forcible occupation of Bessarabia," a territory "belonging to the USSR." The note further stated that the Soviet Union "has never consented and will never consent to regard as legal the occupation of Bessarabia or its annexation by Rumania."[15]

In only one instance, in the summer of 1927, obviously under the combined impact of the tensions with England and France and the internal political crisis, is Stalin reported to have contemplated concessions to Rumania. Grigory Bessedovsky, a high-ranking Soviet diplomat who was reassigned from Harbin to Paris, recalls being summoned to Stalin during a stopover in Moscow. Stalin, worried by the tensions especially with France, thought that he could defuse the situation by an improvement of relations with Rumania. "Give them Bessarabia as a bait," Stalin said; but he also insisted on handling all contacts in great secrecy, so that "our opposition within the Party [does not] get hold of it."

When Bessedovsky's ensuing negotiations with Klimas, the Lithuanian envoy in Paris, whom he chose to mediate with the Rumanians, were intercepted by the GPU, Stalin immediately ordered Bessedovsky to discontinue any further dealings, allegedly "in fear of losing the support of the Ukrainians in the struggle with the Opposition."[16]

The question of Bessarabia also came up in 1929, in connection with the Litvinov Protocol. Here, for the first time, the problem was discussed between Titulescu, then Rumanian ambassador to London, and Litvinov, who tried to win Rumania's support for his project. However anxious Litvinov was to secure the participation of Rumania (which in turn would help him to win the signature of Poland), the commissar's readiness to make any concessions on Bessarabia was very limited. Asked by Titulescu to state clearly the Soviet attitude toward the territorial integrity of Rumania, Litvinov said only that "although Russia's claims in Bessarabia are valid. . . . Russia would not press her claims in any way." Titulescu accepted this formula when Litvinov refused to go further.[17]

The course, and the failure, of Soviet-Rumanian negotiations on the nonaggression treaty between summer 1931 and October 1932 are described by Oprea. His account, however guarded because of the delicacy of the issue in the Socialist Republic of Romania, is nevertheless based on unique primary sources, and gives a sufficient idea about the whole undertaking:

> As early as the initial phase of the negotiations held in Riga, one could notice essential differences of views between the two delegations. In order to smooth the way for negotiations and to bring about the conclusion of the non-aggression pact, Romania's delegation, led by M. Sturdza, considered it a *sine qua non* condition to exclude from the treaty any mention concerning the existence of a litigation between the two states.[18]

Without specifying the actual Soviet position (the name Bessarabia is

[63]

in fact never mentioned) or the litigious issue the Rumanians did not want to have on the record, Oprea says that "the very first confrontations showed that the viewpoints of the two delegations could not be harmonized" and that "direct negotiations were suspended [with] no term for their resumption specified."[19] The problem certainly was not that of the format of the treaty, because according to diplomatic reports from Bucharest, Rumania did not press for one collective pact for all Soviet neighbors, but accepted the bilateral arrangement quite early, probably on French advice.[20]

Another round of these negotiations, in January 1932, also failed to bring any progress, because the Rumanians again asked for explicit guarantees of their territorial integrity, at least in line with the preamble and the conclusion of an analogous Polish-Soviet pact.[21]

Claims that a Soviet concession on this matter was possible during the last round of these talks, held in Geneva in October 1932, are not substantiated.[22] W. E. Scott's suggestion that these negotiations, assisted by Herriot and Colonel Beck, then attending the Disarmament Conference, were spoiled by a "bizzare affair" in Rumanian politics is inaccurate.[23] Herriot, whose cabinet had come to office in June, was of course less disposed than André Tardieu to sacrifice the French nonaggression pact with Russia for the sake of an "unknown country" (to borrow a later term from Neville Chamberlain); he was certainly also prompted to conclude that pact by the Deuxième Bureau reports about the nature and extent of secret German rearmament. Under these circumstances, Titulescu appears to have been afraid that Rumanian negotiators in Geneva might yield to French pressure and sign the pact with Russia without obtaining the crucial guarantee of Rumanian territorial integrity.

That was the real background of the "bizzare affair"—Titulescu's resignation—which resulted in a governmental reorganization in Bucharest. Titulescu himself, ironically the most consistent advocate of Soviet-Rumanian understanding among the interwar Rumanian politicians, was appointed minister of foreign affairs. In two parliamentary speeches, one November 3 and 25, Titulescu explained that the problem was not whether Rumania should or should not have a nonaggression treaty with the USSR, but that such a treaty could only make sense if it contained the essential pledge of both sides to recognize and to respect their territorial integrity.[24] After all, the Soviets even refused, in November 1932, to make the problem of Bessarabia an object of international arbitration—not surprising after the blows the Rumanian case suffered by the desertion of Poland and France, who did not wait for the Soviet-Rumanian settlement and signed their own nonaggression pacts with Russia in July and November 1932 respectively. In short, nothing shows that at any point of these negotiations between July 1931 and September 1932 the Soviets professed their willingness to sign with Rumania a pact similar to those signed with other countries, and no one can seriously blame the Rumanian government for striving for the same guarantees that were not missing in other contemporary treaties of nonaggression.

Titulescu was not discouraged by the failure of previous initiatives to reach a satisfactory agreement with the Russians. Unable to enlist further French assistance in Geneva immediately after his assumption of the office of foreign minister, he turned to the Czechoslovak foreign minister Beneš, an old acquaintance, known to have established good personal relations with a number of Soviet representatives abroad. Beneš's attempts to solve a problem in which his own country was vitally interested, however, brought no results. Beneš discussed the problem first with the Soviet *polpred* (envoy) to Prague, Arosev, and then with the Soviet ambassador in Paris, Dovgalevsky. Czechoslovak archives record Dovgalevsky's answer to Beneš's inquiry, dated March 18, 1933, which stated (in point 3): "Litvinov believes that this moment is not appropriate for the solution of the substance of controversial [Soviet-Rumanian] problems, particularly Bessarabia."[25] It is not without interest that this Soviet position was dated almost six weeks after the presentation of the Soviet draft of the Definition of Aggression, and in a situation generally marked by Hitler's rise to power in Germany. But circumstances aside, Dovgalevsky's reply thwarted Beneš's idea to settle the Soviet-Rumanian dispute by way of a collective nonaggression treaty between the Little Entente and Soviet Russia; it was unthinkable, of course, to leave the statement of recognition and respect for all countries' territorial integrity out of any document of its type.

Titulescu immediately recognized the possibilities of the Definition of Aggression for the Rumanian interests, and he specifically turned his attention to point 2 of the Soviet draft, which defined, as one of the instances of aggression, "the invasion of the territory of another State by armed forces, even without a declaration of war."[26] Titulescu's idea was to supplement this article of the Soviet draft by a clear formula defining the "territory against which aggression should not take place," and he soon submitted a formal proposal to that effect which stated that the territory in question was "the land over which a state actually exerts its authority."[27] Supported by Beneš and the Greek foreign minister, N. Politis, Titulescu achieved the inclusion of his supplement into the draft. In this form—together with other changes adopted in Geneva—the definition was signed by the participants of the Convention for the Definition of Aggression in July 1933, including Rumania. In a conversation with the British ambassador to Bucharest in April 1933, Titulescu made clear his opinion that the definition, in its final version, "should cover the case of Bessarabia."[28] He added, nevertheless, that "there could be no question of an exchange of diplomatic representatives between Bucharest and Moscow until the Soviet government formally acquiesced in Rumania's possession of Bessarabia."[29]

Before he signed the convention, Titulescu was in fact looking for more explicit Soviet assurances regarding the territorial integrity of his country. After several conferences with Litvinov, however, all that Titulescu was able to extract from the Soviet commissar was a verbal gentlemen's agreement, defined by Rumanian sources as "an application of the Convention for the Definition of Aggression onto the sphere of Rumanian-Soviet relations."[30] It is described in these terms:

> Titulescu and Litvinov mutually pledged on behalf of the governments which they represented to adopt, and to keep up in their diplomatic relations, whatever the circumstances, such an attitude as should in no way permit Rumanian-Soviet disputes to be discussed again. In order to render the gentlemen's agreement permanent, the Soviet representative set a sole condition: the strict maintenance of the Rumanian foreign policy along the same line of orientation existing at the moment when this agreement was concluded—a condition which the Rumanian state observed, in spite of many difficulties and vacillations, as long as the internal and international conditions favored that orientation.[31]

The claim of a contemporary Rumanian interpreter of the prewar relations of his country with the USSR, that Bucharest observed the obligations assumed by her foreign minister "as long as conditions favored them," is as resolute as the circumstances allow. It has a special meaning; Bucharest certainly was willing to pay that price for the security of her Dniester frontier, and the Soviet attempts to justify the one-sided renunciation of the agreement a few years later were unfounded.

Another turn in the development of the problem occurred in spring 1934, when Beneš, in line with the general agreement between Barthou and Litvinov on the Eastern Pact (May 18), launched his diplomatic operation aimed at timely normalization of diplomatic relations between the three member-states of the Little Entente and the

USSR.[32] Yugoslavia's response was still negative, but Rumania, together with Czechoslovakia, exchanged full de jure recognition with Moscow in June 1934. During his negotiations with Litvinov on this question, Titulescu again vainly tried to obtain an unequivocal Soviet recognition of the territorial integrity of Rumania. A new compromise formula agreed upon stated only that both countries respected their full sovereignty.[33] According to Rumanian archival sources, however, it was on this occasion that Titulescu, for the first time, suggested the possibility of a Soviet-Rumanian alliance—another of his many variants of how to arrive at a settlement with the Russians. Litvinov's reaction to the Rumanian proposition at this early stage is not recorded in the available sources, but Oprea quotes the foreign commissar's negative reply, a year later:

> The Soviet foreign minister alleged the lack of real reciprocity determined not only by the relatively unimportant contribution which Rumania would have made if the Soviet Union had become victim of aggression, but also by the geographical situation in consequence of which, as Rumania was always the first to form the object of a German attack, it was on the Soviet Union that the obligation to grant assistance devolved first.[34]

This flat Soviet refusal of an offer to complement the recently concluded treaties with France and Czechoslovakia by an agreement with one of the two countries whose territory separated the USSR from the operational area of the new alliances deserves attention, primarily because of its timing: dated December 25, 1935, it shows a considerable early lack of interest in a course of action that would significantly facilitate the solution of the geographical asymmetry of the alliances with France and Czechoslovakia. A Soviet-Rumanian settlement, in addition to its own practical consequences, could also have positively affected the attitude of Poland, an ally of Rumania.

The coincidence with certain trends in Soviet-German relations following the credit agreement of April 1935 (see chapter 5) is a matter that cannot be overlooked: diplomatic correspondence in these months was burdened with no greater problem than reports and speculations based on expectations of an anticipated Soviet-German rapprochement. Soviet attitudes toward the Rumanian offer of alliance, however, warrant attention primarily in the light of parallel Soviet demarches in Paris concerning the Franco-Soviet military convention. The new Soviet ambassador in Paris, V. P. Potemkin, was busy in the summer of 1935 lobbying for this convention,[35] in spite of the fact that the Franco-Soviet pact had not yet been ratified by the French parliament (see note 36). In August 1935, Moscow also urged the Czechs to intervene in Paris for the same purpose.[36] At the same time, however, Soviet diplomacy was also busy ruining the prospects of an entente with Rumania that could, considering the impact it might have on Soviet-Polish relations, provide the key to the geographical problem of the alliance system that the USSR had contracted only a few months earlier.

As already noted, the question of the Soviet access to potential battlefields in case of German aggression against France or Czechoslovakia was discussed on several recorded occasions in 1935, especially during President Beneš's visit to Moscow. Unconcealed Soviet disregard for regularly agreed arrangements for the eventual movements of the Red Army over foreign (Polish, Lithuanian, or Rumanian) territories could not escape Rumanian attention, and it provided an argument for Titulescu as early as May 1935, when he asked King Carol for a mandate to negotiate an alliance with Moscow. According to the well-informed Czechoslovak ambassador to Bucharest, Jan Šeba, Titulescu cautioned the Rumanian monarch—the ultimate constitutional authority in prewar Rumania in matters of foreign policy and national security—that in case of a conflict in Central Europe, Soviet troops would go through Rumania anyway, no matter whether Bucharest would agree or oppose [it]; exactly in view of that, it would be highly advantageous for Rumania to reach an agreement with the Soviet Union to find a proper formulae of affiliation with the pact between Moscow, Paris and Prague, and to get something in exchange for that from Moscow."[37] To overcome the reluctance of the court and of the majority of Prime Minister Tatarescu's government to agree to such an enterprise, Titulescu had to rely heavily on French support and especially on the tireless efforts of Beneš, who had himself been cold-shouldered in Moscow in June when he had offered to mediate between Russia and Rumania to speed up the entente between the two countries.

Titulescu finally got his mandate in August 1935, and opened his talks with Litvinov in Geneva in September, hoping that "within the mutual assistance, the Soviet Union would guarantee the national independence of Rumania and of her allies." Titulescu also intended to achieve a treaty that would be directly aimed not at one country, but rather against any possible aggressor.[38] He also sought "to ensure that Soviet troops proceeding to Czechoslovakia in fullfilment of the engagements arising from the Czechoslovak-Soviet pact should be confined to a single route through Rumania,"[39] and that "after the cessation of hostilities, they [the Soviet troops] would withdraw behind the Dniester''[40]—a very sensible part of the project.

Along these lines, Titulescu drafted a proposal of the Soviet-Rumanian treaty of alliance, which he presented to Litvinov in Geneva in the first half of October. According to diplomatic reports, the ensuing short negotiations centered around three principal questions:

(1). A Soviet demand, formulated in the course of discussions on the Rumanian draft, according to which Rumania would be obliged to render military assistance to the Soviet Union against Poland;

(2). A Rumanian demand, the factual *conditio sine qua non* of Bucharest in the whole undertaking, that Moscow explicitly guarantee the territorial integrity of the Rumanian state.

(3). A Rumanian proposal that the Soviet Union render assistance against Bulgaria, and especially against Hungary in case of the latter country's participation in German aggression against Czechoslovakia.[41]

Litvinov refused points 2 and 3, and Titulescu could not accept point 1, because Rumania had a valid alliance treaty with Poland—something that the commissar of course had to know fairly well in the first place. In the European diplomatic world, busy as it was with the affair of Ethiopia, expectations were very high in the early autumn of 1935, especially when it became known that both sides already agreed that Titulescu would go to Moscow to sign the pact between October 25 and 29. A compromise was probably found in the form of a secret clause, according to which Rumania would simply not oppose the passage of Soviet troops in case of a German aggression against Czechoslovakia.[42] Then, on October 24, Litvinov made a surprise public statement in which he declared that his talks with Titulescu had failed because of disagreement on Bessarabia (which was true), and also because of the alleged Rumanian refusal to permit the passage of Soviet troops to Czechoslovakia (which was false). The Soviet government, said Litvinov, considered the whole pact irrelevant.[43]

Titulescu's mandate to negotiate an alliance treaty with the Soviets was not, according to Oprea, revoked after the setback that the Rumanian foreign minister suffered in Geneva in October 1935. On the contrary, this mandate remained in force for almost another year, and after January 1936—in the context of the coming ratification of the Franco-Soviet pact by the French parliament—Titulescu pursued the issue with a new vigor.[44] In a new offer communicated to Moscow in February 1936, following an exchange of views with Litvinov in January, Titulescu emphasized the primary necessity to reach an agreement on the question of the passage of Soviet troops, as well as the importance of the Soviet pledge that the Red Army would be withdrawn from Rumania after the accomplishment of its mission in Central Europe.[45]

Litvinov's answer to this Rumanian proposal was particularly arrogant. The Red Army was able to march through Rumania even against the will of Bucharest, he declared, because the Rumanian army was unable to offer any resistance.[46] The Soviet foreign ministry even conveyed this response to Prague through diplomatic channels. The Czech foreign minister, Kamil Krofta, confidentially informed the French ambassador to Prague, Victor De Lacroix, on April 15, 1936, that "the USSR made known to Prague that in case of an attack on Czechoslovakia, the Russian Army would come to help through Rumania with or without the consent of the cabinet in Bucharest. M. Krofta knows that M. Titulescu is aware of this [Soviet] intention and that is one of the reasons which urge him to sign a pact of alliance with Russia."[47] The Soviet attitude toward Rumania could not fail to be duly noted in Warsaw, where its effect is not difficult to guess.

The fact that Titulescu was still not discouraged even after this rare exercise of diplomatic tact testifies to the good will and perseverance with which he tried to keep his country in the pro-French camp, and to ensure for Rumania a safe, negotiated status in the uneasy system of alliances. He was willing to overlook another Soviet offense that occurred at the time of the Conference on the Straits in Montreux (June–July 1936), when Soviet officials at a Soviet exposition in Paris exhibited a map of the Soviet Union showing Bessarabia as a part of the USSR. This act, which drew a protest from the Rumanian Embassy in Paris, further weakened the case of those in Bucharest who, like Titulescu himself, believed that it was possible to arrive at a decent agreement with the Russians.[48]

Continuing Soviet sabotage of a settlement with Rumania was by that time causing understandable concern in Paris as well as in Prague. At the conference of the Little Entente in Bucharest on June 6–7, 1936, Czechoslovakia proposed, "in agreement with Paris,"[49] a restructuring of the grouping into a general trilateral alliance. After his return from Bucharest, Beneš informed Ambassador De Lacroix that "it was agreed that from now on, the three states would act collectively as far as the negotiations with the three neighboring powers are concerned. There will be no more tête-a-tête which would get Czechoslovakia into an inferior situation vis-à-vis Germany, Yugoslavia vis-à-vis Italy, Rumania vis-à-vis Russia."[50]

Beneš's account was too optimistic, but the prospect nevertheless displeased the Soviet ambassador in Bucharest, Ostrovsky, who did not hide his very negative view of the conference of the Little Entente. His French colleague, Ambassador d'Ormesson, reported Ostrovsky's comment on the state of Soviet-Rumanian negotiations: "It is nothing urgent. Soviet Russia absolutely does not need this convention."[51]

Titulescu was obviously more realistic than Beneš in his assessment of the prospects of the Little Entente. When he arrived at the Montreux Conference, he was determined to try once more to reach a direct agreement with Litvinov. International tensions were rising. It was a few months after the reoccupation of Rhineland; Ethiopia had been all but strangled and the Spanish Civil War was just about to break out. Not unimpressed by Litvinov's great oratory in Geneva in defense of Ethiopia and of collective security, Titulescu may have thought that Moscow might now be more inclined to consider Rumanian offers.* He was, however, not overly optimistic. A few days before his trip to Montreux, he complained to d'Ormesson about the Soviet attitude toward Rumania, expressing the opinion that the Russians had already wasted the opportunity to sign an alliance treaty with Rumania at the most promising moment, in the summer of 1935.[52]

Before these new, and last, negotiations with Litvinov, Titulescu obtained the renewal of his mandate, and reassured the Soviet foreign commissar during their first meeting that "Rumania continued to remain a firm advocate of her traditional orientation toward the French policy." At the same time, he told Litvinov that maintaining friendly relations with the Soviet Union was a genuine commandment of the Rumanian foreign policy."[53] According to Rumanian sources, these negotiations proceeded quite well and in July in Lausanne,* both men reached a general agreement on the text of the pact.[54] Paul-Boncour, who attended the Montreux Conference, is also of the opinion that this round of Soviet-Rumanian talks was "most hopeful" and that "the framework of a treaty was agreed upon."[55]

The essential Soviet pledge demanded by Rumania was to evacuate the Red Army beyond the Dniester, a formula that left out the word "Bessarabia" and won the consent of King Carol and the conseil privé

---

*It is impossible to disregard, in this context, the impression caused abroad by the internal development in the USSR. The Great Purges were already in motion and the show trial with Zinovev and Kamenev was under preparation exactly at the time of the conference in Montreux. Nevertheless, the full impact of the Great Purges fell upon foreign policy considerations abroad some ten months later. This problem will be discussed in Chapter 6.

*More probably Montreux. Oprea places the Strait Conference in Lausanne.

de cabinet, the supreme council of the state, on July 14, 1936.[56] Titulescu nevertheless seems to have insisted upon some more explicit formulation in respect to the Rumanian territorial integrity, which was interpreted by Litvinov as a demand of "formal abandonment of Bessarabia," something that the commissar termed "unnecessary and impractical."[57]

It is not clear which, if any, of the other problematic issues were left out of this agreement in the expectation that they could be solved by the eventual reorganization of the Little Entente, and by its projected collective alliance with France.[58] Agreement on a draft seems nevertheless beyond doubt. Before the end of the conference, however, Litvinov asked for a postponement of the signature of the treaty until September.[59] The foreign commissar also suggested that instead of sending the draft to Bucharest, Titulescu should submit it to King Carol in person. Titulescu agreed, but before he returned to Rumania, he lost his cabinet post in a reorganization of the government on August 29, 1936,[60] retaining his position as the Rumanian permanent envoy at the League of Nations.

Izvestiya's commentary on Titulescu's fall reads like an obituary. Certain qualities of the man were recognized, rather belatedly.[61] Litvinov, on the other hand, returned from Moscow to Geneva to inform Titulescu that their recent agreement "was no longer valid."[62]

In late summer of 1936, forces unfriendly toward the idea of a Soviet-Rumanian alliance were undoubtedly gaining momentum in Bucharest. It is, however, equally correct to observe that "complicated Soviet intrigues unquestionably contributed to [Titulescu's] downfall,"[63] and that, had the Soviets had sincere interest in a settlement with Rumania, they had had plenty of time to achieve one much earlier. Litvinov certainly wasted no time in affirming the failure of the negotiations, and quickly renounced the 1933 "gentlemen's agreement." In fact he did so twice—in October 1936, in a conversation with Prime Minister Tatarescu; and eight months later at his last known encounter with Titulescu, in Talloires, a small town near Geneva.[64]

Even after Titulescu's withdrawal from the office of foreign minister, Rumania did not lose interest in some arrangement with Moscow. The new foreign minister, Antonescu, had a different, modest approach, understandable after all that had happened to his predecessor's initiatives. In a conference with Litvinov in Geneva on May 28, 1937, Ion Antonescu revived the old project of a simple nonaggression pact between the two countries, similar to a treaty recently concluded between Yugoslavia and Italy. Recognition of both countries' territorial integrity was, of course, part of the proposition. Foreign Minister Krofta of Czechoslovakia and the French delegate to the League of Nations, Paul-Boncour, both pleaded with Litvinov to accept at least this modest settlement, but once more the commissar refused.[65]

Archival documents in the first half of 1937 reveal a marked change in the Soviet attitude toward the problem of passage. As we have seen, in the 1935–36 period Soviet representatives, including Voroshilov, on a number of occasions, professed a rather lighthearted attitude toward the problem of the territorial barrier between the Soviet Union and the areas the Red Army would have to reach in case of German aggression against France or Czechoslovakia. By February 1937, however, Soviet diplomacy recognized the intervening foreign territories as an obstacle; indeed, as an insurmountable obstacle. On February 17, 1937, Soviet ambassador Potemkin visited French prime minister Léon Blum to communicate the Soviet answer to a previous inquiry of the French General Staff concerning the forms and scope of the Soviet assistance to France and Czechoslovakia in case of German aggression. Point 1 of the Soviet reply was affirmative for the hypothetical possibility of Polish and Rumanian consent to the movements of the Red Army through their territories, despite the lack of any specific agreements on that matter. Point 2 was more relevant: "If, for incomprehensible reasons, Poland and Rumania would oppose rendering assistance by the USSR to France and to Czechoslovakia, and if they would not permit transfer of Soviet troops through their territories, in that case the assistance of the USSR will be inevitably limited."[66]

Asked whether the Soviet government had considered the possibility of the passage of Soviet troops through Lithuania via East Prussia, Potemkin again replied in the new line of argumentation: "The passage through states friendly toward France has been counted on. If there are any other hypotheses possible, it is up to France, in agreement with the USSR, to prepare them."[67]

This statement was tantamount to the announcement of a new doctrine. From that point on, until September 1939, the Soviet government would officially rule out any possibility of a Red Army move westward without the explicit consent of the countries in question. France (or to some extent Czechoslovakia, in case of the Rumanian route) would be solely responsible for ensuring the arrangements. To send the Red Army across the Rumanian or Polish border would now "look like aggression."[68]

By taking this position, the Soviets showed even more clearly their indifference to a solution of the passage problem: neither France nor

Czechoslovakia could negotiate an arrangement that was so obviously outside their jurisdiction. The conditions of passage could be agreed upon only by countries directly involved, that is, the Soviet Union, Poland, and Rumania. The most France and Czechoslovakia could do—and both countries did it repeatedly between 1935 and 1938—was to use their influence in Moscow, Warsaw, and Bucharest in tireless efforts to keep the problem on the diplomatic agenda. France, for instance, did not quite give up the possibility of a Polish-Soviet settlement of the problem of passage before December 1937, and more probably April 1938; the French Embassy in Bucharest was reported to have pressed for Rumanian concessions as late as mid-September 1938.[69] Czechoslovakia's actions also sharply contrast with those of the Soviet Union. Assuming that under the circumstances presumed by the pacts of 1935 Rumania would, in the end, consent to the transfer of Soviet troops to Czechoslovakia, Prague intensified its financial support for the improvement of the railroad system in Bukovina. The general hypothesis proved correct,[70] but because of mismanagement and misuse of funds (not unusual in the Balkans) the construction of the second track of the railroad from Vatra Dormei to Vizaul proceeded too slowly. However, the fact that Rumania agreed to the improvement of this railroad connecting western Ukraine with Ruthenia (then part of Czechoslovakia) can be taken as a clear indication of the Rumanian attitude at a time when Germany tried hard to lure Bucharest away from the French camp.

It is characteristic of Soviet behavior that even in mid-1938 Moscow did not refrain from acts that were bound to deepen Rumanian apprehensions concerning the possibility of the entry of the Red Army into their country. On June 7, 1938—amidst an unending flow of news from the USSR about executions and mass deportations—the Soviet government announced that the Rumanian minority living in the USSR on the eastern banks of the Dniester, the only group of Soviet population speaking a Romance language, "voluntarily decided" to adopt the Russian *azbuka* instead of the Latin alphabet.[71] In July, according to Georges Bonnet, "Rumanian sources pointed to explicit and repeated declarations of Soviet representatives in Bucharest to the effect that Moscow's claims to Bessarabia are valid and will never be surrendered."[72]

There appear to be certain discrepancies in King Carol's position on the question of passage in 1937,[73] but during the crucial period in 1938, "Rumania held well," to use Paul-Boncour's words.[74] A hitherto unpublished Rumanian official note transmitted to the Soviets on

September 24, 1938, supplies pieces of information up to now missing both to the story of passage and to the story of Munich. According to this document, the question of Red Army passage through Rumania was discussed between N. P. Comnène, the Rumanian minister of foreign affairs, and Litvinov in Geneva between September 9 and 13. By the 13th, Moscow awaited only formal Rumanian approval of the agreement. According to the note of September 24, the Rumanian government, King Carol, and the Rumanian General Staff decided to open the Rumanian territory, in case of German aggression against Czechoslovakia, for the transfer of Soviet troops through Bukovina (including the aerial route).

It can be assumed that even at this high point of the drama of collective security, Comnène had not been any more successful than Titulescu in obtaining Soviet guarantees regarding the Rumanian territorial integrity, because the Rumanian decision to permit the passage of Soviet troops explicitly renounced "all conditions and Soviet guarantees."[75] Considering the risks involved, the Rumanian decision was a remarkable act of international responsibility.

It was obviously at Rumanian initiative that the question was taken up on the Soviet-Rumanian agenda on September 9, because during earlier exchanges with Litvinov held both by Dianou, the Rumanian ambassador to Moscow, and Foreign Minister Comnène in Geneva, the foreign commissar did not touch upon the possibility of passage at all, confining himself to general problems of international tensions.[76] The fact that her government explicitly renounced Rumania's well-deserved traditional guarantees of territorial integrity testifies to Soviet reluctance to make, even in September 1938, the elementary concessions that had burdened the Soviet-Rumanian relations since 1919. Accessible sources indicate that Moscow made no effort to open negotiations on the basis of the Rumanian offer. The preliminary Soviet answer of September 25 did not touch upon any practical aspects of the Rumanian initiative. Published Soviet sources say nothing at all about the case, and German and Polish intelligence reports reveal no relevant movements of Soviet armed forces in the western military sectors of the USSR in September 1938.[77]

The conclusions that the story of passage makes rather apparent have ultimately to be seen in the broader context of other issues and developments, some of which have already been very thoroughly researched (such as, for example, French and British policy of appeasement). Some, on the other hand, have still not been evaluated in any depth, such as the impact of Soviet internal factors upon the fate of collective security; and others still leave substantial room for reevaluation (e.g., the German factor in the Soviet foreign policy consideration in the 1935–38 period). One can nevertheless say that within the scope of the concept of collective security, the ability and willingness to establish neighborly relations based on mutual trust and respect were the fundamental criteria of each European country's international behavior. Between 1934 and 1938, Soviet Russia failed to establish such relations with any of her European neighbors, and it would not be difficult to prove the same about her neighbors in Asia, even those with which her relations were then most of the time relatively relaxed (Afghanistan, Persia, Turkey). The prevailing feelings of neighboring states toward the Soviet Union were mistrust and fear, and internal events in the USSR, especially in the second half of 1930s, continued to feed these apprehensions.

A step-by-step examination of the passage problem does not support the assumption that Moscow's increasingly detached attitude toward the alliances with France and Czechoslovakia after the early months of 1937 resulted from the French failure to oppose the German march into the Rhineland a year before, as well as other professions of the policy of appeasement. Chances to regularize Soviet relations with Poland and Rumania had been systematically sabotaged well before March 1936, and that cannot be simply explained by Soviet disappointment with their ally's performance in defense of the Versailles system. In fact, the recent entry into the League of Nations and the assumption of the obligations following from the covenant should have prompted the Soviets to adopt a more conciliatory policy especially toward Rumania, where Soviet insistence on the "right" of annexation of a clearly non-Russian, non-Slavic people had no place in the international system to which the USSR had adhered. The obvious absence of such a policy even after the conclusion of the alliances with France and Czechoslovakia, therefore, hardly indicates a serious intention to stand by the obligations assumed both in September 1934 and in May 1935. The initial gestures of readiness for enforced passage (a posture abandoned two years later) testifies to a very early disregard for the Covenant, and accurately illustrates Soviet attitude toward negotiated settlements of this problem. This attitude, so clearly demonstrated in the long story of the efforts of Rumania to obtain Soviet recognition of her territorial integrity, could not fail to further corroborate the known distrust of Soviet Russia in Poland, whose territory was the real key to a full solution of the passage problem.

It can therefore be concluded that the Soviet Union was substantially responsible for the failure to overcome the geographical handicap of the alliances of May 1935, of which the Franco-Soviet pact could otherwise be considered, in many respects, the backbone of the whole collective security system in Europe between 1935 and 1938.

[4]

The Comintern and the Short Life of the United Front

For reasons that follow from the organization's specific status and structure, the activities of the Comintern, as an instrument of the Soviet foreign policy, in the 1934–38 period require separate examination. A comparison of the genesis of its "United Front" political line (promulgated in summer 1935) with the gradual adoption of the new orientation of Soviet foreign policy in 1934 and 1935 may help to clarify the circumstances under which the Soviet Union adhered to the Versailles camp.

The activities of the Comintern and of its national sections cannot, of course, be examined on the basis of such primary sources as the diplomatic correspondence. For the period after August 1935, no records of the internal dealings of the Comintern's leading organs are available, and the archives of the Communist parties are not renowned for their accessibility. Nevertheless, there is some documentary evidence that can be used.

In the first place, it has to be noted that in contradistinction to other instruments of the Soviet foreign policy, such as the Narkomindel or the Commissariat for Foreign Trade, the Comintern was not composed just of paid professional personnel, but also of large memberships of the national sections whose loyalty was voluntary, based on fixed ideological precepts and subject to moods and pressures that the Soviet leadership had little power to control.

The changes that the Comintern had undergone in 1928–32 were similar to the internal transformation of other Soviet institutions, and above all of the Soviet Communist party itself. "Bolshevization" resulted in the installment of new and obedient leaderships in all national sections of the Comintern (with the notable exception of the Communist party of China), which in turn assured a docile complement to the five Soviet members of the executive.[1] The outward expression of this process was the political course of the Sixth Congress of the Comintern (1928), characterized by the sectarian policy of struggle against the Social Democracy as the main enemy.

The fact that this policy was practiced until late 1934 and not officially called off before summer 1935 can only be explained by the successful imposition of the Soviet control over the leading bodies of the national sections of the Comintern. The Bolsheviks could not be overly sensitive to the fate of labor and democratic freedoms abroad: they had themselves destroyed the emerging parliamentary system in Russia, in 1918; the Soviets as freely elected councils in 1921 at the latest; and the independence of the trade unions a year later. And between 1927 and 1929, Stalin even wiped out the last remaining internal freedoms in the Bolshevik party. The Soviet leadership was perfectly ready to tolerate the destruction of democracy and the labor movement in Germany, and even the destruction of the Communist organization in that country, if only the Nazis were willing to preserve good interstate relations with the Soviet Union. It was therefore not the internal practice of fascism that was causing alarm in Moscow—at least, not before the Nazi regime manifested itself as a direct threat to the Soviet Russian state.

In contrast to this frame of mind of the Soviet leadership that prevailed in the ECCI and the new leaderships of the national sections, the rank-and-file memberships of European Communist parties were in no way apathetic to the rise of totalitarianism. And whereas leaders were easy to replace, it was not such a simple operation with the rank and file.

Numerically, the memberships of most European Communist parties declined in the 1928–32 period. Nowhere was a Communist party a majority force of the Left any longer, as had been the case in 1920 in France and Czechoslovakia, for example. Even these reduced memberships, however, in spite of a gradual change in the rank-and-file basis following both from the "Bolshevization" and from the mass unemployment after 1929, were still largely composed of former left-wing Social Democrats. These old Socialists had usually come from parties distinguished not only by older socialist traditions than the Bolsheviks, but also by a spirit of democratism that the Bolsheviks had never experienced. Genuine internationalism was another distinctive trait of European socialists, including many of those who had, after 1918, joined the Comintern. And whereas Soviet Russia emerged from the Stalinist Revolution as a totalitarian and increasingly nationalistic state—a fact that many rank-and-file Communists were unable to verify and unwilling to concede—the Comintern still contained large memberships bound to the democratism and internationalism of the original European socialist movement. As long as Moscow was not prepared to get rid of the Comintern completely (individual parties were easier to sacrifice), this Social Democratic heritage in the mass of the rank-and-file Communists represented considerable political weight.

Various sections of the Comintern reacted very quickly to the rise of Nazism in Germany and to the blatant failure of the policies pursued by the Comintern since its Sixth Congress. This response was largely in the traditional line of defense of the achievements of the European labor movement and of democracy in the broader sense, as it had already professed itself more than a decade earlier at the Third and Fourth Congresses of the Comintern, in 1921 and 1922. The principal element of this earlier course—which had been decisively emphasized especially at the Fourth Congress, a few weeks after the Fascist victory in Italy—was the idea of the United Front; that is, the idea of political alliances with other forces of the Left, and primarily the Social Democrats.

The rise of Stalinism and its application on the Comintern, the so-called bolshevization, ruled out a parallel policy of cooperation with the Social Democrats, and this policy was dropped in 1928 at the Sixth Congress. On the contrary, these natural allies in the labor camp were declared the main enemies of the Communists. Thus, at the time of mortal struggles to preserve democracy in Germany as the fundamental precondition of peace and security in Europe, the Comintern and its German section pursued a policy completely divorced from the political reality of the continent.

The fast revival of the idea of the United Front in the national sections of the Comintern after the Nazi victory in Germany was an important development that also throws additional light on the circumstances under which, in the period 1933–35, Soviet foreign policy was formulated.

The United Front was the labor movement's form of resistance against the totalitarianism of the Right, and against fascism in particular (however inaccurate the application of the term frequently was). The Great Depression and its accompanying mass unemployment were also factors pressing for a new policy. A tendency to depart from the sectarianism prescribed by the Comintern asserted itself in the Czechoslovak Communist party as early as 1931, for example, in connection with the strike movement, in which the CzCP dropped the absurd demand for its "leading role" as a precondition of joint

[80]

actions with the Social Democrats. For the first time since 1928, a member of the Comintern also discontinued (at least temporarily) the use of the term "Social Fascism." Both steps were harshly criticized by the Soviets and by the KPD.[2]

Political considerations appear to have been powerful factors of growing doubts about the wisdom of the line of Sixth Congress, particularly after the Nazi victory in Germany. Rank-and-file Communists in countries with strong Communist parties, such as France or Czechoslovakia, shocked by the fate of the even stronger Communist party in Germany, were leaning toward a return to the United Front policy well before it was identified with the security interests of the Soviet Union. Party functionaries found themselves under increasing pressure to revise the policy of hostility toward the Social Democracy. The Comintern, and the Soviet leadership, were confronted with this development as early as at the Twelfth Plenum of the ECCI in March 1933.

This "revisionist" trend erupted again in the CzCP and found strong expression at the plenary session of the Central Committee of this party held shortly after the Nazi takeover in Germany. The policy of the KPD, and ipso facto of the Comintern, was sharply criticized in the political report presented by Guttman, member of the Presidium and of the Secretariat of the Comintern and chief editor of *Rudé právo*. Josef Guttmann, Jan Šverma, and Pavel Reiman, the party's delegates at the March Plenum of the Executive in Moscow, launched an attack against the old course. According to Rupnik, this was the "first criticism of the suicidal line of the Comintern, coming from the leadership of an important party of the Communist International."[3] Their criticism, however, was rejected. Between April and August 1933, the leadership of the CzCP was forced by the Comintern to return to the old course, and Guttmann, who refused to recant, was expelled from the party.

In the course of 1933, dissatisfaction with the political course of the Comintern was also growing in the French Communist party (PCF). Its publications, including the daily *L'Humanité* and the monthly *Cahiers du Communisme*, ran a number of articles criticizing the policy of the Sixth Congress, specifically its application in Germany. Maurice Thorez observed in his report before the Thirteenth Plenum of the ECCI in Moscow (November–December 1933) that the French Communists gravitated toward the United Front policy.[4]

Nevertheless, the Thirteenth Plenum, like the Twelfth in March, remained overwhelmingly faithful to the old policy. It made "Soviet Power" the central political slogan for the political activity of all sections of the Comintern—a decision whose relevance can well be judged by the situation of the German or Italian parties. Social Democracy was characterized as the main support of the Nazi dictatorship, Franklin D. Roosevelt's New Deal was marked as an exercise in Fascist economics, and England was declared the chief warmonger in Europe.[5] The Executive, and the Soviet Politburo as its spiritual mentor, gave no encouragement to more flexible attitudes toward the concept of the United Front against Fascism.

The development in France after the events in Paris on February 6, 1934, which led to the general strike jointly sponsored by the SFIO and the Communist party, shows clearly how other factors than a political turn in Moscow were affecting the attitudes of the national sections of the Comintern. Vexed with the continuing depression and alarmed by the rise of the extreme Right, the PCF rank and file were simply joining other forces of the Left, especially the Socialist, and demanding unity of action with these forces. Under the existing circumstances, and also in view of the events in Germany, to continue to claim that the chief enemy was the Social Democrats became increasingly absurd and virtually untenable. The PCF leadership was hard pressed from within to respond positively to the initiatives of the SFIO, and to come up with own proposals.

Such a course, however, had not been sanctioned by the ECCI, and the leadership of the PCF was consequently moving very slowly and very reluctantly. Even during the contacts with the SFIO in spring 1934, which the Communist leadership could not avoid if they did not want to commit political suicide, they were so wedded to the old viewpoints that the use of the discredited term "Social Fascism" was not discontinued.[6] A few weeks later (July 27), the PCF signed with the same "Social Fascists" the Pact of Action Unity.

Typical of this attitude of the PCF leadership was their negative reaction to Jacques Doriot's criticism of the conclusions of the Thirteenth Plenum of the ECCI, as well as toward his practical initiative in signing the first agreement between the PCF and the SFIO, in March 1934.

Doriot's rebellion had the significant effect of reimposing upon the agenda of the ECCI a discussion about the substance of the problem, that is, about the rationale of the whole policy practiced since 1928. It can be assumed from the known outcome of the affair that the Soviet leadership was not prepared to sanction any changes to be adopted by the ECCI at that time (May 1934). Instead, the PCF leadership was instructed to take disciplinary action against Doriot for his "fractional activity." His propositions were not clearly rejected, however, which left some maneuvering ground for the hard-pressed PCF leadership. A partial explanation of this inconsistency can be found in the fact that the French Communist party was not the only section of the Comintern affected by the same development.

At the time of the Thirteenth Plenum the Czechoslovak Communist Party was the second largest legally functioning section of the Comintern, operating in a country that had been showing interest in good relations with the USSR. The leader of this party, Klement Gottwald, was a full member of the Executive. The Czechoslovak Social Democracy was a member of most of the "red-and-green" coalitions governing the country in the whole interwar period, and it can be assumed that the situation, and the views of the CzPC, were not ignored in Moscow.

The events in Vienna in February 1934 led to feverish efforts to reunify the Austrian socialist movement, centered around Austrian Socialist and Communist leaders who had found refuge in Czechoslovakia.[7] This development also affected the Italian Left. At the initiative of the Italian Socialist party, contacts with the Communists (both parties were illegal in Italy, and their leading organs were in exile) were established in spring 1934, and in August a pact of action unity between the PSI and the PCI was signed in Paris.[8]

Growing doubts about the sectarian course of the Comintern also existed among German Communists. Many of them believed that the ECCI and the KPD leadership had in advance reconciled themselves to the Nazi victory in Germany, as it was reflected in the "preparations for a long underground existence in decentralized groups."[9] The resolution of the Thirteenth Plenum, emphasizing the necessity to oppose the "rightist opportunism" (i.e., the efforts to soften the Communist attitude toward the Social Democracy), singled out two KPD leaders, Heinz Neumann and Hermann Remele, together with the Czech Guttmann, as its symbols.[10]

According to two Soviet authors who refer to sources otherwise not accessible, the ECCI showed the first signs of retreat from their position between June and August 1934. The important question here is the extent to which this development reflected a change of mood in the Soviet leadership.

In June 1934, Georgi Dimitrov circulated a confidential letter among the members of the Preparatory Commission of the Seventh Congress in which he suggested the possibility of a "revision of tactics." This letter is also interesting because, probably for the first time in this body, it questioned the use of the term "Social Fascism."[11] It is difficult to assess to which extent the document already reflected Soviet

[83]

views. *Pravda* was still liberally using the old terminology in regard to the Social Democrats, and *The Communist International*, the organ of the ECCI, still called for "Soviet Power" everywhere as late as November 1934.[12]

In July, the ECCI continued in their deliberations on the subject of the United Front, obviously in connection with the necessity to give their consent to the pact between the PCF and the SFIO. This consent had to be granted in all probability in the first half of July; the PCF then signed the agreement on the 27th.

During these discussions in the ECCI, D. Manuilsky suggested that the political basis of the United Front should be extended to the right of the Socialists. Manuilsky's view was seconded by P. Ercoli-Togliatti.[13] Echoing Manuilsky's views was the right thing to do in the ECCI, because Manuilsky was Stalin's principal representative in that body. Thorez—hardly on his own initiative, of which he was never suspected—came up with Manuilsky's concept during a coordinating meeting between the PCF and the SFIO delegations on October 9, 1934.[14]

The idea of the inclusion of a strictly "bourgeois" party into the combination, such as the Radicals in France, can be interpreted in two ways. Anxious to avoid a *Klassenbruderschaft* with the Socialists, the Soviets thought that a proper extension of the United Front would take away from the Socialists the clout of the exclusive partners of the Communists. It is of some importance that during the preparations of the program of the Popular Front, Thorez refused the SFIO-proposed nationalization of banks and heavy industry, arguing that such a measure could only be taken by a government of the "dictatorship of the proletariat"; in other words, by a strictly Communist government. This reasoning is in obvious disagreement with the thesis that by refusing the nationalization program of the SFIO, the Communists were simply anxious not to discourage the Radicals. The PCF only agreed to the state takeover of the armament industry. Supported by the Radicals, the Communitst prevailed with their views over the SFIO.[15]

The idea of the extension of the United Front can also be seen in the context of the traditional Soviet preference for foreign-policy partners of established status (when political lackeys were not available). After all, Barthou and Laval were no more Leftists than Walther Rathenau or Heinrich Bruening. This second explanation is, however, less probable in summer 1934 than the first.

In August 1934, according to Soviet sources, the Executive was still divided on the whole problem of a new orientation. Changes were supported by Manuilsky, Dimitrov, Gottwald, Otto Kuusinen, and Palmiro Togliatti. S. A. Lozovsky, V. G. Knorin, Ye. S. Varga, and Béla Kun are reported to have defended the old doctrine, which classified the Social Democrats as the principal enemy.[16] This information is important because it shows that the representatives of the CPSU themselves were still divided, which could not occur had the Politburo already decided one way or the other. The consent of the ECCI to the French experiment was therefore granted as a political exigency. The idea of the United Front "from above" was still rejected by O. Piatnitsky in the November 1934 issue of *The Communist International;* only "cooperation" was cautiously sanctioned.[17] Again, that Piatnitsky would propose a standpoint different from that of the Politburo of his party is out of the question.

Opposition was still very strong against any change in the general line of the Sixth Congress. After all, the whole "establishment" of the Comintern had been recruited after 1928, and it was still not certain whether a new course would not call for a new personnel. Opposition was naturally very stiff in the ranks of the KPD, still the second most influential constituency in the Comintern. According to Wilhelm Pieck, a more flexible attitude did not prevail in the Central Committee of the KPD before January 1935.[18] During the plebiscite in Saarland, however, which also took place in January, the ECCI still approved the slogan "Red Saar in Soviet Germany," coined by the KPD, which obviously reflected the situation not just in the KPD and the ECCI, but also in the Soviet leadership, for whom it was still difficult to decide which to prefer—France or Nazi Germany.[19]

Pressures for a change, nevertheless, continued to grow in the second half of 1934. In Spain, the Communist party leadership could not refuse the offer of the Socialists to enter the Workers' Alliances (Alianzas Obreras), which the rank-and-file Communists were joining anyway; in September, Communist participation was agreed upon.[20] In France, the cooperation with the Socialists brought substantial electoral gains for the PCF in cantonal elections in October, almost trebling their representation. That, of course, was a very strong argument in favor of the new policy.

A thorough examination of accessible sources points to the probability that the Soviet leadership conceded to the necessity to accept the replacement of the general line of the Comintern, and to formalize it, in January or February 1935. The coincidence of the decisions to contract the alliances with France and Czechoslovakia and to permit the Comintern to decree a new course, is obvious. For the Soviet leadership, the reorientation of the Comintern may not in fact have appeared as an indispensable complement of the adherence to collective security, and the slow and reluctant approach to the problem[21] also indicates that the "rectification" was accepted with no zeal. Stalin's attitude can only be surmised; in his speeches, any mention of the subject of the Seventh Congress of the Comintern is prominently missing. Without his consent, however, the changes would have been unthinkable. That Stalin edited Dimitrov's opening speech at the Congress (July 25) is also beyond question.

On the other hand, it cannot be overlooked that the relaxation of the stiff line of the Comintern, however corresponding with the parallel foreign-policy adjustments, did not match with the upcoming internal development in the USSR, as it was foreshadowed at that same time (December 1934) by the assassination of S. M. Kirov.

All these factors counted, the most urgent consideration that pressed for a change in the Comintern's tactical line was the political survival of its main sections in Europe. Foreign policy concerns played a certain role, but the international position of the Soviet Union and her alignment with the Versailles camp did not depend upon the Comintern's change of attitude toward the Social Democracy; and in fact, the new course might eventually become a source of embarrassment. The phenomenon of the Seventh Congress cannot be explained simply by Soviet foreign policy requirements. The activization of the Comintern in the indicated direction (defense of democracy) was in fact bound to tie up, or at least complicate, the maneuverability of the Soviet foreign policy as a whole, and as we know from the Soviet-German agenda, the possibility of a return to Rapallo with no regard to the nature of the regime governing Germany was contemplated very seriously by the Soviet leadership at the time of the Seventh Congress, and most probably even earlier.[22]

The principal characteristic of the Seventh Congress, its compromise between old policy and new, seems to reflect the complexity of factors affecting the event and its outcome. The old course was neither repudiated nor condemned, which would require substantial personnel changes or at least a thorough and humiliating self-criticism of all those who had for years preached the "class-against-class" doctrine, including Stalin himself. Instead, the Congress was asked to approve "the political line and practical activity of the ECCI" in the whole period since the Sixth Congress, and that became the opening phrase of the resolution voted by the assembly.[23] At the same time, the resolution approved the cooperation with the Social Democratic parties and even with the Socialist International, as well as the conclusion of agreements on unity of action, but it also declared that "the main attention should be paid to local mass actions, carried out by local organizations on the basis of local agreements." This, of course, amounted to parallel promotion of the old policy of the "United Front from below."[24]

A very significant achievement of the Seventh Congress was the termination of the use of the term "Social Fascism" and of the characterization of the Social Democrats, especially those of the Left, as the main enemies of the working class. On the other hand, the Congress did not give up the doctrine of the unique and self-redeeming role of the Communist parties, which was particularly endorsed in the formulation of five conditions under which a Socialist party could unite with a Communist party. These conditions, which can be viewed as an abbreviated version of the old Twenty-One Conditions, presupposed a total acceptance of the Leninist theory and Stalinist practice by the Social Democrats.[25] The old policy was also restated in the conclusion that the United Front tactics implied "no reconciliation with Social-Democratic ideology and practice."[26]

The way in which the Seventh Congress circumscribed the government of the Popular Front was similar to the definition of the "Workers-Peasants' Government," defined thirteen years earlier, when the Comintern had for the first time been confronted with the phenomenon of Fascism. The anti-Fascist function of the Popular Front, and of the whole concept of political blocks with non-Communist parties, was specified as their primary meaning. This tendency was further emphasized by the acceptance of "the necessity to defend the remnants of bourgeois democracy" which, in Togliatti's words, was "still better than open Fascist dictatorship."[27] This aspect of the Congress can be seen as an assertion of the original Marxist concept of indivisibility of democracy and socialism, and it certainly represented a noteworthy Soviet concession to the ideas of European Communists, specifically in view of the fact that the defense of democracy was given temporary preference over the struggle for "Soviet power." Togliatti tried to narrow the meaning of this matter somewhat by saying that "the choice now is not between the proletarian dictatorship and bourgeois democracy, but between bourgeois democracy and Fascism."[28]

Before examining the practical application of the conclusions of the Seventh Congress, some observations are in order. The congress failed to produce a thorough analysis of the causes of the bankruptcy of the old policy. The new course was more a complement than a replacement. Whether such an approach provided a suitable basis for the successful realization of the new course, which in fact amounted to a change in strategy and not just tactics, is doubtful. That it offered

[87]

a comfortable ground to the latent opponents of the new course, in the Comintern's bureaucracy and in its sections, is quite certain. Soviet consistency in promoting the new course, the fundamental precondition of its success, is still to be examined. A strange phenomenon, however, was the fact that the stenographic protocol of this congress, in sharp contrast to previous practice, was not published until 1939, when it appeared in a shortened version.[29] Some of the speeches,— those of Togliatti, Palme Dutt, and Campbell, for example—which were more penetrating and more principled than the opening report and the resolution, were thus effectively withheld from the public and from the Communists during the crucial period that followed.

No particular impression of the Seventh Congress upon foreign governments can be traced in diplomatic archives. The Comintern was viewed as a strictly Soviet enterprise, and ideological reshufflings of the agency appear to have been of limited interest to foreign diplomats in Moscow. In one known case, the Seventh Congress brought diplomatic complications, between Moscow and Washington. Ambassador Bullitt viewed the Congress as an open breach in the agreement on the basis of which Soviet-American diplomatic relations had been established in 1933.[30]

On the other hand, the Seventh Congress strengthened the positions of those in the French Socialist Party who were in favor of the Soviet alliance. The support of the Socialists in the Chamber of Deputies was important for the ratification of the Franco-Soviet Pact.

The most important achievement that the new course made possible, however, was the formation of the Popular Front in France (July 1935) and in Spain (January 1936); both carried the next parliamentary elections in February and April 1936 and became the bases for leftist governments, committed to broad social reforms. The Communists did not enter the Popular Front government in France, and at first they did not do so in Spain, either. Their support was essential in France, however, and not without some importance in Spain even before the outbreak of the Civil War. Furthermore, efforts were made beginning in early 1936 to establish regular contacts and cooperation between the Comintern and the Socialist International, which reached their most hopeful point in October, when both organizations agreed to take parallel actions in defense of the Spanish Republic.

This course of events was facilitated by the relatively peaceful internal development in the Soviet Union during most of 1935 and the first months of 1936. In this period, the international prestige of the Soviet Union was growing, aptly promoted by a special propaganda outfit in Paris, which had been built around the International Workers' Aid of the 1920s and was financed by the Comintern. This agency, called "the Muenzenberg Enterprise" after its director, former KPD deputy in the Reichstag Willy Muenzenberg had won an international reputation by publishing the "Brown Book" in 1933; in 1935 and the first months of 1936, the organization was very successful in the "propaganda boosting of the new Soviet constitution." According to Arthur Koestler, who at the time worked for Muenzenberg, "the liberal and progressive-minded section of the European public was completely taken in" by this campaign about the "democratization of the Soviet Union."[31]

Not everything that the agency did to propagate the "rise of democracy" in the Soviet Union need be interpreted as the fulfillment of explicit Soviet instructions. No Russians were employed in the agency, where the boss was a German and his deputy a Czech. Wishful thinking and idealization of the Soviet reality by West European leftist intellectuals accounted for more of the production of the enterprise than instructions from Moscow. The Soviet constitution itself, which in some circles inspired uncritical praise, soon provided a cover-up for the purges.[32]

The rebellion of Spanish generals, known to be supported by Germany and Italy, inspired a widespread movement of solidarity with the Spanish republic. Dozens of national organizations, particularly the trade unions, and thousands of individuals responded to the Spanish government's appeal for material help, for armament and trained military personnel. The Comintern acted swiftly to take lead and control of this movement. A delegation of the Comintern, led by Luigi Longo, came to Madrid in September 1936 to offer the Spanish government the formation of International Brigades. The offer was accepted, and the Brigades were established in October.[33]

The Comintern's action obviously followed from a parallel decision of the Soviet leadership to provide the Spanish government with military aid.[34] The motivation behind this decision can, of course, only be deduced from known facts.

At the time when the Soviet government took the decision to help the Spanish Republic, it was also engaged in continuous efforts to arrive at a political agreement with Germany, which was a power behind the generals' revolt in Spain. The Soviet decision also roughly coincided with the first Moscow show trial, the immediate starting point of the Great Purges. V. Krivitsky testifies that simultaneously with the Comintern's action in Spain and weeks before any Soviet military aid reached Spanish ports, the Politburo also decided to create a Spanish Department of the GPU and to invest it with complete control over all spheres of Communist activities in Spain; which would include both the Spanish Communist party and the International Brigades.[35] The picture of Soviet assistance to Spain would be incomplete without the story of the Spanish gold in the value of 100 million prewar dollars that was shipped to the USSR in December 1936 and never returned, including the Spanish bank officials who accompanied the shipment.[36]

On the whole, it can be assumed that the decision to aid the Spanish Republic was very significantly stimulated by the national sections of the Comintern in Europe, whose rank-and-file members' spontaneous support for Republican Spain was overwhelming. Thousands of young Communists were coming to Spain on their own, particularly from France. It is in fact difficult to imagine that the Soviet government could, in the late summer and fall of 1936, show indifference to a conflict that so aroused the feelings of the whole European Left. Only with reservations can the Soviet decision be viewed as part of a maneuver to induce Germany to a political deal with Moscow.[37] The decisions of the Soviet leadership have always had a more exigent and short-term nature; the idea of far-reaching, long-term plans of action constantly pursued is more a fantasy than a reality.

Least of all, however, does the ensuing course of Soviet actions show the intervention in Spain as a consistent step in line with the concept of the United Front or as the primary Soviet contribution to the cause of collective security and defense of democracy. As Koestler observed, the era of hope that the USSR would really become a power in the defense of freedom "ended with a bang in August 1936. The death sentences in the first Moscow Trial marked the transition from camouflaged terror to stark and open terror."[38]

The international repercussions of this "bang" followed both from the events in Soviet Russia and from their extension abroad. The latter took two main forms: first, in a campaign launched by the sections of the Comintern to "popularize" and advocate the purges in the USSR; second, in acts of physical terror against selected opponents of Stalinism. In at least one known case, that of the Unified Marxist Labor Party of Catalonia (the POUM), it led to random mass executions.

Instructed to advocate and promote the Soviet purges, the Comintern's national sections soon ran into serious difficulties in the parallel pursuit of the general line of the Seventh Congress, that is, of the United Front policy. The Social Democrats, not bound by any allegiance to Moscow, adopted a critical attitude toward the first Moscow trial, and naturally failed to endorse the witch-hunt that followed. Their doubts and criticism drew immediate fire of the Communists.

In the November 1936 issue of *The Communist International*, leaders of the Socialist International and of the (Social Democratic) Trade Union International were accused of "joining their voices to that of the reactionary and Fascist press" in their "suprise and indignation because the Trotsky-Zinoviev terrorists have been ruthlessly exterminated in the USSR."[39] Socialist leaders, "from Schevenels to Otto Bauer, from Citrine to de Brouckere, the Social Democrats of Czechoslovakia, Switzerland, Holland, and the Scandinavian countries" were ridiculed for demanding legal guarantees and for appeals to prevent the infliction of the penalty on the defendants in the first show trial.[40]

The inevitable controversy that followed between the Communists and the Socialists inevitably grew ever more bitter during 1937, when the purges in Soviet Russia reached monstrous proportions. In the heat of the dispute, the Comintern declared in its authoritative manifesto published on the twentieth anniversary of the Bolshevik Revolution that it was, after all, "necessary to put an end to Social Democracy in the labor movement."[41] And this stance of course returned things, in essence, to the situation before the Seventh Congress, when the ECCI, in its May Day Manifesto, put the "revolutionary overthrow of capitalism" on the order of the day again.[42]

The new policy of the United Front therefore did not last very long, victim of the Great Purges and of the Comintern's violent advocacy of them. The anti-Trotskyist campaign was a particularly striking expression of the renewed Communist intolerance, and its introduction into the fragile structures of new-born democratic alliances in the fall of 1936 had destructive impact by itself. This campaign led to the belief that only a "positive attitude" toward the USSR—in other words, approval of the purges—could qualify for membership in the anti-Fascist alliances. Disagreement with the show trials was characterized as a service to fascism. The terms "Trotskyism" and "Fascism" were combined into one,[43] to make it quite clear that the Comintern would tolerate no reservation in regard to the Soviet purges.

It hardly needs saying that this whole campaign had nothing to do with the purpose and spirit of the United Front, and Andrei Vyshinsky's constructions could not be imposed upon the independent partners of the Communists in the anti-Fascist coalitions. The whole campaign could only result in the destruction of the political alliances concluded in 1934 and 1935. By the end of 1937, all prospects of effective united actions by the anti-Fascist forces were ruined. It was a repetition on an international scale of the catastrophic policy of the German Communist party in 1928–32.

In contrast to the initiatives leading to the political alliances with the Socialists in 1934 and 1935, the course taken by the Comintern and its national sections in the second half of 1936 was clearly imposed upon the agency by the Soviets. The dominance of the Comintern by the Soviet government at that time was complete. In Enrique Castro-Delgado's authoritative judgment, the Comintern was an integral part of the Soviet Russian state: in the ECCI, there was no longer even any voting—Manuilsky simply made a "resumé."[44] Moreover, the whole international network of supervisors, couriers, instructors, and the all-powerful representatives of the ECCI appointed to the central committees of individual sections was gradually taken over by the organs of the GPU.[45] This last process was completed before the outbreak of the Spanish Civil War.[46]

It can be concluded that the purges were followed not only by a gradual decline in the Soviet interest in foreign affairs, but also in growing insensitivity toward the opinions and attitudes of the leftist forces abroad, which had for years been sympathetic toward the Soviet Union. This generalized intolerance was finally applied to the sections of the Comintern and the purges fell upon the Communist International itself, especially on its personnel in Moscow, on the representatives of foreign parties, and on the thousands of foreign Communists who had found refuge in the USSR when their parties had been outlawed in their own countries.

Louis Fischer testifies that the onslaught of the GPU on the Comintern had already begun at the time of the first show trial in August 1936, when two German Communists were accused of an attempt, in the service of the Gestapo, to assassinate Voroshilov.[47] During 1937, "the whole of the full-time Comintern functionary staff was cruelly decimated. . . . Whole departments of the ECCI dwindled down to a few members."[48] At the beginning of 1938, the Comintern's headquarters in Moscow were reduced to a skeleton of the most indispensable services, operated by a few dozen terrified survivors.[49] The extent of the purges in the Comintern can be illustrated by the fact that in the spring of 1938 the ECCI was even forced to close down its famous Lenin College for high Communist officials, which had been attended by such students as Ulbricht, Axen Larsen, Karl Ackermann, Edvard Kardelj, and Slánský because of a shortage of both teachers and students.[50] Not even the International Brigades in Spain, still fighting for a cause that appears to have been otherwise abandoned, were spared the rage of the terror.[51]

How the ECCI actually functioned in the last years of its existence can only be surmised from the scanty memoirs of a few men and women, none of whom was a member of the Executive itself. Reports about the proceedings of the body, which had served as the principal guide for theoretical orientation and practical action of the national sections of the Comintern, ceased to appear in the Comintern's publications after the Seventh Congress. The whole publishing activity of the Comintern was cut down to a general information bulletin, *The Inprecor,* or *World News and Views* since July 1938. *The Communist International,* the official organ of the ECCI, shrank from a weekly into a monthly whose editors, one after the other, were arrested and slain or, in the luckier cases, sent to concentration camps.[52]

The fact that the general line of the Seventh Congress was not formally recalled before September 1939 led to a Kafkaesque paradox, an incongruous mixture of sterile appeals for unity against fascism on one side and systematic repulsion of all potential allies on the other. The entire Soviet foreign policy, equally paralyzed by the purges and continuing lack of options reflected this situation.

The Comintern's commitment to the policy of the Seventh Congress lasted about a year. Franz Borkenau is of the opinion that the Soviet (and the Comintern's) retreat from the United Front course was begun in July 1936 by the wage movement in the French aircraft industry, organized by the PCF, which had the strongest positions in this sector.[53] To launch this movement only a few weeks after the "Matignon Agreements," which had already assured a rise in wages by 7 to 15 percent,[54] was unmistakably directed against both the government of the Popular Front and the French armament program. At this point Stalin's attitude toward the Popular Front seems to have already been negative. In August 1936, at the time of the Zinoviev-Kamenev show trial, Thorez introduced the term "Front Français" instead of "Front Populaire," another attempt to extend the political basis of the Popular Front to the right, this time to the right of the Radical party.[55] Such a maneuver would make it easier for the Communists to disassociate themselves from a grouping definable as "bourgeois."

The Czech historian Miloš Hájek draws attention to a speech by Manuilsky, Stalin's principal agent in the ECCI and in most informed accounts a reliable source regarding Soviet intentions, shortly after the Seventh Congress before a gathering of Moscow and Leningrad CPSU officials. In this speech, Manuilsky made serious efforts to reconcile the new course of the Comintern with Stalin's earlier thesis (1924) that Fascism and Social Democracy were "twins." That would indicate a rather special understanding of the United Front line, and hardly as a new policy.[56]

On the whole, the Comintern, as an organization built on Leninist conspiratorial principles, was probably not at all fit for effective and lasting performance along the lines of the policy of the United Front, even without the blow which that policy suffered from the Soviet purges. The internal structure of each section of the Comintern was subordinated to the special needs of a policy that ran counter to the concept of fair cooperation, and there is no indication in available sources that the Comintern ever contemplated the abolition of the various subversive and terroristic *Apparaten* in the national sections. On the contrary, there is strong evidence that these secret bodies functioned with growing intensity all through the period after the Seventh Congress.[57]

It can be concluded that the commitment toward the policy of the United Front was a short-lived tactical variant, which was primarily a Soviet concession to the grass roots of the memberships of the national sections of the Comintern; it was found convenient, or at least acceptable, at the time of the Soviet adherence to the collective security system and to the alliance with France. Neither the structure of the Comintern nor the compromising character of the decisions of the Seventh Congress provided a suitable basis for successful and consistent pursuit of the United Front policy. In the whole, the activities of the Comintern, especially in the period following the first Moscow show trial, contributed significantly to the failure of the efforts to unite the democratic and anti-Fascist forces for joint effective opposition against Nazi aggressiveness.

[5]

Germany and Russia, 1934–37: Not-So-Incompatible Adversaries

Soviet-German relations in 1934–38, when Soviet Russia was associated with the League of Nations' collective security system and Germany was opposed to it, present a problem that has not ceased to puzzle students of the interwar era. The feud between Nazi Germany and Soviet Russia, then largely confined to noisy campaigns of mutual public incriminations, stood in striking contrast to the flourishing economic cooperation of both regimes, based, strangely enough, on a generous German credit policy.[1]

Some authorities have regarded this discrepancy as a significant element of the prewar Soviet-German relationship.[2] Contemporary diplomatic observers like the British Embassy in Berlin, on the other hand, were inclined to translate the Soviet-German economic cooperation into political potential.[3] Diplomatic correspondence of the whole era shows widespread and persistent doubts about the nature and possible duration of the controversy between Nazi Germany and Soviet Russia.

A number of factors were believed to lead, sooner or later, to a reconciliation between Berlin and Moscow. One of them was the objective similarity of both systems and the lack of direct conflicts of interest between them. As before 1914, Russia again had more in common, in terms of her internal structure, with her adversary than with her ally, but the similarity did not have the same meaning in the 1930s. The Hohenzollerns and the Romanovs had been replaced by various types of *Fueherprinzips* and *Gleichschaltungs* that could not fail to impress and attract each other. On top of that, the absence of common borders and of territorial disputes (rather rare in interwar Europe) was depriving the "irreconcilable conflict" of an immediate rationale. It does not seem that in 1937, for example, Stalin still took

Alfred Hugenberg and Rosenberg very seriously; and Hitler is known to have believed as early as 1935 that Bolshevism had never been a serious threat for Germany.[4]

In any case, the state of the Soviet-German relationship was a very considerable component of the 1934–38 era. The system of which the USSR had been formally a part since September 1934 was significantly affected, through the years, by both the real and rumored qualities and dimension of the Soviet-German agenda.

As we have seen, the Soviets reconciled themselves to the dissolution of the "community of fate" with Germany very reluctantly, seeing no comparably suitable replacement for this tried relationship. Statements by marshals Voroshilov and Yegorov to German diplomats in Moscow in January 1934, as noted in chapter 1, show this unfortunate state of mind very clearly.[5] The efforts of the short-term German ambassador in Moscow, Rudolf Nadolny, to ward off the final break (he resigned in June) probably made the impression on the Soviet leadership that all was not yet lost. The Soviet proposal in March 1934, of a Soviet-German guarantee pact for the Baltic region certainly still falls into the Rapallo frame of mind. At a dinner in Ambassador Otto Nadolny's residence in Moscow toward the end of March, Krestinsky, then deputy commissar for foreign affairs, explicitly interpreted the proposed agreement as a means of improving Soviet-German relations, a step "to eliminate existing mistrust." Voroshilov, who was also present—a not unimportant detail—approved of Krestinsky's explanation.[6]

Adolf Hitler, however, was adamant in his unwillingness to enter into any political arrangements with the Soviets at that time. On the other hand, he must have approved the preparations of a new German-Soviet economic arrangement which was, according to British sources, "hastily worked out in the Wilhelmstrasse" in spring and early summer 1934[7] and signed in August. During that time, the French noted, in Léger's words, "a noticeable cooling-off" in Soviet attitude toward France, and the Quai d'Orsay was worried that "Germany and Russia might get together and conclude some form of alliance."[8]

The German-Soviet Protocol of August 1934 gave only partial substance to French apprehensions, but it nevertheless threw further doubts on the real nature of the war of words between Berlin and Moscow. The protocol extended the trade and credit agreement between the two countries, which had been signed only five months earlier. Had the Germans been more businesslike at that point, the new agreement might even have been much larger. According to the head of the Russian Department of the German Foreign Ministry, Herr Brautigam, Soviet negotiators then pressed hard for a very substantial further extension of Soviet-German trade.[9]

The Soviet decision to maintain broad economic cooperation with Germany regardless of the state of mutual political relations, and regardless of the fact that a security arrangement with France was already seriously discussed, is certainly noteworthy. In this connection, Soviet perception of the durability of the Nazi regime in Germany may not be unimportant. According to Krivitsky, this perception was significantly affected by the massacre of the SA leadership in Germany on June 30, 1934. This event, according to Krivitsky, made a very strong impression on Stalin, who then concluded that Hitler would, after all, stay in power. Shortly after the Roehm affair, the Politburo decided "at all cost to induce Hitler to make a deal with the Soviet government." On the basis of this decision, Stalin's foreign policy in the next six years was, in essence, "a series of maneuvers to place him in a favorable position for a deal with Hitler."[10] In all events, an examination of the Moscow press in 1934 reveals the strikingly prominent attention given to Hitler's speech in the Reichstag on July 15, 1934. *Izvestiya*, for example, reserved four columns on its front page for the Fuehrer's account of the Roehm affair,[11] and during the second half of 1934, of twenty-nine editorials and editorial commentaries in *Izvestiya* on foreign affairs, twenty-one dealt directly or indirectly with Germany. None showed any particular interest in France.

A strange episode marked the second stage of Soviet rapprochement with the collective security system in the spring and summer of 1934. The only available documentary account of the talks between Barthou and Litvinov in May 1934 indicates that both were to undertake the task of informing the projected participants of the Eastern Pact about the plan sponsored by France and the Soviet Union.[12] No detailed draft appears to have been produced on this occasion, but the project was nevertheless officially characterized as "the result of the exchange of views between M. Barthou and M. Litvinov."[13] It was particularly specific as far as the exchange of guarantees between France and the USSR was concerned: in the case of France, a guarantee for the Eastern Pact or, as it was called in the outline, "Treaty of Regional Assistance"; in the case of the USSR, a guarantee of the Treaty of Locarno.[14]

France informed Berlin about the project through Ambassador André François-Poncet on June 7. Litvinov, in his turn, arrived in Berlin (for what turned out to be his last visit) a week later, and personally informed Foreign Minister Neurath about the same plan. The Germans later complained that both presentations were too vague to be acted upon, but more interesting is the fact that between François-Poncet's version and Litvinov's was one quite substantial difference: the Soviet foreign commissar failed to mention the fact that the French guarantee for the Eastern Pact would be balanced by the Soviet guarantee for the Treaty of Locarno,[15] and for reasons of his own characterized the project as a "French conception,"[16] obviously keeping open a line of diplomatic retreat.

More than a month later, after the British-French conference in London during which Barthou won British support for the plan, and after a number of clarifications exchanged between Paris, London, and Berlin, the Soviet ambassador in Berlin, Suritz, finally appeared in the Wilhelmstrasse and formally complemented Litvinov's initial version of the Eastern Pact by the missing part.[17]

It is not difficult to see through this calculated omission; only the reciprocity of guarantees clearly revealed the purpose of the project, that is, to hold Germany safely at bay. Litvinov did not feel ready to go that far with Neurath in June 1934, obviously reflecting his master's still unresolved reservations. Ambassador Nadolny's conclusion seems to be substantiated that until the end of 1934, the collective security orientation in the Soviet foreign policy was not yet fully embraced in the Kremlin.[18]

Diplomatically it was a faux pas, but that never mattered too much in the Soviet diplomatic practice. Barthou, who was probably not very anxious to see the Germans enter the pact anyway, was of the opinion that Litvinov was doing his best to see the plan through, knowing that "a number of his colleagues disapproved the whole business [of rapprochement with the West] and considered that Russia's future lay in an alliance with Germany."[19]

Soviet vacillation was seen again in October 1934, when the Soviet delegation in Geneva (together with the Hungarians, the Poles, and the Turks) abstained from voting for the resolution of the Disarmament Conference in response to the German explanation of its withdrawal from the conference. The heart of the matter being the fate of the Versailles Treaty, Soviet abstention was a telltale expression of their uncertain mood. Although the USSR had entered the League of Nations a few weeks earlier, it was still reluctant to join the Western camp in this unfriendly act toward Nazi Germany by putting their imprimatur on the Versailles Treaty.

Without access to Soviet sources, the role of foreign trade in external policy considerations of the Soviet leadership can only be deduced from other known facts. In line with the Marxist-Leninist doctrine, commercial interests could hardly substantially affect any decision on the general orientation of the foreign policy of the Soviet state. Advantages following from the trade with a foreign country could therefore only provide secondary additional weight to other considerations. Germany's value as the main foreign policy partner of Soviet Russia had already been recognized, and it seems to be a safe deduction that temporary fluctuations in Soviet-German trade, often caused by technical factors, could not by themselves substantially affect this basic cognizance. Continuing Soviet efforts to build the economic cooperation with Germany on solid political grounds, as will be shown, sufficiently confirm this conclusion. The Soviet government did not take such pains to achieve a similar arrangement with any other foreign country, and France was no exception.

International trade statistics show that in the 1934–38 period, Germany was not in fact Soviet Russia's leading foreign trade partner. England's consistent participation in Russian trade and relatively extensive imports from the USSR made her the most important Soviet business partner in this period, taking 21.1 percent of the total volume of Soviet foreign trade (25.5 percent of Soviet exports, 16.8 percent of Soviet imports). Germany came second, with only 12.6 percent (12.5 percent and 12.6 percent respectively). These figures, however, reflect the sharp decline in Soviet imports from Germany in 1934 and 1935, resulting from the exhaustion of previous German credits as well as from the declining total volume of German imports after 1936. On the whole, Germany stood as the main foreign trade partner of Soviet Russia between 1925, when the relevant figures start to be available, and 1938, taking almost 20 percent of Soviet foreign commerce (England 18.2 percent). Especially significant in this long period was the German share in Soviet imports, reaching 22.9 percent (the corresponding figure for England in the same period was only 12.5 percent).[20]

Soviet-German trade in the 1934–38 period deserves attention for other reasons besides its volume. First, Soviet-German trade remained unaffected by the noisy feud between the two regimes. Second, this trade was strongly stimulated by government actions on both sides, including German-government-guaranteed long-term, low-interest credits unparalleled by any other Soviet trading partner.[21] Third, the actual volume of Soviet-German trade in this period represented the maximum limits of the Reich's industrial and financial possibilities, whereas the Soviets persistently pressed for further and further extension of the economic cooperation between both

[99]

countries. Finally, the Soviets repeatedly used the commercial and economic contacts with German authorities to further the idea of a revival of the old political relationship, eventually of a direct alliance.

Germany had been a traditional business partner of imperial Russia; she occupied the leading position in Russian foreign trade even before 1914, when both countries had a common border. In the 1920s, when they were separated by Poland and Lithuania, Germany nevertheless assumed again her position in the Russian trade, "practising an intelligent policy" of easy credits, which contrasted with the tough conditions laid down by other Western countries.[22]

When Hitler came to power, Soviet Russia had an outstanding debt in Germany—1.2 billion marks, of which 700 million was due.[23] The sharp decline in Soviet imports from Germany in 1934 resulted from this situation more than from any other political considerations. In March 1933, Hitler had to grant the Russians a new (refinancing) credit of 140 million marks to ease the pressure on the Soviet treasury. During the next two years, increased Soviet exports to Germany and decreased imports marked Soviet effort to pay the debt. In December 1934, it still amounted to 250 million marks.[24]

Nevertheless, as early as May 1934, Moscow began negotiations for a new German loan of 200 million marks. These negotiations were first conducted by the German state secretary, Posse, and a Soviet trade delegate in Berlin by the name of Weizer. In the summer of 1934, Weizer was recalled to Moscow, where he disappeared without a trace. His place was assumed by F. W. Friedrikson, later a deputy of the better-known David Kandelaki, Stalin's compatriot, fellow seminarist, and personal friend.[25] Negotiations concerning the duration of the new credit were concluded in April 1935 by an agreement signed by Kandelaki and Hjalmar Schacht, president of the Reichsbank and minister of economic affairs. According to this agreement, the USSR was granted a new five-year, 2 percent credit of 200 million marks, "a far longer credit than anything [the British] industrialists could contemplate," observed a British diplomat in Berlin, who complained that the Germans "were always ready to give the Russians better terms than we were."[26] Within a few days the Soviets signed two important foreign treaties—the new credit agreement with Germany and the alliance treaty with France. In practical terms, the first was to make more sense than the second.

This new Soviet-German arrangement fell within the rules of Hjalmar Schacht's "Foreign Trade Program," introduced in September 1934. According to Schacht himself, it represented a centralization of trade whereby imports were compulsorily regulated according to the means of payment available.[27] The primary purpose of the new system was to secure raw materials and foodstuffs for Germany through a bilateral trading scheme.

The Soviets did not like this system, in spite of the fact that it resembled their own foreign trade organization; Russian exports to Germany, under the new arrangement, could only be converted into German products and currency. This disadvantage, of course, was sufficiently offset by low-interest, long-term German credit.

Oil and lump ores figured prominently among Soviet exports to Germany. Machinery of all kinds, particularly heavy machinery, constituted the larger part of German exports to the Soviet Union. Railway equipment was also a very important item among German exports. Soviet railroads were so dilapidated that a complete reconstruction was thought necessary.

Some of the hardware that the Russians were interested in, however, caused a certain confusion. Already in the course of the negotiations of the 200 million DM credit, in January 1935 (a significant date), the Soviet Trade Delegation in Berlin sent to the Reichswehr Ministry "a long list of items which the Russians wanted to buy." This list has disappeared, but German archives contain an inquiry on this matter by a Major Ehsebeck from the Ministry of War to the Ministry of Foreign Affairs.[28] During Anthony Eden's visit to Moscow in the spring of 1935, Stalin, in a conversation with the then lord privy seal, asserted that "the Germans had agreed to supply war material in connection with their credit."[29] The general secretary was not bluffing.

The five-year credit negotiated in April 1935 was only eight months old when Kandelaki, not later than December 1935 and probably earlier, initiated talks on another German loan, this time of 500 million marks.[30] A memorandum on an interdepartmental conference convened by the Reich Ministry of Economic Affairs and held in Berlin January 4, 1936 indicates that conversations between Schacht and Kandelaki on the subject of this new loan had been going on for some time.[31] These negotiations were assuredly at an advanced stage when Kandelaki, upon his return from a trip to Moscow at the end of December 1935, produced a "strictly confidential" list of new Soviet orders that would be covered by the new loan, including the following items:

1. Deliveries of naval vessels, in particular submarines;
2. The closest scientific and economic cooperation with the I. G. Farben Industry; purchase and use in the Soviet Union of I. G. Farben patents;
3. The same cooperation with the German optical industry, in particular with the firm of Zeiss.[32]

Considering the state in which Soviet-German political relations

[101]

were at that time, at least outwardly, this was a very daring proposition, but it did not come out of the blue. This side of the story, however, will be discussed in its own context.

For the Germans, who were at the time waging loud propagandistic campaigns against the growing military power of the Bolsheviks (to cover their own war preparations), it was certainly difficult to agree, without some face-saving operation, to supply the Soviets with the military hardware that Moscow wanted to buy. The fact that the Russians were supplying Germany with vital materials like manganese and chromium ores badly needed for the German armament production could not, of course, be ignored. The problem was solved by a decree of the Fuehrer"forbidding all transactions in war material with Russia," accompanied by this interpretation: "The Reich Ministry for War is of the opinion that war material should be taken to mean only what is laid down in the Law of November 6, 1935,"—the Law on the Export and Import of War Material, known to offer a sufficiency of loopholes. On the basis of this arrangement, the "Russia Committee of the German Industry" advised the Wilhelmstrasse "not to break off current negotiations regarding military machinery" for the Soviet Union.[33]

When the Final Protocol on the German-Soviet Economic Discussions and the Commercial Treaty were signed on April 29, 1936, they did not amount to any further extension of German credits. Of the 200 million DM placed at the disposition of the Russian Trade Mission in Berlin, only a small portion was exhausted, and the credit was open until June 30, 1937. In fact, until the end of 1937, it was only used to the extent of 183 million marks.[34] The extent to which Soviet purchases of war material were settled during the negotiations of this treaty is not clear. The document, however, reconfirmed mutual most-favored-nations rights and stated that "the two contracting parties will endeavour to extend their mutual exchange of goods as much as possible."[35] In addition to the existing agreements, a system of short-term trade and payment agreements (clearings) was also adopted and practiced, especially in 1937 and 1938 in the absence of other regular arrangements unbelievably disrupted by the purge of the Commissariat of Foreign Trade.

The fact that Germany and Soviet Russia supported different sides in the Spanish Civil War, which broke out in mid-1936,[36] did not result in any significant changes in Soviet-German trade. Nor did the signing of the Anti-Comintern Pact between Germany and Japan in November bring any dramatic effects. A few weeks after the conclusion of the Anti-Comintern Pact, the secret clauses of which were well known in Moscow, M. I. Kalinin still did not hide from Ambassador Robert Coulondre that Germany was selling war material to Russia.[37] In the first half of 1937, Soviet imports from Germany were still rising at a rate of 125 percent, in machinery only, over the first half of 1936, a substantial growth considering the relatively high levels of German exports to Russia in 1936.[38] In the second half of 1937, a combination of factors led to a gradual slowdown and decline of Soviet-German trade: growing pressures of armaments on the economies of both countries, as well as the shortage of foreign currencies, played their role. In the USSR, the disruptive effects of the purges added another serious factor. This in fact appears to have been the most important element in the situation. As we read from a German document:

> The Economic Treaty [between the USSR and Germany] could not be renewed for 1938 on time, because the Russians were unable at first to appoint plenipotentiaries for negotiations either in Berlin or in Moscow. The deliveries and orders from Russia, therefore, have been at standstill since the end of 1937, to the detriment of Germany economy. Not until January 5, 1938, did the Russian Trade Mission here declare that it was prepared and authorized to enter into negotiations.[39]

The Soviets, usually prompt with their payments, fell behind in their obligations and had to ask for an extension beyond the December 31 due date. This was granted December 22, 1937.[40]

As soon as the new round of negotiations started, the Soviets asked for "an additional credit of 200 million Reichsmarks or more," but they were not ready to speed up the repayment of the old debt of 183 million marks. An interdepartmental conference was convened by Rudolf Hess in mid-February 1938 to consider the possibility of selling the Russian bills of exchange abroad, but that scheme was rejected because it might kill trade with Russia completely; trade that meant for Germany primarily the importation of strategic raw materials without paying in hard currencies.[41] After the January prelude, negotiations with the Soviets were formally started in March 1938 in Berlin, but for a number of reasons yet to be discussed they were not concluded before the end of the year. Soviet-German relations in 1938 are part of the story of the crises of 1938, and will be discussed in chapter 7.

Political relations between Moscow and Berlin in this period were marked by a barrage of invectives, exchanged regularly between the Soviet and German media and, somewhat less harshly, between the representatives of each country. Denunciation of German behavior constituted the substantial part of Soviet activity in the League of Nations. Performed with a great skill and persuasive power by Maxim Litvinov, this criticism was particularly emphatic in 1935 and the first half of 1936, between the reintroduction of conscription in Germany and the reoccupation of Rhineland. Later on, Soviet criticism of Germany became gradually less accentuated and aggressive. This phenomenon is most frequently explained by Soviet disappointment over the Anglo-French reluctance to uphold the Versailles order in Europe by all means, including military. We are still to examine significant internal factors that fell upon the Soviet foreign policy, affecting not only its outlook but even the practical ways of carrying it out. These factors became especially onerous after the second Moscow show trial, in January 1937. The purges then became such a dominant feature of Soviet life that interest in foreign affairs inevitably declined, especially in any international actions in defense of the status quo that might call for active Soviet participation. These circumstances also partially explain the intensified Soviet efforts to arrive at a political agreement with Germany.

Neither British archives and available French diplomatic documents nor relevant memoirs show that Paris and London were aware of Soviet wooing in Berlin. Suspicions about secret Soviet-German contacts cropped up again and again, but no facts were positively established. The Wilhelmstrasse, for reasons of its own, was entirely discreet about the matter; and in Moscow, most of the Soviet-German agenda of the prewar period has never been revealed. The Soviets at times hinted at some (nonexistent) German interest in an entente with Moscow. In any event, both the British and French governments followed the development of Soviet-German relations with cautious attention. Entente between the USSR and Germany was at no point of the 1934–38 period ruled out by these powers; on the contrary, it was considered entirely feasible. Its symptoms were therefore thoroughly analyzed and forces presumably sympathetic to Soviet-German rapprochement were realistically appraised. A British document composed in February 1935 may well exemplify the educated perception of the problem of German-Soviet relations in the West at a very early point of Soviet cooperation with the collective security system:

As regards Germany, a possibility of detente with the Soviet Union cannot be neglected, in spite of Herr Hitler's anti-Communist obsessions and the extent to which anti-Communism is a fundamental tenet for the National-Socialist Party. . . . It is difficult to see what advantages can Germany hope to achieve in the long run by antagonism to Russia. On the Russian side, there is understood to be a party in Moscow which would be prepared to bring about a detente in Soviet-German relations for the sake of a free hand elsewhere. Main reasons for its lack of success hitherto have been the fanatical anti-Russia attitude of the Nazi Party and of Herr Hitler himself, and the schemes of Herr Rosenberg which have long been regarded as fantastic.[42]

The British chargé d'affaires reported from Berlin in March 1935 that "it was untrue that there was complete political discord between Germany and Russia;"[43] Edouard Herriot noted in his diary after the signing of the Soviet-German commercial treaty in April that it "inaugurates the tradition of Rapallo;"[44] Werner von der Schulenburg, from his outpost in Moscow, found it "extremely difficult to determine how the Russians really view the [Franco-Soviet] Treaty" when it was signed May 2, 1935.[45]

SOVIET WOOING IN BERLIN

The first positively recorded Soviet initiative in the direction of Soviet-German political reconciliation can be found in a minute of a conversation between Schacht and Soviet trade delegate Kandelaki, which occurred July 15, 1935. Kandelaki himself later claimed that the Soviets had approached Berlin in this matter earlier; but whom they had approached, and exactly when, is not quite clear. Most probably it was in February. During his conversation with Schacht in July, Kandelaki specified that the earlier Soviet feeler had been sent out at the time of the negotiations of the Franco-Soviet alliance.

A French intelligence report from Berlin in February 1935 describes a mysterious visit of three Soviet officers, in company with the German military attaché in Moscow. The three officers—Kolenkov, Orlov, and Provorotov, whose ranks are not recorded—held conversations with German generals F. W. von Fritsch, Werner von Blomberg, and Walter von Reichenau.[46] The purpose of their visit is not known, but under no circumstances would they have made the trip except on the highest Soviet instructions. It is equally improbable that they discussed other but very important problems of the Soviet-German agenda. Nevertheless, the first regularly recorded Soviet proposition to solve the problems between Germany and the Soviet Union by way of a political settlement occurred during Kandelaki's above-mentioned conversation with Hjalmar Schacht, in July 1935.

According to the minutes of the conversation, Kandelaki took the time, first of all, to make his full credentials absolutely clear. In Moscow, he emphasized—whence he had arrived shortly before this meeting—he had spoken not just to his personal superior, A. P. Rosengolz, the commissar for foreign trade, but also with Molotov and especially Stalin. Kandelaki stated that they had all approved of his previous conversations with Schacht (which are not recorded). Finally, he proposed to take steps toward the improvement of Soviet-German political relations.

Schacht, who at least according to his own reports did not distinguish himself as a particularly friendly and sympathetic negotiator with the Soviets, immediately referred Kandelaki to the services of the Wilhelmstrasse, whereupon the Soviet Trade Delegate indicated that Schacht might "help a little" himself.

The record shows quite clearly that Kandelaki had been instructed to bypass the German Foreign Office (and for that matter, the Soviet Embassy in Berlin as well), and to establish a direct access, through Schacht, to the Fuehrer himself. Schacht, however, appears to have been adamant in his insistence that the Wilhelmstrasse was the only proper agency for this transaction, and he brought Kandelaki's "good deal of embarrassed circumlocution" to an end.[47]

Why the Soviets singled out Schacht for the purpose of gaining a direct line to Hitler can only be guessed at; but Schacht himself, in his otherwise detailed memoirs, tells little about his interviews with Kandelaki. The whole business with Russia is dismissed in a marginal remark regarding a conversation with the Belgian monarch in 1937.[48] His communications stored in German archives as well as his memoirs give the impression that he really was not disposed to act according to Soviet expectations, and was unable to overcome his general dislike of his Soviet business partners. Speculations about his sympathetic views concerning a political entente with Moscow appear to be completely unfounded; he seems to have viewed the whole trade with the Soviet Union as a useful and inevitable evil. The Soviets may have arrived at the same conclusion after Kandelaki's unsuccessful attempt to recruit Schacht as an intermediary, for they later tried other channels.

The next recorded approach was entrusted to Marshal Tukhachevsky who, quite unexpectedly, arrived at the farewell reception offered by Ambassador Schulenburg for Councillor Twardowsky in October 1935. It can be safely deduced that Tukhachevsky neither came on his own initiative nor made his eloquent observations without intensive consultation with the Kremlin. In the Russia of 1935, such things did not occur otherwise.

This was Tukhachevsky's first visit to German premises in Moscow since 1933, and his tête-à-tête conversation with Twardowsky, with "General Koestring [the German military attaché] joining in from time to time," lasted about an hour. According to Twardowsky's report, Tukhachevsky, "generally reputed to be pro-French,"

> was unusually frank and cordial. He emphasized that General Koestring was cordially welcome to the Red Army, and observed that the Red Army still felt great sympathy for the Reichswehr. His remarks were full of the greatest respect for the German Army, its officers' corps and its organizational capacity. . . . He remarked several times that he was very sorry that Germany and the Soviet Union were not working together. . . . He cherished the profound hope that Germany and the Soviet Union would come together again.[49]

Tukhachevsky's appearance in the residence of the German ambassador, and his repeated expression of friendship toward Germany, contrasted with his broadly publicized anti-German article in *Pravda* in March the same year, which had even drawn a formal German protest.[50] But German reports show no particular surprise. Even before Tukhachevsky's sudden appearance in Schulenburg's residence, Norbert von Baumbach, German naval attaché in Moscow, told his Swedish colleague that "the Jews in the *Narkomindel* were really the only obstacle to more friendly relations" between the USSR and Germany, but "their position would be overcome before long and in a year or two, there would be a close cooperation between the two countries again."[51] Whether Schulenburg himself shared his naval attaché's theory about "the Jews in the *Narkomindel*" is not certain, but he was nevertheless taken by surprise to see Litvinov, at the state dinner commemorating the October Revolution in 1935, raise his glass and hear him say to the German ambassador: "I drink to the rebirth of our friendship!"[52]

Shortly thereafter, Schulenburg left for Germany. Accessible documents indicate nothing of any particular importance for the Soviet-German agenda in connection with his trip to Berlin. It is therefore interesting to see S. Bessonov, a councillor of the Soviet Embassy in Berlin, himself arriving from Moscow toward the end of November "after several months of absence," and making an urgent inquiry at the Wilhelmstrasse about Schulenburg's audience with the Fuehrer. The report on Bessonov's demarche (December 2) notes that the Soviet diplomat "let it be understood that the Soviet Russian Embassy were particularly interested in this audience. . . . M. Bessonov then broached the question of German-Russian relations. He considered that efforts should be made to achieve a détente in these relations."[53]

Schulenburg was received by Hitler on December 11, but no record of their conversation has been found, or any other document that would reveal the actual purpose of Schulenburg's trip to Berlin and the reasons the Russians were so interested in his reception by the Fuehrer. In the context of the previous Soviet initiatives, however, it is reasonable to assume that Schulenburg was carrying a similar message.

Anyway, the Russians did not wait for the outcome of Schulenburg's visit. At that time, Twardowski was assuming the office of deputy director of a department in the Foreign Office. In his new position, he made an appointment to pay a courtesy call on Soviet ambassador Suritz. To Twardowski's surprise, immediately after the appointment was arranged, Bessonov telephoned and asked to be received by him before he saw Suritz. This juxtaposition provides an interesting insight into the inner mechanics of the Soviet Embassy. Whereas Suritz was directly following the instructions of the Narko-mindel (and of Litvinov, with whom he also was on close personal terms), Bessonov, as a representative of the GPU, had his own line of command. Both agencies, we can assume, had been instructed to pursue the same issue, and in their zeal to be the first to bring the boss in Moscow the good news he was waiting for, Suritz and Bessonov acted in a way as competitors. Twardowski saw both men, separately, on December 10, and they indeed came with the same objective.

Bessonov opened the conversation with a straight question: "How could German-Soviet relations be improved?"[54] Twardowski tried to avoid the subject, arguing that political relations between the two countries were no longer his responsibility, but Bessonov "insisted on discussing this question." Suritz, some hours later, "also led off his conversation by saying that he would ask me, as an old acquaintance and an expert in German-Russian relations, to give him my advice as to what should be done to improve German-Soviet relations and above all what he personally could do to achieve this end."[55]

One specific suggestion Suritz made in his conversation with Twardowski deserves attention: it concerned the possibility of "a development of the Berlin Treaty" of 1926. In Twardowski's opinion, "It emerged very clearly from this whole conversation that M. Suritz has strict instructions to do everything in his power to bring about, at least outwardly, an improvement in mutual relations. In parentheses I should like to add that he repeatedly emphasized that the idea that

M. Litvinov was an opponent of German-Soviet relations was entirely mistaken."[56]

The idea of "developing the Berlin Treaty" was further pursued by Bessonov during his visit to Roediger, the acting head of Department 2 of the Wilhelmstrasse, on December 21, 1935. Emphasizing that "some way out of the deadlock must be found," Bessonov proposed "the idea of supplementing the Berlin Treaty by a bilateral non-aggression pact between Germany and the Soviet Union," which "was a question that had [already] been spoken of in a private German-Soviet Russian conversation at the beginning of this year."[57]

It is not quite clear how a Treaty of Neutrality and Non-Aggression (the actual title of the Berlin Treaty) could have been supplemented by another nonagression pact; this agreement could only be "developed" in the logical direction of an alliance. In any case, the practical conclusion that follows from this episode is that the Soviets were willing to neutralize (if not directly denouce) their alliances with France and Czechoslovakia, signed only eight months earlier, if Hitler was willing to accept the proposed "development of the Berlin Treaty." It also appears that Moscow had already been contemplating the same idea at the beginning of 1935, before the final round of the negotiations with Paris. That, of course, offers an interesting view of the frame of mind in Moscow at the moment of the Soviet accession to the collective security cause.[58]

In the development of Soviet-German relations in this period, a number of events still cannot be sufficiently clarified, or reconstructed, on the basis of available sources. One of them is Tukhachevsky's stopover in Berlin on his way to London to attend the funeral of King George V in January 1936, and in Paris on his way back. In Paris, Tukhachevsky was a guest at a dinner offered by General Gamelin, where the Soviet marshal also met the French officers with whom he had shared German captivity during World War I; Tukhachevsky's conduct was anti-German at this gathering (it could hardly be otherwise).[59] A day later, however, he attended a dinner at the Soviet Embassy in Paris where the French guests, as witnessed by Geneviève Tabouis, were "alarmed at his display of enthusiasm" for the Germans: "They are already invincible."[60]

It seems most probable that at least during his first stopover in Berlin, Tukhachevsky had some conversations with German officers, and probably was also shown some sample of the new Reichswehr's capabilities. However, no documents have been found to throw more light on this episode.

At the annual reception for the diplomatic corps in Berlin in January 1936, Hitler went down the line during the formal presentation of the accredited envoys and to the surprise of the assembled diplomats, including the American ambassador, William Edward Dodd, spoke with the Soviet ambassador more freely than with others.[61] On those days, Molotov made this statement before the Central Executive Committee: "during the last few months, representatives of the German government had raised the question of a new and larger credit scheme, covering a ten-year period, which is still under consideration of the government of the Soviet Union."[62]

This assertion cannot be substantiated by available documentation, which shows that initiatives toward new German credits were invariably coming from the Soviet side. German banks and industry, whose interests Schacht represented more than those of the Fuehrer, agreed to the "credit schemes" as a way to secure the importation of essential raw materials paid for by finished German products. German archives contain no documents in support of Molotov's theory; on the contrary. But a statement in Molotov's speech that it was "up to the German government to draw practical conclusions" from the economic cooperation of both countries seems to point in the same direction as the discreet initiatives pursued by Soviet representatives in Berlin.[63]

In December 1935, the British Embassy in Berlin was so alarmed by the possibility of Soviet-German rapprochement that it dispatched to London an extensive report, based partially on information from secret sources, indicating a deal in the making between Berlin and Moscow in connection with the activities of David Kandelaki.[64] This report was evaluated in the Foreign Office, whose "non-secret informations afforded valuable confirmation of secret reports," and the whole file was sent to Viscount Chilston in Moscow for consideration and comment.[65] Chilston and his staff at the British Embassy in Moscow composed, in the course of 1936, two comprehensive analyses of the state of Soviet-German relations as it then appeared to the British diplomats in Moscow on the basis of the admittedly limited information obtainable in the Soviet Union. The first report was written in February, the second in November. Both were skeptical about the possibility of an imminent entente between Berlin and Moscow. The first report observed that an anti-German stand had two significant advantages for Moscow:

1. It gives the Soviet government a perfect excuse, internally as well as externally, for an unlimited program of armaments;
2. It attracts into the Soviet orbit all powers who are afraid of Ger-

many, and it makes them inclined to forgive the Soviet Union a multitude of sins.[66]

The report nevertheless noted that "the widest difference of doctrine" did not affect Soviet foreign relations.[67] The second report concluded that "neither my military attaché nor myself [Chilston] can throw much light on the probable attitude of individual personalities of the Soviet government and of the Soviet High Command, to German overtures."[68] Not Moscow but Berlin was suspected of initiatives toward Soviet-German rapprochement; the report seems to confirm that the Soviet initiatives in Berlin were largely unknown. It is surprising, however, that neither Molotov's speech in January 1936 nor his interview with *Le Temps* of Paris in March,[69] shortly after the reoccupation of Rhineland, both of which hinted at Soviet-German reconciliation, were found worthy of note. The diplomatic community in Moscow appears to have been inclined to take Soviet public pronouncements with very limited confidence.

The signing of the Soviet-German Commercial Treaty in April 1936 was followed by new Soviet efforts to lure the Third Reich into a political agreement. To interpret this activity as a reaction to the feeble response of the Western powers to the reoccupation of Rhineland,[70] however, would mean to disregard the fact that Soviet initiatives in this direction had been very consistent since at least July 1935. The Germans themselves viewed the conversations that took place in May 1936 as being "occasioned by the signing of the Commercial Treaty" or placed "in connection with that Treaty."[71] Propositions brought up by the Soviet representatives at this time show full continuity with those presented in the previous year.

On May 4, 1936, the Soviet Trade Mission in Berlin gave a luncheon for German officials who had taken part in the negotiations of the Commercial Treaty. On this occasion, Bessonov and Gnedin, a secretary of the Soviet Embassy, chose Andor Hencke (the future chargé d'affaires in Prague, in 1938) to communicate the willingness of Moscow "to revise the Soviet government's present attitude" if that would be required as "one of the pre-conditions of (Soviet-German) détente."[72] Specifically, Rhineland was one of the issues on which Soviet attitudes were susceptible to revision. In March, Litvinov had delivered one of the key addresses in Geneva on the subject of Rhineland; now the Russians made it clear in Berlin that they were not, after all, so serious in their criticisms of German actions. Soviet opposition could be easily changed into a benevolent indifference if only Hitler were willing to make a deal with the Soviet Union.

[111]

Two weeks later, Kandelaki's efforts to win access to high Nazi personages were finally successful. Through the services of a cousin of Hermann Goering who happened to be a high official in the German Ministry of Economic Affairs, Kandelaki obtained an audience with the Prussian minister-president on May 20, 1936. Accompanied by his deputy Friedrikson, Kandelaki was, according to a German report, in every respect delighted by Goering's charming manners. Goering characterized the Soviet-German Commercial Treaty as a "pacemaker on the road to further political understanding between these two great nations," and declared that "all his efforts were directed toward making close contacts with Russia again, politically, too."[73] Whether Kandelaki brought up his earlier suggestions with Goering is not certain. Goering, on the other hand, seemed to know perfectly well what the Russians wanted to hear. In any event, immediately after this audience, Kandelaki hurried to Moscow to report on his achievement.

During the conversation with Goering, the Russians managed to complain about some difficulties they were encountering in their purchases of war material in Germany. Specifically, they mentioned shortwave radio transmitters. Goering explained in a friendly way that the Germans "could not supply what [they] were manufacturing in strict secrecy for themselves and for their own use and were not exporting at all," but he thought that this situation would soon improve: "Altogether, if the Russian gentlemen encountered difficulties or were faced with questions with which they were making no headway, he most cordially invited them to turn to him at any time. . . . He was convinced that the time was ripe to set in train more friendly relations between Russia and Germany all along the line, in both the economic and political sphere."[74]

In the long run, Goering did not fulfill the expectations he obviously aroused on the part of. Kandelaki, whose report in Moscow was probably very positive. This channel upstairs yielded little further progress for the Soviets, who ultimately had to turn their sights to lower levels again. In October, Goering took over the whole Russian trade in his hands in an effort to centralize an agenda that was growing in importance for Germany because of the ever-increasing demand for strategic raw materials. Goering, however, as it is reported in a memorandum on economic policy, decreed that, first, business with Russia "should be rendered completely non-political"; there could be "no question of granting a [new] credit to the Russians at present"; the German conception was "a purely compensation trading: German deliveries of industrial products . . . against Russian deliveries of raw materials on the basis of world prices."[75]

This decision to maintain a strictly nonpolitical character of the German-Soviet trade amounted to the exclusion of a political agreement, at least for the foreseeable future; it was in fact to remain the German policy until summer 1939. In his conversation with Kandelaki on May 20, Goering obviously played a game, trying to exploit the Soviet desire for political rapprochement with Germany for his own ends, such as increased Soviet deliveries of strategic raw materials.

Goering also had to take a stand on continuing Soviet demands for German armament. The Russian shopping list, in October 1936, included aircraft catapults, armored plates, and underwater listening devices, commodities which the Germans agreed to deliver. The Soviets, however, also "desired deliveries of warships to the value of 200 million Reichsmarks," to which Goering himself "was favorably disposed, but it was doubtful whether his view would prevail." The principal currency with which the Soviets were paying for everything was manganese ores.[76]

Goering received Kandelaki and Friedrikson once more, toward the end of October. Further working contacts with the Soviets were then entrusted to Herbert Goering, the cousin in the Ministry of Economic Affairs. Kandelaki was stymied. He could expect nothing in terms of the political negotiations that he had been furthering so persistently; this Goering was just a cousin, nothing more. Certain decisions exceeding Herbert Goering's authority, however, were to be referred to either the minister-president or to Reichsbank president Schacht. Of the two, Kandelaki preferred Schacht for his next exercize of high diplomacy in November and December 1936 and in January–February 1937. Schacht did not have the charming personality of the future Feldmarschall, but at least he seemed to be more businesslike. The Germans were not offering many choices, anyway.

The picture of these contacts is probably very incomplete, because part of this ticklish agenda may have already been handled by the Dienststelle Ribbentrop (the Ribbentrop Bureau), a shadow foreign office of the Nazi party. That this outfit did not merely gather information is sufficiently clear. The absence of Ribbentrop himself (he was ambassador to London from mid-1936 to January 1938) did not mean any deactivization of this agency. We know from Dirksen's memoirs that the Anti-Comintern Pact (November 1936) had been negotiated between Oshima, the Japanese military attaché in Berlin, and the Ribbentrop Bureau, since December 1935 without the knowledge of the Wilhelmstrasse.[77] There is no reason to rule out the possibility that a deal with the supervisors of the Comintern was discussed at the same time and with the same discretion—ideological principles had never had much bearing on either side of this combination. Even after his takeover of the Wilhelmstrasse, Joachim von Ribbentrop did not dismantle his Dienststelle; it remained in separate operation and, as we know from Peter Kleist's account, played crucial role in Soviet-German relations after September 1938.[78] Kleist himself, however, joined the agency only at the beginning of 1939. In the absence of positive evidence, there is no reason to disregard the possibility of earlier contacts with the Soviets, who must have been attracted by this organization, so similar to their own all-powerful *mezhotdel* in the CPSU Central Committee apparatus. "Continuation of a Russian policy," according to Rauschning, "was by no means unpopular among the National Socialist leaders. . . . Goebbels was not the only one who, during the years of struggle, had been wellnigh exultant over those relations between National Socialism and Bolshevism. There were a number of *Gauleiters* who saw in a German pact with Russia the only political solution."[79]

Ambassador Schulenburg, when he was returning from his summer leave in October 1936, was quite surprised by the extraordinary friendliness professed by all Soviet officials whom he encountered on his way from the border to Moscow, "as if nothing whatever had happened." His surprise is natural considering the events between July and September—in July the Spanish Civil War broke out, and in September, at the Nuremberg Congress of the Nazi party, the principal speeches, including that of the Fuehrer, were distinguished by wild anti-Communism. In Moscow, however, even N. N. Krestinsky, the acting head of the Commissariat for Foreign Affairs, was "too extremely friendly and did not refer to the events at Nuremberg at all."[80]

This stands in marked contrast to the attention paid by Voroshilov to the speeches at the Nazi congress in his conversations with the French general Schweissguth, who attended the Red Army war games in September. Voroshilov, and probably Tukhachevsky, tried hard to convince their French guest that Germany's next move would be to attack France, not the Soviet Union.[81] They did not, however, mention the quantities of the manganese and chromium ores they were shipping to Germany at that time. Those shipments were no secret to the French, however; nor was the fact that Germany "was supplying Russia with large quantities of arms."[82] And it has more than an illustrative value, in the context of the Soviet policy toward Germany in the fall of 1936, that the French Communist Party at that time adopted a distinctly hostile attitude toward the government of the Popular Front, which could only have followed from instructions from Moscow. Just when Count Schulenburg was so favorably impressed by the expressions of Soviet friendship, Ambassador Coulondre of France was busy delivering energetic protests of his government against the activities of the PCF, which in Léon Blum's words were designed "to ruin the Popular Front."[83] That view, of course, is at odds with the Soviet action in Spain. The Popular Front government could only be replaced by one entirely unfriendly to the cause of the Republic, which Moscow was trying to salvage. This whole period, however, is characterized by a number of contradictory developments that should be included in any examination of Soviet-German contacts in November–February 1937.

INTERNAL CONCERNS

In the fall of 1936, the most important concern of the Soviet Politburo, and especially of the general secretary and his staff, was not foreign policy or foreign trade, but the preparations of the second show trial. These preparations were launched in August. Karl Radek was arrested in September, G. L. Pyatakov in October. The drafting of the scenario of the trial (in which, initially, as many as fifty defendants were slated to be put in the dock) took at least four months.[84] The enterprise was as demanding as the shooting of a grand historical movie, and Stalin was the principal director of the show. The international importance of this trial lay in the inclusion of the espionage charges (implying Germany), and in the fact that this process was preparing grounds for the onslaught on the Red Army High Command (with Radek's implication of Marshal Tukhachevsky). The decision to accuse the defendants at this trial of treason in the service of Germany had to be taken not later than November 1936.[85] The traffic with forged accusations of Tukhachevsky and his colleagues must have begun at least in the first half of December, when the first information on the case reached President Beneš and was sent by him to Léon Blum, if not in November.

Alexander Orlov's detailed and unquestionably authentic account shows that Stalin was substantially occupied by this business, conferring daily with G. G. Yagoda, N. I. Yezhov, and leading interrogators on the progress of the preparations for the trial. It was Stalin who provided the final editing of all principal "testimonies." Proceedings of the Eighth Congress of the Soviets toward the end of November show clearly that external problems were not the Soviet leadership's primary concern at the time.[86]

At the same time, however, certainly not later than in November 1936, the Politburo (or at least Joseph Stalin himself, and a Politburo approval is more probable) decided to reactivate Kandelaki and to recall Suritz.[87] The latter was to be replaced by a non-Jewish envoy, more suitable for the job of ambassador to Hitler.[88] That these decisions were prompted by the conclusion of the Anti-Comintern Pact is doubtful. Assuming such a simple rationale behind Soviet foreign policy decisions can be very misleading. Had he been really alarmed by the signing of the Anti-Comintern Pact, Stalin would probably have called off his preparations for the extermination of his best military men. Pact or no pact, he must have felt quite safe to do what he was going to do in 1937.

In December 1936, V. Krivitsky "received orders to throttle down our work in Germany." In January 1937, he "was engaged in demobilizing large sections of our intelligence service in Germany."[89] Litvinov's failure to persuade Stalin to publish Mussolini's letter to Engelbert Dollfuss containing a humiliating characterization of Hitler also falls in this period.[90] All in all, the broader framework of the Soviet-German contacts in December 1936 and January 1937 (when the Radek-Pyatakov show trial was in progress) was extremely complex, and it is not easy to see how all the various events fit together. It is, for example, not very clear why the implication of Germany in the January show trial could not be moderated when the Germans were supposed to consider Soviet propositions favorably. Stalin, of course, may have thought that the Germans, who knew best that the accusation was false, would not mind and that his fellow dictator would not be fussy about such things. He doubtless was not; probably more serious considerations prompted him to postpone his deal with Russia.

It is nevertheless very characteristic that the Soviet intelligence operations in Germany were called off, in coordination with the expected diplomatic *rochade*, but the absurd accusations of the defendants before the Moscow tribunal had to stand. Stalin needed this heavyweight charge to be brought up exactly at this stage of the purges, and obviously everything else mattered less. Foreign policy, including the delicate operation entrusted to Kandelaki in Berlin, was then obviously overshadowed by the business of the purges, which were, of course, preparing grounds for the "great reorientation" of 1939.

KANDELAKI'S LAST FEELER

Formal framework of the Soviet-German talks in the last weeks of 1936 was provided by the negotiations of the Commercial Treaty between the two countries for 1937. Only incomplete information can be drawn from available documents, which can be found in German archives; nevertheless, the existing evidence is very valuable.

At some point in the talks, which were resumed by Kandelaki and Schacht in Berlin in December (or perhaps November) 1936, the head of the Soviet Trade Mission tabled a proposal for another, presumably quite substantial extension of Soviet-German economic cooperation. That is clearly implied in a later communication from Schacht to Neurath.[91]

In reply to Kandelaki's proposition, Schacht declared that "he saw no possibility of an active development of trade between Russia and Germany unless the Russian government made a clear political gesture and offered guarantees . . . that it would abstain from all Communist agitation outside Russia."[92]

Schacht's statement is notable not only for its surprising lack of interest in the Soviet trade, but also for its clearly political nature. Considering Schacht's previous reluctance to address himself to any aspect of the Soviet-German political relations, his last statement indicates that he had, in all probability, been advised before his talks with Kandelaki what stand to take in case the Soviet representative came back with some proposition of a political nature.

Kandelaki showed his sympathy for Schacht's view of the Comintern, and left immediately for Moscow, obviously to consult his superiors. This trip to Moscow must be seen within the context of the time. Kandelaki stayed in Moscow during the immediate preparations for the Radek-Pyatakov show trial, which took place in the last week of January, and probably had to attend at least the opening day of the process. On the 28th, he returned to Berlin. From all we know about the background of the trial and Stalin's personal involvement in it, we can assume that Kandelaki had difficulty getting the general secretary to consider the case at all. He obviously succeeded, however, because on January 29, when he called on Schacht again, he brought with him an official Soviet statement which he formally presented "in the name of Stalin and Molotov." This seems to have somewhat impressed the otherwise very cool Schacht, who noted that Kandelaki was Stalin's "Jugend-Schulkamerad."

Kandelaki stated in his communication that his government "had never demurred in political negotiations with Germany." On the contrary, the Soviet government had, in the past, made "specific political proposals."

At this point, Schacht interrupted his guest to ask when these specific political proposals had been made. Kandelaki promptly answered, "at the time of the negotiations of the Franco-Soviet Pact," or most probably between February and April 1935.[93]

Returning to the text of the message he had brought from Moscow, Kandelaki further declared that "it was not the attitude of his government to be opposed to German interests." On the contrary, the USSR was ready "to enter into negotiations with the government of the Reich on the improvement of mutual relations and general peace."

Schacht reminded his guest of the existence of normal diplomatic channels, but did not directly refuse to pass the message along. In doing so, the Reich's minister for economic affairs exhibited a remarkable lack of haste—his letter informing Neurath about the Soviet proposition is dated eight days later. It is doubtful that Schacht tried to see the Fuehrer before turning to Neurath; he was simply *dienstordnungsmaessig*. Neurath brought the affair to the attention of the Fuehrer on February 10, and a few days later replied to Schacht that Hitler had decided to decline the Soviet offer. Hitler's attitude appears to have been strictly in line with the Pact against the Comintern. Neurath noted the continuing connection between the Soviet government and the Comintern, a circumstance that promised "no success for political negotiations between Germany and Soviet Russia."[94] This answer was then presumably communicated to Kandelaki by Schacht, so that the Wilhelmstrasse was formally left out of the whole affair.

Kandelaki's operation in Berlin in winter 1936–37 does not appear to have offered any more realistic chances of success than the earlier Soviet initiatives. It is therefore difficult to explain why expectations were so high in informed Soviet circles, and particularly in the Soviet intelligence community, even after the rebuff. One explanation could be that in winter 1937, the earlier Soviet feelers in Berlin were not widely known to the GPU operatives abroad, in spite of the direct involvement of the agency in some of them (Bessonov). Krivitsky learned about the case as late as March 1937, when attending a conference with Yezhov in Moscow, but he was told that nothing had come of the negotiations.[95] On the contrary, the information he received from Slutsky, then head of the Foreign Department of the NKVD, made a Soviet-German deal look quite probable. Litvinov appears to have learned about the last Soviet initiative in Berlin from Suritz also in March, but we know, of course, that the commissar had been informed about one of the earlier feelers in which Suritz played a role. What was news to Litvinov was the fact that Stalin worked through Kandelaki and outside the usual channels, that is, the Narkomindel and the GPU. Kandelaki's last mission appears to have been a personal diplomacy of Stalin.[96]

Foreign diplomats in Berlin and Moscow knew nothing about this affair. Their attention was rather attracted by a continuing period of relative moderation in the way the media in Germany and the Soviet Union were treating one another, a situation that extended until the beginning of June. It is difficult to avoid the explanation that the coming onslaught on the Red Army High Command was a factor both in Moscow and in Berlin. Reinhard Heydrich, in Walter Schellenberg's version, did not rule out the possibility of Tukhachevsky's contacts with the Reichswehr when the information came from the White Russian general Skoblin in Paris about the generals' conspiracy in Moscow. Heydrich was equally uncertain whether the information had not been planted by the GPU, however, and he asked Hitler to decide what to do. Hitler, allegedly, "decided to back Stalin instead of Tukhachevsky," which then led to the actual transaction with forged documents.[97]

In any case, the strange cease-fire in the Soviet-German war of recriminations aroused great nervousness in the diplomatic community, which had no knowledge of any contacts beyond the trade negotiations between Germany and the Soviet Union.[98] The French were especially concerned, because at that time (February–April 1937) they were engaged in talks in Paris with Potemkin about the military cooperation, and both French ambassadors, in Berlin and in Moscow, were on the alert.[99] Coulondre repeatedly reported "indications of détente in the German-Soviet relations," and François-Poncet in Berlin did the same, calling attention to the fact that in the Nazi presentation of Soviet Russia, an interesting change had occurred recently in that "a distinction is being made between Russia and the Jewish clique controlling the Comintern."[100] Litvinov's long and friendly talk with Ambassador Schulenburg at an American reception in Moscow was also duly noted, as well as the fact that the Soviet government did not ask for the recall of the two German diplomats (military and press attachés) who had been implicated in the January show trial. A scaling down of German involvement in the Spanish Civil war was also noticed,[101] whereas the fact that Moscow too started to cut back its assistance to the loyalists[102] was not immediately obvious.

The Soviets must have become aware of the intensity of the rumors concerning their relations with the Third Reich, because the Soviet ambassador in Prague, M. Alexandrovsky, was instructed to inform Czech foreign minister Krofta that "stories about a rapprochement between the USSR and Germany had no substance," and that the Soviet government had no intention to send replacements for Kandelaki, who had been recalled from Berlin in March, and for Suritz, who was reassigned to Paris shortly afterward.[103] The new Soviet ambassador to Berlin, Yurenev, was nominated only a few weeks later, and Kandelaki was certainly well replaced by G. Astakhov, a GPU operative who later negotiated the pact of August 27, 1939. Litvinov's diary also mentions a member of "the Molotov clan," Soviet commercial attaché in Berlin Babarin, as one of those Russian representatives working for an entente with Hitler.[104]

Soviet-German relations did not undergo any visible changes owing either to the January show trial or to Hitler's rebuff of Soviet offers in January. The Tukhachevsky affair was followed by a certain revival of the standard exchange of invectives, whereas in the economic arena, business was as usual. "In 1937, Russian obligations arising from bills that fell due that year, were paid before maturity by delivery of goods which were foreign exchange assets to us," stated a relevant German report in January 1938.[105]

Berlin was cautious not to disclose anything about Soviet feelers, which introduced an element of complicity in the relations between both governments. The reception of the new Soviet ambassador in Germany, in July 1937, was another indication of the shallow ground of the presumed antagonism between the two regimes.

The new envoy, Yurenev, former Soviet ambassador to Japan, was invited to present his letters of credence not in the Reichskanzlei in Berlin, but rather in Hitler's private residence on the Obersalzberg, which in itself, according to François-Poncet, was a sign of détente.[106] In addition, Hitler "had taken the trouble to make quite a friendly speech" to Yurenev,[107] whose "Aryan" appearance pleased him; the Fuehrer's aversion toward the Soviet regime was, after all, in Rauschning's testimony, "not ideological in character," but rather inspired by his pathological anti-Semitism.[108]

The fact that Yurenev was later not spared in the purge of the Narkomindel enraged Hitler, and brought a tension in mutual relations in the first months of 1938 that otherwise would have had no objective causes. The ambassador whom Hitler had so benevolently received in Berchtesgaden was summoned to Moscow in December 1937 and probably shot without trial shortly afterward. Neurath informed Count Schulenburg in mid-January 1938 that the Fuehrer was so angry that "it was no good encouraging the Soviet government to send a new Ambassador to Berlin in the near future, as it would be by no means as easy a matter to get the Fuehrer to give his agrément." As an expression of Hitler's displeasure, Schulenburg was even instructed to take a two-month leave of absence from Moscow.[109] Yurenev's episode offers a characteristic example of the indifference in the Kremlin at that time to external policy concerns in general, and to European affairs in particular: the purges had top priority.

As a prelude to the exercise of foreign policy during the crises of 1938, the last months of 1937 were marked by continuing decline in direct interest and active involvement of the USSR in European affairs. In November and December, foreign observers in Moscow noted a shift in the criticism of Germany from specifics to generalities ("Fascism" with no adjectives added for closer national identification). V. M. Molotov and A. A. Zhdanov, in their speeches before the annual session of the Supreme Soviet, were more critical of France than of Germany.[110]

Before the end of the year, the Moscow correspondent of the Parisian newspaper *Le Temps* Luciani, was granted an interview by the foreign commissar, which was followed by an off-the-record conversation, the contents of which Luciani reported to Ambassador Coulondre. Here, Litvinov offered a rather accurate picture of Soviet foreign policy attitudes at the high point of the Great Purges. Answering the correspondent's question whether German-Soviet rapprochement was possible, Litvinov said:

> Perfectly. . . . It is you, the French, who are interested in the preservation of the territorial clauses of Versailles. We, however, have won nothing in Versailles. Therefore, we have nothing to give up. . . . The USSR will not be harmed by a territorial revision. That is why we can disinterest ourselves. It [the eventual rapprochement with Germany] will not be a question of signing new treaties. Things can go otherwise.[111]

Thus, on the eve of the crises that delivered their fatal blow to the collective security system, Soviet foreign policy was steadily closing the circle along which it had been moving since 1933. One principal fact emerges from a close inquiry (at least as close as is possible on the basis of available evidence) into Soviet-German relations of that period. Its membership in the system and obligations following thereof notwithstanding, the Soviet government was striving for a political agreement with Germany, the main adversary of collective security. This effort was not limited to the episode in winter 1937 which might, in a way, look like a variation of the Bjoerke affair; on the contrary, the Soviets had been launching initiatives in that direction persistently at least since July 1935, and probably since February. One might almost say that parallel to each of the grand speeches of Maxim Litvinov in Geneva during those almost two years, there was a try in Berlin or in Moscow by some other representative of the Soviet government to achieve exactly the opposite of what the foreign commissar was publicly pleading for in the League of Nations. Some of those quiet Soviet gentlemen who were, without publicity, selling the idea of a Soviet-German Axis were Litvinov's subordinates, and he could not be unaware of it. Suritz, for example, very obviously acted on the Foreign Commissar's instructions in December 1935.

Soviet propositions were never too specific, because no negotiations on the subject ever seriously started before summer 1939. Nevertheless, certain indications are documented—first of all, the proposed "development of the Berlin Treaty" of 1926, formally still in force after Hitler's ratification of the protocol (May 1933).[112] To develop a treaty must reasonably mean to extend the obligations arising from its clauses. It is not difficult to guess in which direction a treaty of neutrality and nonaggression could possibly be extended, and how that extension would be bound to affect the security clauses of other treaties that the Soviet Union had meantime signed, including the Covenant of the League of Nations. Furthermore, we know that certain "changes of attitudes" were offered by the Russians as part of the proposed political détente with Germany, and one of these changes was specified as concerning the reoccupation of Rhineland. That seems to be clear enough to shed light on what kind of a deal the Soviets had in mind in their approaches to Germany. It does not appear accidental that official Soviet textbooks of the prewar foreign policy of the USSR leave the story of Soviet-German relations out of the picture.[113] It is particularly characteristic for these relations that in their economic sphere, both countries were significantly contributing to the war preparations of the other side. The Soviets were supplying the Germans with large quantities of strategic raw materials, indispensable for armament production, and the Germans were selling finished war machinery and even sophisticated devices for the Soviet armed forces that were helping their modernization. This last fact was no secret in Paris and in London, and could not fail to arouse serious doubts about the stand Soviet Russia would take in case of a German assault on her allies, France or Czechoslovakia.

The fact that no Soviet-German political agreement was signed in this period that would effectively annul Soviet membership in the League of Nations and the alliances with France and Czechoslovakia can be attributed solely to Hitler's refusal to enter into any but economic arrangements with the Russians, at least as long as anti-Communism could be employed as a useful device to soften the Western resistance to German plans in Central Europe. The Soviets, on the other hand, considering how early they started wooing Hitler after the break of 1933–34, seem never to have thought of their association with the League of Nations and with France as a suitable replacement for their past relationship with Germany. They continued to be ruled by the general axiom that other powers had to be prevented from allying themselves against Russia, and from that perspective, to go as far as Geneva and Paris had to look like a blatant miscalculation. Discreet initiatives soon followed to correct this error. They failed, and the ensuing policy was more or less the result of inertia and of a lack of alternatives.

Accessible evidence yields no proof that Soviet initiatives were known to other powers at that time, although information about the case almost certainly did reach some governments through non-diplomatic channels. Soviet-German relations were generally analyzed on the basis of more or less publicly known or officially reported facts, and Soviet overtures in Berlin or in Moscow were not among those facts. Germany was assumed to be more interested in a rapprochement than the Soviet Union, but on the whole there was no factual basis to assume that either Germany or Russia was striving for a mutual political settlement.

Even the loud public campaigns waged in Germany against the Soviet Union, however, and in the Soviet Union against Germany, failed to provide sufficient assurance that a German-Soviet rapprochement or entente was not in the making. Not even assistance to the Spanish Republic, the most impressive single act of the USSR as an advocate of collective security, diffused the suspicions of a potential collusion with Germany. This may of course have followed from the parallel fact of the purges in Russia, the least assuring background for an exercise of the defense of democracy. And yet the fact that these purges, in addition to providing Stalin with unrestricted personal power, performed a specific role in asserting the pro-Nazi orientation in the Soviet foreign policy was not understood at the time, and even nowadays does not seem to be sufficiently acknowledged.[114]

At any event, deduced partly from the economic cooperation between Germany and Russia and partly from the memory of the previous close relationship before 1933, and fed by each of the unexplained periods of sudden mutual moderation in public treatment, doubts never fully abated in Western ruling circles that Berlin and Moscow were close to a friendly political settlement. Even Viscount Chilston, the most skeptical of foreign observers in the Soviet capital regarding the possibility of a Soviet-German rapprochement, warned: "Whatever treaties, loans, and other favors we and the French may give to the Soviet government, so great is the moral and physical influence of Germany in Eastern Europe that I have little doubt that they would not weigh for a moment with Litvinov if Hitler were to offer him a German alliance."[115]

Attention was usually focused on "political undercurrents" in both countries that were supposedly sympathetic to the idea of a Soviet-German entente. As far as the Soviet Union was concerned, however, it was not a problem of an undercurrent: in the 1930s there was no longer a place for undercurrents in Russia. The search for a deal with Hitler was directed from the very top of the pyramid of power.

[6]

The Great Purges and
Collective Security

Between 1934 and 1936, Soviet Russia's international esteem reached its peak. The Soviets were accepted in the respectable world of Western democracies, admitted into the League of Nations, and linked with the Versailles system by alliances with France and Czechoslovakia.

The Soviets were still acclaimed, even idolized, by significant segments of leftist and liberal intellectual circles in Europe as pioneers of socialism. The extent of this support was manifested by the International Writers' Congress in Paris in 1935. Organized behind the scenes by the Comintern, the congress was attended by such world-renowned literary figures as André Gide, Henri Barbusse, André Malraux, J. R. Bloch, Louis Aragon, Bertold Brecht, Heinrich Mann, Lion Feuchtwanger, Johannes R. Becher, Robert Musil, Anna Seghers, Aldous Huxley, Martin Andersen-Nexoe, and many others. The support of leftist and liberal intellectuals significantly eased the admission of the Soviet Union into the democratic club. This process was also facilitated by a parallel relative moderation in the internal development of the USSR and by the gradual relaxation of the political course of the Comintern, which was officially enunciated by the Seventh Congress in the summer of 1935.

In 1935, many friends of the Soviet Union in the West believed that Russia was on her way toward developing a genuine system of democratic socialism. André Gide expressed the opinion that "on the high road of history . . . the Soviet Union has taken the lead in a glorious manner. No doubt a period of mass affirmation was necessary," he added in an effort to explain past violence; but in Gide's view that period was over. "Taking into account the particular idiosyncracies of each individual" was now under way, and eventually Communism would prevail.[1]

When the news became public that a new Soviet constitution was being drafted in the Soviet Union, hopes were widespread in foreign leftist and liberal circles that the hour of democracy in Russia had arrived. Louis Fischer remembers that he "always looked forward to the growth of democracy [in Soviet Russia] at the expense of the dictatorship."[2] The potential of such a development in Russia for the international situation in the fateful 1930s was tremendous as Fischer suggested:

> Democracy inside Russia would have been very relevant to the policy of collaboration for peace with the Western democracies against Hitler. A democratic Russia would have helped anti-Fascist forces in England and France unseat their Neville Chamberlains and Daladiers. A democratic Russia would have avoided the Stalin purge and the Moscow trials, which weakened Russia economically and militarily. A democratic Russia would not have signed the 1939 pact with Hitler. A democratic Russia, in other words, might have prevented the war which the totalitarian Soviets helped to precipitate.[3]

To draft a new constitution was a formal decision taken at the Seventh Congress of Soviets convened in February 1935—a few weeks after the ominous murder of Kirov, but also halfway between the Soviet entry into the League of Nations and the conclusion of the Franco-Soviet alliance. The constitution, which was promulgated in November 1936, was a farce. Its impressive list of civil rights was supported by no constitutional mechanism to safeguard them. All the high-toned declarations of the new constitution (Bukharin and Radek were among the members of the Drafting Committee of the Supreme Soviet) were rendered virtually meaningless. The fact that the peasantry, which represented a majority of some 70 percent, was given voting rights and thus formally accepted into the Soviet "socialist family" was debased by the complete absence of electoral choice. The existing dictatorship was as strong as ever, merely decorated with a more elaborate system of "transmission handles" in line with the old Leninist prescription, which had of course been designed for a different time and situation. "Under a patina of constitutional and legal procedures lay the dead hand of Nicholas I's official nationalism and some of the macabre touches of Ivan the Terrible."[4]

In other words, Stalin's new foreign policy course was accompanied by no corresponding change in his methods of governing Russia. On the contrary. Soviet Russia's new association with Western democracies was accompanied by the launching of the horror of the Great Purges. And the impact of this internal Soviet development upon foreign public opinion, foreign governments and general staffs—including that of Germany—in a period crucial for the fate of collective security, was catastrophic.

The starting point of this ghastly era appears to have been the murder of Sergei Kirov in December 1934, which was very probably engineered by the GPU itself. By the second half of 1936 the purges were in full swing, and did not recede before 1939.

Western observers had noticed the atmosphere of fear in Moscow before the real horror broke out. President Beneš remembers his and Massigli's astonishment in Geneva in the summer of 1934, when Maxim Litvinov suddenly exclaimed during an exchange of views on the modalities of the Soviet entry into the League of Nations: "Do you not realize that if I do not return to Russia with an unquestionable success, I'll be put before a firing squad?"[5] During Georges Bonnet's visit to Moscow in August 1934, Ambassador Alphand informed him about the bugging devices in Litvinov's quarter in the Commissariat for Foreign Affairs. When received by the commissar, Bonnet "gladly gave satisfaction to [his] informer. In fact, from the moment when I took a seat by his side, I recognized that his tone changed and Stalin's name appeared more frequently in his speech, always accompanied by the most flattering epithets."[6]

George F. Kennan, who was assigned to the U.S. Embassy in Moscow in mid-1930s, notes in his memoirs that foreign representatives in Moscow had to deal with two separate governments, of which the formal one, including the Foreign Office, was in fact powerless; the real power lay with the GPU.[7] "Extensive damage has been done to the fabric of Soviet foreign relations over the years by this vicious system." With the outbreak of the purges, "the atmosphere for the conduct of any sort of diplomatic work in Moscow, by anyone, [further] drastically deteriorated."[8]

The fact that Soviet diplomatic personnel became an early target of a prolonged pogrom of the GPU had, of course, special importance for the state of foreign relations of Soviet Russia. Foreign relations of any country are primarily conducted by its officially appointed representatives. In the USSR, only the Commissariat for Foreign Affairs had the license to maintain political contacts with foreign governments and their missions in Moscow. The effect upon foreign diplomats in the Soviet capital and upon the chancelleries abroad of the systematic extermination of their Soviet counterparts, with whom in some cases they had established personal relationships, was an inevitable and significant component in all deliberations concerning international relations whenever Soviet Russia played a part, potential or actual.

Litvinov complained about the GPU's mistreatment of the personnel of the Narkomindel as early as 1931. "Members of our staff have been arrested. . . . In charge is a certain Shkiryatov. . . . Jews are obviously purged first."[9] The assault on the Commissariat was launched in the second half of 1936, and continued with unrelenting intensity through 1937 and even later. The Czechoslovak ambassador to Moscow, Zdeněk Fierlinger, whose sympathies for the Soviet Union are well known, observed: "The atmosphere in Moscow was heavy. Contacts between the diplomatic corps and the Soviet society were interrupted. Every day, the press printed news about acts of sabotage. Officials, with whom the diplomatic corps had been in contact, were disappearing from government offices overnight."[10]

In May 1937 French ambassador Coulondre, describing himself as "stricken by the extent of the repressive actions" (even before the executions of the Soviet military leaders), complained to Yvon Delbos about the disappearance of General Goekker and M. Steiger, two Soviet officials who had been in charge of the liaison between the Politburo and the foreign missions in Moscow.[11] Until recently, the French envoy explained some time later, he had had other channels than the Narkomindel through which to communicate with the Politburo, but these possibilities were destroyed during the *tourmente terroriste* of recent weeks.[12]

Purges were simultaneously affecting dozens of Soviet missions abroad, such as the important embassy in Paris. "Principal officials of the [Soviet] Embassy were disappearing one after the other, victims of the frequent purges. . . . An atmosphere of distrust and fear descended heavily upon the salons."[13]

Litvinov himself, during his stay in the United States between 1941 and 1943, partially disclosed the extent of the decimation of Soviet foreign service to Arthur U. Pope in Washington. Among the diplomatic victims of the purges were Litvinov's two deputies, G. Yu. Sokolnikov and N. N. Krestinsky; his personal secretary, Gershelman; almost all heads of departments of the Commissariat together with, among many others, ambassadors to China (Bogomolov), Germany (Yurenev), Poland (Davtyan), Turkey (Karakhan), Latvia (Karsky), Finland (Asmus), Spain (Rosenberg), Lithuania (Brodovsky), Afghanistan (Shkvirsky), Denmark (Tikhmenev), Hungary (Bekzadian), Bulgaria (Raskolnikov), Norway (Yakubovich), Estonia (Ustinov).[14] Soviet officials attending diplomatic receptions in

Moscow in the early fall of 1937 were of low rank, sheepish, intimidated, standing together aside, visibly afraid to show that they had anything in common with their hosts.[15]

Accompanied by a wave of nationalism and xenophobia that even drew an official French protest,[16] the decimation of the Soviet foreign service was followed by a decision to close down as many as twenty-two foreign consulates. This action affected not just unfriendly countries like Germany and Japan, but also Great Britain, Czechoslovakia, Turkey, Scandinavian and Baltic countries, and others. Count Schulenburg called the closing of the Czechoslovak Consulate in Kiev, which had been opened only a year before, "particularly amazing."[17]

An early fallout of the purges was the disenchantment of many liberal fellow travelers. Some of them, like André Gide, decided at once to break with Moscow completely; others postponed their divorce only because of the outbreak of the Spanish Civil War in July 1936, "swallowing their bile and waiting for the day when . . . Russia and the Comintern [would be] ready to become democratic institutions."[18]

Stalin soon extended the purges to the Iberian front line of the anti-Fascist struggle, which even *Pravda* openly reported in December 1936 in its coverage of the Spanish war.[19] One after another, leading Soviet representatives sent to coordinate the aid for the Loyalists were recalled to Moscow and shot, including Ambassador Rosenberg, General V. E. Goriev, and the almost legendary commander of the International Brigades, General Kléber.[20] André Gide's *Retour de l'URSS*, which appeared in November 1936 (followed by *Retouches* three months later), expressed the shock and disillusionment of many liberal intellectuals, both those who were already abandoning the ship and those who were still on board, waiting for some miracle that would return their dreams. Gide's verdict, in the most widely read political pamphlet in leftist and liberal intellectual circles in Europe in 1937, sounded like the cry of a betrayed lover:

> From top to bottom of the reformed social ladder, the most favored are the most servile, the most cowardly, the most cringing, the basest. All those who refuse to stoop are mowed down or deported one after the other. . . . Soon in the heroic and admirable people who deserved so well our love, there will be left only executioners, profiteers and victims.[21]
>
> And I doubt whether in any other country in the world, even in Hitler's Germany, thought is less free, more bowed down, more terrorized, more vassalized.[22]

[129]

Contrary to the impression that the falsity of the show trials was immediately obvious, the fact is that diplomatic observers in Moscow took the accusations very seriously—in some cases right up until the last of the trials, in March 1938. With the passing of the time, their interpretation of the accusations and verdicts departed from the official Soviet version, and came to differ quite substantially; but it was not based on the assumption that the whole enterprise was a fraud and a witch-hunt. Besides, the purges were followed by far-reaching consequences—disruption of industry, weakening of the armed forces, general political malaise. These stark facts could not be interpreted in any uncertain terms.

Two reports of the French Embassy in Moscow, both filed in January 1937, reflect the seriousness with which the official version presented in the show trials was accepted by the principal Soviet ally in Europe:

> Opposition in the USSR is a serious matter. This opposition is not counterrevolutionary, as they are trying to tell us here, but it is the expression of—within the framework of the Revolution—various nonconformist and anti-Stalinist tendencies. . . . In any event, there exists an attempt at a collusion between Germany and Japan on one side, and Trotskyism on the other.
>
> As far as the Reich is concerned, this trial has revealed, in both countries, the persistence of an undercurrent the importance of which it is impossible to ignore.[23]

> In this drama, it is difficult to separate the part played by the Russian soul and that played by the GPU. If it is possible to be uncertain about the motives of their [the accused's] acts and attitudes, it does not, on the contrary, appear to be a matter of doubt that the accused headed a terroristic organization, which spread its ramifications all around the country and whose membership extends into the highest levels of administration.[24]

The report concludes that the opposition in the Soviet Union, which had been minimized, had in fact been gaining in strength during the last three years and acquired a terroristic character, which is not unusual in autocratic regimes. "So we see the reappearance of one of the most specific traits of old Russia."[25]

That there had been at least "a loose form of conspiracy and actual plot to overthrow the government," the failure of which had largely been "the result of a lack of resolute and bold leadership," was the opinion of the American ambassador, Joseph E. Davies, as late as June 1938.[26] It was not an uncommon opinion among foreign diplomats in Moscow.

President Beneš, who may unwittingly have played a role in the complicated traffic of fraudulent documents between Heydrich and Yezhov that precipitated the action against the Red Army High Command, never ceased to believe that the conspiracy was real. His "persistent, tenacious and cautious effort in the direction of rapprochement between Prague and Moscow" effectively ended with the trials of 1937,[27] and his attitudes vis-à-vis the Russian alliance in 1938 was largely due to the impression created by the internal turmoil in the USSR. After all, as Deutscher observes,

> Whether Western statesmen and military men believed the charges levelled against the defendants to be true or not, their conclusions could not but detract from Russia's value as an ally. If so many outstanding politicians, administrators, and military men had in fact formed a monster fifth column, it was asked, then what was the morale of a nation in which this could happen? If the charges were faked, then was not the régime that indulged in such practises rotten from top to bottom?[28]

British diplomatic correspondence from Moscow in 1937 and 1938 reveals an effort to avoid a direct assessment of the substantiation of the accusations brought against the victims of the show trials, but it covers the course of the purges in great detail, and on an almost daily basis. The consternation of both the diplomats on the spot and their colleagues in the Foreign Office in London is undisguised in questioning "the century in which the political values of contemporary Russia should be situated."[29] The remark was hardly out of place, considering the contents of the typical reports that had to be filed from Moscow during those years. To cite just one example:

> The competent authorities have achieved what must be a record number of executions during the first days of October [1937]. The total number of death sentences reported in the Moscow and provincial press for this period is no less than 314, whereas the total for the whole September was just under 200 and the total for August about the same.
>
> As you no doubt realize, the figures which we give you from month to month only cover quite a small proportion of the total number of executions which take place in this country.[30]

THE TUKHACHEVSKY AFFAIR

Of all the arrests, deportations, and executions, the Tukhachevsky affair, in June 1937—the starting point of the assault of the GPU on the Red Army—was the most shocking, and the most damaging to the Soviet reputation abroad. The previous purge of the GPU itself, following the fall of Yagoda, had produced false expectations abroad that the worst might be over. As Nadezhda Mandelstam noted, the victims, who had meantime "ceased to believe in natural causes of death," did not share that hope. The "new GPU" soon proved that they were right.[31]

Headed by a team recruited in the highest echelons of the party apparatus, with Yezhov as the new boss, the GPU fell upon the armed forces with unrestrained fury, fed by the fact that in the previous purges the Red Army had been left virtually intact. The reaction abroad was immediately vehement, even before it became clear that the affair was not limited to two marshals and a few generals, but was to affect some 50 percent of the entire officer corps of the Soviet armed forces, including three of five marshals, thirteen of fifteen army commanders, fifty-seven of eighty-five corps commanders, and so on—altogether thirty-five thousand officers (90 percent of all generals, 80 percent of all colonels).[32]

The executions of Tukhachevsky and the other leading Red Army commanders had a particularly strong impact in France, "a country with a conscript army which, it was realized, might have found itself taking the field with a power whose high command was conspiring with the common enemy."[33] Ambassador Bullitt reported from Paris that "the executions of Marshal Tukhachevsky and six generals of the Army High Command for the crime of betraying military secrets to Germany caused great consternation" in French military and political circles.[34] Coulondre in Moscow visited Litvinov two days after the announcement of the executions of the military leaders to inform the foreign commissar of "the deplorable impression produced by the massacre show [jeu du massacre]" in France and other countries friendly to the USSR, especially now that the Red Army was affected.[35] Two weeks later the French ambassador repeated his demarche, this time informing Potemkin (who was on his way up, over the corpse of Krestinsky, to the position of deputy commissar) that France, as an ally of Soviet Russia, was naturally concerned about the treason affair in the Soviet High Command and demanding information on "how far the executed officers had been involved in the conspiracy with Germany." Potemkin replied that the generals had organized a coup d'etat with the intention of concluding an alliance with Germany.[36] In spite of Potemkin's obvious effort to play down the charges of the generals' direct collusion with Germany, the allegation that a pro-German conspiracy had taken place in the Soviet High

Command was confirmed through diplomatic channels, and soon thereafter, the progress of the Red Army purge showed that the conspiracy was also widespread in lower commands.

The case could not fail to affect relations between the French and Soviet general staffs. A secret note of the French Ministry of War in April 1937, summing up the contacts between the two armies, testifies to the French interest in some regularization of the military cooperation. A similar conclusion can be drawn from a note of the General Staff of the Army, compiled for the French government in May 1937.[37] Shortly thereafter another document of the French General Staff, entitled "Note . . . Concerning the Eventuality of Franco-Soviet Military Contacts," dated June 9, 1937, took note of the probable consequences of Tukhachevsky's transfer to a provincial command (shortly before his arrest and execution). This document stated:

> The internal situation of Soviet Russia, and especially the complete lack of stability of the military High Command have substantially reduced the authority of those Russian military men designated to establish contacts with the representative of the French General Staff. . . . It [therefore] seems to be better to wait until the uncertainty of the purges which are raging in the USSR will be over. To act differently would mean to court the risk of seeing the military men with whom negotiations would be conducted and arrangements possibly concluded, disappear shortly afterwards.[38]

That was not an unfounded consideration, as the experience of the Czechoslovak General Staff may illustrate. The two armies reached an agreement, in the summer of 1936, to establish practical cooperation in the field of intelligence work against Germany. (It may be noted, as a less important detail, that the Soviets tried to direct their intelligence operations from Czechoslovakia more against Poland than against Germany.) During the Czechoslovak General Staff delegation's stay in Moscow that summer they were received by Tukhachevsky, and conferred with a group of Soviet officers headed by General M. S. Uritzky. On this level, the agreement on the cooperation in the field of intelligence against Germany was concluded. The Soviets then sent a "courteous and well educated former Tsarist officer"[39] to Prague, who started to work in cooperation with the officers of the Czechoslovak Military Intelligence. A few months later (March 1937), this Soviet officer, code-named "Rudolf" by the Czechs, was suddenly ordered to Moscow, were he was in all probability executed. In June, General Uritzky himself was shot. A Soviet Intelligence delegation arrived in Prague in the fall to resume contacts. None of those who had concluded the agreement of summer 1936 were among them. Clearly, they had all been shot.[40]

The alleged treason case in the Soviet High Command was still affecting the attitudes of the Czechoslovak General Staff in 1938, as can be seen from a German diplomatic report from Prague in March 1938. This report, obviously based on intelligence sources, states:

> After the shooting of Marshal Tukhachevsky and other very high-ranking officers of the Soviet Army, the Czechoslovak General Staff lost its confidence in the Red Army staff. On this account mutual relations assumed an abnormal form, especially because the Government on their part adhered to their friendly treaty relations with Moscow. On January 28, 1938, the Czechoslovak General Staff . . . turned down the proposal of the Red Army Staff for the appointment of a mixed commission to examine the defense plans of both states. The Czechoslovak General Staff did not reveal secrets regarding the operational plans and armament of Czechoslovakia, as well as the plans for mobilization and their latest aircraft engines. The fears of the Czechoslovak General Staff are shown by the fact that, up to now, it is not yet convinced that, as Moscow maintains, Tukhachevsky was not in contact with the German General Staff, and so might have betrayed to the latter all the Czechoslovak defense secrets, and because it is not sure that some representatives of the Red Army General Staff might not again hand over such secrets to the German General Staff.[41]

These fears of the Czechoslovak General Staff were far from unsubstantiated, because the Red Army purge was by no means discontinued in spring 1938. At the end of February, quite a short time before the German military attaché compiled his report in Prague, two very high-ranking Red Army commanders were shot-admirals Orlov and Sirkov. The French reaction was similar to that of the Czechoslovak General Staff. Ambassador Bullitt reported from Paris a few weeks after the execution of the Red Army commanders: "Orders were issued to the French ministries and are strictly observed that henceforth no information is to be given to any Soviet representative. . . . An uneasy feeling exists here that information of confidential nature which had been made available to Soviet military leaders may have found its way into German hands."[42] The Abwehr may have had a more direct access to French military secrets at that time, but the impact of the accusation that the executed Soviet military leaders had worked for Germany could not fail to cause great concern. There is little doubt that the GPU's assault on the Red Army

High Command in June 1937 hampered the prospects for a broadening of the cooperation between the French and Soviet general staffs, which until then was the trend, however slow and still lacking a properly negotiated framework. It was agreed in April 1937 to open technical conversations between the two general staffs, which certainly constituted an important step toward such mutual cooperation. This agreement followed a round of talks on the subject between Léon Blum and Ambassador Potemkin, and was understood as the beginning of a process in that direction.[43] Then came the announcement of the arrest and the execution of Tukhachevsky and his "accomplices." No technical talks, of course, ever took place.

In the eyes of the French General Staff, the treason case in the Soviet High Command did not appear improbable, in view of the previous close cooperation between the Red Army and the well known Reichswehr, in high French military circles. According to Georges Castellan, the French Deuxième Bureau had informed the French General Staff regularly until 1933 about the numbers of Soviet officers trained in German military institutions—at least 120 senior Soviet officers in early 1930s.[44] Some of these officers (Tukhachevsky, Uborevich) were then accused of collusion with Germany; others, like the chief of the Soviet General Staff, Marshal Yegorov, retained their positions. On the whole, the blow that the affair inflicted upon the confidence of the French military in their Soviet counterparts could not possibly be redressed in the short period then remaining before the Franco-Soviet alliance would be put to practical test.

Diplomatic correspondence from Moscow, including reports filed by the military attachés, shows that foreign observers soon recognized the continuous and systematic nature of the purge, with its inevitable consequences for the commanding structure of the Red Army.[45] All through 1937 and 1938, the progress of the military purge was reported in great detail. Strong emphasis was put on the fact that the extermination of the Soviet officer corps did not slow down in the summer of 1938 or at the time of Munich.[46] In this last development it was the Soviet Air Force that was particularly affected. Although the previously held radical views about the decisive role of aircraft in modern warfare had to be corrected in the light of the war in Spain, the Soviet Air Force was still considered a formidable factor at the beginning of 1938, believed to be numerically the strongest in the world.[47] In 1938, the Soviet Air Force was purged of its most distinguished commanders (Generals Alksnis and V. V. Khripin and thousands of lower officers; even Tupolev was imprisoned).[48] The reaction of the French air minister in Daladier's government, Guy La

Chamber, expressed in May 1938, may be quite characteristic of French and British views:

> The Russians killed every airplane engineer and constructor they had. They have no new planes and the best they have are their imitations of American models four or five years old. . . . In addition, the officers' corps of the Russian Air Force had been annihilated so completely that the Russian Air Force could not be considered an effective fighting force in spite of the number of planes it contained.[49]

The British government, on the eve of the final stage of the Czecho-slovak crisis at the beginning of September 1938, received from its ambassador in Moscow a report that not only presented a picture of complete administrative disarray, but included a description of the situation of the Soviet armed forces:

> At the beginning of the year, I reported that during 1937 at least 65 percent of the officers over the rank of Colonel, or the equivalent, in the Red Army, Navy and Air Force, had been liquidated. There is every reason to suppose that this year in the fighting services the successors of those who were liquidated are themselves being liquidated at an equally alarming rate.[50]

The broadly publicized desertions of Soviet officers fleeing from the purge to the West, across the Pripet River to Poland, and even to the Far East—(a particularly ominous sign, considering the reputation of the Japanese in the Far Eastern Red Army in respect to their treatment of prisoners of war)—further underlined the desperate situation of the Soviet armed forces.[51]

THE SOVIET PURGES AND THE MILITARY PLANNING OF OTHER POWERS

This whole development could not fail to affect the strategic consid-erations of all parties involved, directly or indirectly, in the crises of 1938. "That hecatomb of generals," wrote Coulondre in his memoirs, "caused abroad, and especially in France, a catastrophic impression, which I myself was unable completely to escape."[52] Sir Samuel Hoare noted in his memoirs that in 1938 "the Great Purge seemed to have left the Soviets incapable of any military action."[53] Ambassador Bid-dle reported in April 1938 that President Beneš had given up his expectations that Soviet Russia could be counted upon as an ally:

Beneš "did not regard Soviet Army any longer as an effective force for Western actions."[54] In Biddle's opinion, Moscow "was slipping in her foreign policy line and potentially facing isolation at a moment when [the Soviet] internal structure had registered a new low in terms of stability."[55] In one of his reports in March 1938, Ambassador Coulondre observed: "Emphasizing the thesis of capitalist encircle-ment, the Kremlin reserves a justification for its abstention in foreign affairs."[56] Litvinov in fact expressed Soviet readiness to be isolated in a conversation with American ambassador Davies as early as Novem-ber 1937.[57] The French ambassador to London, Charles Corbin, re-ported from the British capital also in November 1937 that in British opinion, the Soviet Union was not only weakened by the purges, but her reputation in Western Europe was declining and "her diplomatic action is already stricken by sterility."[58] Ambassador Chilston charac-terized the general Soviet attitude toward the Czechoslovak crises (both in May and September 1938) as "noncommital"; not very sur-prising at a time when, by conservative estimate, every eighth Soviet citizen was in jail, in a concentration camp, or on his way before a firing squad. Chilston concluded: "It is indeed permissible to doubt whether, in existing conditions, the Soviet government would be capable of maintaining the country's vital industries and admin-istrative machinery on a war footing. . . . The severity of the re-pressive measures which they have taken cannot have failed to aug-ment the latent hostility of large sections of the population."[59] Alexander Werth, who placed almost the entire responsibility for the failure of the anti-Nazi alliance on France and Great Britain, nev-ertheless noted "the deplorable effect created in Western Europe by the purges in the Red Army, and the belief that a 'decapitated' army could be of little use."[60]

Ambassador Bullitt noticed the heavy effect of the Red Army purge upon French political and military circles very shortly after the execu-tion of Marshal Tukhachevsky and his comrades. In June 1937 he reported that the recent events in Russia

> greatly strengthened the case of the opponents of the Franco-Russian entente, for the belief now is widespread that the military power of the Soviet Union has been so greatly impaired that in an emergency, the Soviet Union either would not, or could not give France serious armed aid.[61]

In his second report in July 1937, Bullitt stated:

> The emotional reaction in France has been considerable, but the mental

response to recent Russian development has been no less important. The two have combined to produce certain definite changes in France's internal politics as well as in her international position.[62]

In Ambassador Coulondre's opinion, the French political and military establishment (in 1937–38) judged the Soviet factor of the international situation "primarily in view of the Soviet internal crisis; it made them feel that the USSR was not part of the game anymore."[63] According to Ambassador Davies, "Stalin destroyed the confidence of Western Europe in the strength of his government; that also weakened the confidence of both England and France in the strength of the Russian army and weakened the democratic bloc in Western Europe."[64] Winston Churchill, never inclined to justify the folly of the appeasement policy, confirmed that "to Mr. Chamberlain and the British and French General Staffs, the purge of 1937 presented itself mainly as a tearing to pieces of the Russian Army, and a picture of the Soviet Union as riven asunder by ferocious hatreds and vengeances."[65] The whole problem cannot be objectively assessed without considering the alternative—a peaceful internal development in the USSR in the 1935–38 period, in line with Soviet diplomatic action in Geneva at the same time. The complete inconsistency of one with the other was in itself woeful; after all, in the struggle of the epoch, collective security was essentially the cause of democratic forces, opposed by the totalitarian regimes. By its external, diplomatic action, Moscow had associated with the first.[66] By its internal policies, on the other hand, it surpassed all the horrors that Fascist regimes were themselves practicing at the time. This discrepancy affected the Soviet relationship with friends and allies, actual or potential, in the most detrimental way.

The German diplomacy, which did not fail to recognize this inherent defect in the opposing camp, does not appear to have exploited it with any visible success, at least before 1938. Unable to reconcile German revisionist goals with the decisively antirevisionist attitude of France and, to a lesser degree, England, the Wilhelmstrasse had little to offer to the Versailles powers. As for the Soviet Union, objective lack of meaningful differences with Germany and the growing economic interdependence of the two countries were overshadowed by the ideological dispute; which, however, neither side took too seriously. Hitler himself, according to Hermann Rauschning, viewed Bolshevism in his own special way: in essence, he believed it was a brand of National Socialism that needed to be rid of its Marxist-Jewish coating.[67] Had he applied this view to the purges in Russia, they might appear to him as the kind of "purification" he thought necessary. He obviously did not accept Soviet offers of rapprochement in 1935–37 because he would have had to moderate the traditional Nazi anti-Communism which he still needed vis-à-vis the Western powers.

The fact is that Hitler specified, for the first time, his war aims in November 1937, as they are in their *pünktlich* way recorded in Major Hossbach's memorandum. No such specification can be read from Hitler's instructions for the Four-Year Plan, which simply demanded the accomplishment of readiness for war by both the German industry and German armed forces.[68] In November 1937, Hitler narrowed his goals to the Anschluss of Austria and the elimination of Czechoslovakia. That he viewed these two goals as a necessary prerequisite for a campaign against Poland Hitler disclosed to his generals only two years later, after Munich. This chronology of Hitler's planning shows, first of all, that during the Great Purges in the Soviet Union, and especially the Red Army purge, the Fuehrer was refining his expansionist schemes. It also shows that he gave priority to the southerly direction, against Austria and Czechoslovakia, instead of the more predictable drive against the Polish Corridor and Silesia, the territories that Germany had lost in 1919 (Austria and Bohemia had never been part of Prussia or Germany). In November 1937, the fact that Czechoslovakia was protected by a Soviet guarantee, as embodied in the pacts of May 1935, does not seem to have worried the Fuehrer anymore.

A number of factors were involved in Hitler's decision, but his low assessment of the Soviet capability and readiness to intervene militarily outside their own territory was certainly among them. The contribution that the Sicherheitsdienst is suspected of making to the Tukhachevsky affair is of relatively limited importance in this context; the purge of the Red Army officers' corps seems to have followed inevitably from other purges, anyway, with or without Heydrich's assistance.[69] Besides, as Ambassador François-Poncet reported from Berlin as early as March 1937, "trials against the Trotskyists as well as, undoubtedly, intelligence reports from agents, gave the Hitlerite leaders the idea that the USSR was undergoing a deep crisis and that it would soon become a theater of great upheavals."[70] Rumors then circulating in European capitals may have been of various origins, but two months after the Radek-Pyatakov trial and three months before the Tukhachevsky affair, rumors could not have been wilder. It is not difficult to imagine the impression that the extermination of the Red Army commanders must have made in Berlin, when the earlier purges had already produced the effect described by the French ambassador.

One of the first benefits the Nazis drew from the new wave of executions in Soviet Russia was a not improbable theme for Joseph Goebbels's propaganda machine, which claimed that those in the West who had thought that Soviet Russia would become a normal partner in the system of collective security, suffered a moral catastrophe. More important, however, was the obvious encouragement that this self-inflicted mutilation of France's ally would inevitably produce in Berlin. Those most directly affected recognized the danger immediately; shortly after the execution of Tukhachevsky, the Czechoslovak ambassador in Washington observed to Under Secretary Sumner Welles that "this sudden development might bring a more belligerent attitude on the part of Germany."[71]

Ambassador Schulenburg's correspondence from Moscow testifies that neither the Wilhelmstrasse nor the ruler of the Third Reich missed any important detail in the constant flow of obituaries from Russia. Unlike his French, British, American, or Czech colleagues in the Soviet capital, of course, Schulenburg was not disposed to accept with any degree of confidence the Soviet accusation of Tukhachevsky (or, six months earlier, of Pyatakov and Radek, and then Rykov and Bukharin) as working for Germany. For the German ambassador, it was "not clearly discernible where the wave of terror sweeping over the Soviet Union had its origin and what is its aim." At the same time, he reported to Berlin the course and the results of the purges as effectively as the other foreign envoys. Whereas the Paris or Prague, however, the news from Moscow was unqualifiedly bad, in Berlin it made quite a different impression to learn that, for example, "there is no doubt that the wave of murder and persecution that is still [November 1937] unspent has gravely shaken the organism of the Soviet Union. . . . Today the Soviet Union is politically and economically heading for a depression."[72] Schulenburg advised his government that the purges in the USSR "reduced the specific weight of the Soviet Union in world affairs to such an extent that any of Litvinov's attempts to win over other countries for the Soviet viewpoint would be doomed to failure from the very beginning."[73]

In 1938, Schulenburg's conclusions drawn from the unconcerned Soviet reaction to the Anschluss with Austria and the May crisis concerning Czechoslovakia represented a qualified interpretation of the purges from the point of view of German interests. The German General Staff drew its conclusions, too. A detailed "Strategic Study," drafted by the Supreme Command of the Wehrmacht (OKW) in June 1938, the center of which was *Fall Gruenn* (invasion of Czechoslovakia), did not reckon on any Soviet intervention; it only presumed the intervention of France and, rather surprisingly, of Great Britain.[74] This assessment obviously underwent no changes during the summer months, in spite of the fact that the Soviet diplomacy became more visible than in the previous year and a half. On September 9–10, Hitler held a conference with his principal military advisors, generals H. A. H. W. von Brauchitsch, Wilhelm Keitel, and Franz Halder. In a detailed overview of the preparations, and of the battle plan for *Fall Gruenn*, none of the participants touched upon the possibility of a Soviet intervention, either by land or air forces,[75] even though German diplomatic sources reported from Prague three days before the Nuremberg Conference that Rumania accorded its permission for the overflights of Rumanian territory by Soviet aircraft en route to Czechoslovakia.[76] Hitler and his generals simply did not believe that the Russians would fly, permission granted or not. A few days before that, Ambassador François-Poncet informed Paris from Berlin, as if adding color to the Nuremberg Conference, that "the conviction that Soviet Russia will tumble down has reappeared among the leaders of the Reich. According to them, Stalin is seriously ill; revolt rumbles everywhere; war would serve as a signal."[77]

Amid a continuing flow of reports about "unveiling" of conspiracies and punishment of traitors in July 1938, Litvinov quietly concluded an oral agreement with Schulenburg to tone down mutual recriminations of leaders of both countries. This, according to Hilger and Meyer, was the first step to the pact of August 27, 1939, which "was prepared by the Great Purges and [the removal of] the Bukharins, Krestinskys, Radeks and so forth."[78]

This last assumption represents an interesting point. The Bukharins and the Krestinskys, not to mention the Radeks, had not been known to oppose cooperation with Germany before 1934, and their real stand on the possibility of a return to that policy in late 1930s is very difficult to ascertain, if one does not want to take seriously Vyshinsky's fairy tales. Leon Trotsky did oppose the Soviet collusion with Nazi Germany, which he in fact predicted in December 1937,[79] but the connection between himself and the defendants in the show trials was a trumped-up charge.

On the other hand, the general background of many of the Old Bolsheviks killed between 1936 and 1939 does substantiate the opinion that they "would have found it very hard to stomach" any alliance between Nazi Germany and Soviet Russia, as finally happened in August and September 1939. Stalin "visualized the coming pact with Hitler as more than merely a way of securing temporary safety from invasion. . . . What he contemplated . . . was a kind of

Moscow-Berlin axis, an active collaboration of the two dictatorships of influence in Eastern Europe, the Balkans, and even the Middle East."[80] That would presumably have been too much for the Old Bolsheviks, and naturally for most of the foreign Communists in Moscow as well; hence the active external aspect of the politics of the purges. The case of Bukharin supports this thesis. Bukharin's general profile, analyzed by Cohen,[81] shows a man who could not agree to the policy of the pact of August 1939. Both his speech before the Seventeenth Party Congress in 1934 and his last editorial in *Izvestiya* on July 6, 1936 are clear indications of his principled opposition to Nazism, with which Stalin was then seeking an agreement.[82]

Although all that was not immediately understood at the time of the purges, their overall impact upon the outside world was catastrophic.

Seen in the light of the impression created by the internal events in Soviet Russia, the collapse of collective security does not appear as a series of naive assumptions and diplomatic blunders. The purges destroyed the emerging Soviet reputation as a stable state with growing potential to function effectively in the role of one of the principal sponsors of the international status quo. Paradoxically, the terror launched in 1936 coincided with the time when collective security was passionately defended by the official Soviet foreign policy and its chief spokesman in Geneva, Maxim Litvinov. The fact that internal Soviet life became a scene of mass persecution, deportation, and extermination of millions of innocent people rubbed Litvinov's brilliant oratory of most of its credibility. Further, the fact that so many people so highly placed in the civil and military administration of the Soviet Union were routinely accused of treason could not fail to undermine Soviet credibility as an ally. "As a subject of discussion," a London *Times* editorial observed in September 1937,

> treason in Russia shares with weather in England the quality of rueful banality. The deposition, almost invariably followed by the execution, of officials holding positions dimensionally analogous to those held, under imperialism, by a colonial governor or by the head of a government department, is of weekly occurrence nowadays. . . . The horrible routine of trials and killings has become so normal a feature of the daily news that it is easy to forget, or to overlook, how in the course of a year, the image of Russia in men's minds has changed.[83]

The "treason case" in the Red Army High Command, and the prolonged massacre of the Soviet officer corps, had a particularly damag-

[142]

ing effect upon the value the West placed upon the Soviet Union as a possible ally against Germany. From mid-1937 on, conditioned both by the negative and denouncing response abroad and by the objective internal consequences of the purges, Soviet foreign policy gradually moved into semi-isolation. In view of the Soviet offers in Berlin spurned by Hitler, this state also reflected an obvious lack of options.

In Germany, where the purges in Russia met with more complacency than contempt, the gradual apostasy of the Versailles camp by its ally in the East could not fail to result in the encouragement of the Fuehrer to move faster, and more openly after his morbid goals. So, by the totality of their effects abroad and at home, the Great Purges became a critical factor in the fatal processes leading to the Second World War.

[7]

The Soviet Union and the Crises of
1938: The Politics of Withdrawal

Compared with the British and French foreign policy course in 1938, the Soviet role in European affairs in that year has drawn relatively little criticism.[1] One explanation could be that Soviet treaty obligations toward France were not activated by the actual events of the year, and obligations toward Czechoslovakia were activated only if France acted first. As for the Anschluss with Austria, the USSR could not be expected to do more than other members of the League of Nations, who collectively did almost nothing. All in all, the Soviet government could not be accused of breaching its treaty obligations or be directly blamed for the failure of the alliance system, which under the circumstances, it had no power to activate.

On the other hand, close examination of the passage problem, of the purges, of the policies practiced by the Comintern, and of Soviet overtures toward Nazi Germany all demonstrate that meaningful Soviet intervention in any conflict covered by the alliances of 1935 was highly improbable in 1938, and had to appear so to the Western powers. Finally, the outcome of an engagement of the Red Army in a war with Germany had to be regarded with dubiousness because of the disorientation of the commanding structure of Soviet armed forces.[2] Soviet behavior in 1938 does therefore deserve a careful look. The essential question is whether Soviet foreign policy practice departed, in 1938, from the pattern it had assumed in the second half of 1936 and especially during 1937.

Soviet historiography claims that the USSR was the only power in the world that faithfully stood behind Czechoslovakia in the crises of 1938 and that was ready and willing to provide full-scale military assistance even if France failed to fulfill her more directly binding treaty obligations.[3] The question therefore also is to what extent this theory is substantiated by the facts.

At the beginning of 1938, Soviet attention was almost completely absorbed by the trial of Bukharin. Among his codefendants was Krestinsky, who until his arrest in the fall of 1937 had been Litvinov's first deputy. Another deputy foreign commissar, Sokolnikov, had already been shot in connection with the Pyatakov trial, and the imprint of this continuous affair upon Soviet diplomacy need not be restated. The latest show trial coincided with the Anschluss with Austria. Foreign affairs were given less than marginal attention in Soviet media at that time; *Izvestiya*, the principal organ of the Soviet government, devoted not a single editorial to foreign policy in the whole first half of 1938, a characteristic example of "a policy of abstention in foreign affairs" as it was defined by the French ambassador in Moscow.[4]

In terms of treaty commitments, the Anschluss was more test for Paris than for Moscow, of course, but considering the existing Soviet formal endorsement—since 1934—of the European status quo based on the Paris Treaties, it was of interest to both France and Germany to see how the Soviet government would react to the death of Austrian independence. The Anschluss, after all, significantly altered the strategic situation in Central Europe, exposing to eventual German assault the unfortified southern border of Czechoslovakia, a country allied with Moscow. The gradual escalation of the Czechoslovak problem in the course of 1937 had made Germany's motives quite apparent.

Soviet-German relations were undergoing another spell of marked moderation in the way the media of each country treated the other. Always an intriguing phenomenon for foreign diplomats in Berlin and Moscow, this time it was especially puzzling for those stationed in the Soviet capital because it contrasted so sharply with the xenophobic propaganda campaign pursued since spring 1937, when the Soviet *Staatsidee* was officially supplemented by Russian nationalism. Relations between Berlin and Moscow were still clouded by the Fuehrer's anger over the Yurenev affair, and diplomatic correspondence offers no other explanation for the media restraint aside from economic concerns. At all events, the German chargé d'affaires in Moscow, councillor Werner von Tippelkirsch, was visibly pleased with Soviet indifference with respect to the Anschluss, and especially by the fact that the Soviet press "treated the Czechoslovak question with great reserve. As a rule, they [the Soviets] mention only French obligations to Czechoslovakia."[5] That it was not just a coincidence is clear from Litvinov's remark in a conversation on March 19 with the British ambassador to Moscow, Viscount Chilston, that for the Soviet government the Lithuanian affair (Polish pressure on Kaunas to re-establish diplomatic relations) was a much more serious matter "than any German menace to Czechoslovakia."[6]

The fact that Moscow was so absorbed by its internal affairs and that it "shifted aside [external] political problems in which it should be engaged" was a matter of growing concern to President Beneš,[7] who had already been worried by angry Soviet protests against the critical tone of a large section of the Czechoslovak press in relation to the Soviet purges, and who could not easily explain the unfriendly Soviet act of closing down the Czechoslovak Consulate in Kiev along with the consulates of Germany and Italy. We cannot know whether or not Beneš knew the contents of Zhdanov's spiteful speech that provided a general rationale for the closing down of foreign consu-lates in the USSR,[8] but the facts themselves were enough to cause very serious concern. In February 1938, Beneš recommended in Paris the activation of contacts with Moscow,[9] the probable result of which was Delbos's instruction to Coulondre to visit Litvinov and to remind him that "the French government had no intention to modify the policy which had found its expression in the Franco-Soviet Treaty."[10] Zdeněk Fierlinger, the Czechoslovak ambassador to Moscow, visited Deputy Foreign Commissar Potemkin in a parallel action, but was assured that the USSR was ready "to render assistance to Czechoslo-vakia in line with the pact of mutual assistance."[11]

Litvinov's declaration of March 17, the first Soviet reaction to the Anschluss,[12] however, showed that things were not so simple, and that the French and Czech worries had not been out of place. Litvinov proposed to convoke a conference of great powers and interested parties, "within or outside the League of Nations," to deal with urgent problems threatening peace.[13] Inasmuch as the problem in question was obviously that of Czechoslovakia, the most striking as-pect of Litvinov's declaration was the fact that it completely ignored the existence of the Franco-Soviet-Czechoslovak alliance system and proposed instead to call together an international conference to deal with the problem. (Coincidentally, the method was later used, with-out Soviet participation, in Munich.)

Aside from Soviet displeasure with the criticism of the Soviet pur-ges in the Czechoslovak press—which cannot be underestimated, given the importance Stalin attached to the issue—Soviet-Czechoslo-vak relations at the beginning of 1938 were probably better than Soviet relations with any other European country. To claim that Soviet attitudes toward Czechoslovakia were animated by special feelings for a "brotherly Slavic people,"[14] however, is an obvious overstatement. As Kennan caustically, and accurately, observes, "the jealous and intolerant eye of the Kremlin can distinguish, in the end, only vassals and enemies."[15] The circumstances under which the Czech Consulate in Kiev was closed had no trace of brotherly affection. In the Leninist concept, Czechoslovakia was primarily a capitalist country, the unfriendly role of which in the Russian Civil War was repeatedly harped on in Soviet history textbooks.[16] Thomas G. Masaryk, Czechoslovakia's founder and its president from 1918 to 1935, fared no better in Soviet propaganda than Marshal Pilsudski. The fact that thousands of Russian émigrés had found refuge in Czechoslovakia after the war was also resented in Moscow. The strong Czechoslovak Communist party, enjoying constitutional freedoms found nowhere else in Central Europe after the death of the Weimar Republic and the Dollfuss coup in Austria, followed an openly hostile course toward the government of the Republic until 1935, and continued to be a problem in mutual relations between Prague and Moscow even after the Seventh Congress of the Comintern.

Beneš himself, in agreement with Masaryk, always believed that participation of the USSR in European affairs was necessary and useful, and opposed its policy of isolation.[17] Relations between Czechoslovakia and the Soviet Union were established at Beneš's initiative at the Genoa Conference in 1922, but de jure diplomatic recognition was postponed until 1934 because of strong resistance of the Czechoslovak Right. Long before 1934, however, when he significantly contributed to the diplomatic operation that brought Moscow into the League of Nations, Beneš had cultivated friendly personal relations with a number of Soviet representatives in Europe, including Litvinov. Conclusion of the alliance treaty of 1935 was a logical outcome of his policy, which had of course been seriously handicapped by the corrections in the Curzon Line. The original line would have provided Czechoslovakia with two hundred kilometers of common border with the USSR, an optimal element in the security system of Czechoslovakia, in Beneš's view.[18]

Beneš returned from his visit to Soviet Russia in 1935 with very favorable impressions. "He had found the Russian leaders sincerely desirous of peace and anxious to collaborate with all to that end," reported British ambassador Addison from Prague after his conversation with Beneš in June. "It had been necessary to attract Russia westward, in order to re-establish equilibrium in Europe."[19] Not unlike the French, Beneš applauded Soviet alliances with France and Czechoslovakia primarily for "the merit of drawing Russia away from Germany."[20] Beneš was also uncritically impressed by the internal conditions in Russia; he thought that the country was moving away from Communism to some more tolerable political system.[21] The fact is that at least until the fall of 1936, even as president (since December 1935), he worked sincerely for a many-sided rapprochement with Soviet Russia—always, however, considering France the principal pillar of the international position of Czechoslovakia.

In January 1937, according to his own account, Beneš informed Stalin of what he believed was a German conspiracy with Tukhachevsky to overthrow the Soviet government.[22] In later years he lived with the illusion that he had deserved Stalin's gratitude, but he turned out to be another leader duped into believing in the conspiracy theory that was the justification of the purge of the Red Army High Command. Beginning in the fall of 1936, however, Beneš became more and more dubious about the role Soviet Russia could play in European affairs. Greatly disturbed by the catastrophic impact of the purges both internally and externally, he nevertheless tried to play the issue down in his conversations with foreign visitors, anxious to maintain at least the illusion of an effective defensive union with Soviet Russia, or at least of the possibility "to head off Poland and the USSR making a deal with Germany."[23]

In January and February 1938, the Soviet Union placed large armament orders in Czechoslovakia, the result of recommendations by a Czechoslovak military mission that had attended Red Army war games in September–October 1937. The Soviets particularly needed specialized infantry weapons and heavy artillery pieces, for which they sent additional orders in April and July 1938. The contract concluded in April amounted to an "almost general re-equipment of Soviet artillery." Dozens of Soviet technicians were trained in the Škoda Armament Works in Pilsen, where some of them remained even after the German occupation of the rest of Bohemia and Moravia in March 1939, until June 1941. The Soviets were thus in the critical year 1938 acquiring from Czechoslovakia types of armaments that they were unable to obtain from Germany, France, or elsewhere.[24]

Soviet delivery of a small number of medium-sized bombers in summer 1938 made a partial recompense for Czech cannons. The Soviets highly valued Czech technical assistance in the reequipment of their artillery, as witnessed by the fact that when a delegation of Škoda technicians visited the USSR in June 1938, the deputy commissar for war, General Fedko, welcomed them at the Moscow railway station, and later came again to take leave of them—a marked departure from ordinary protocol.[25]

As already noted, French and Czech demarches in Moscow in February 1938 were primarily expressions of the uneasiness caused by the closing of foreign consulates in the USSR, including those of friendly countries. The possibility of Soviet-German rapprochement, again widely rumored at the beginning of 1938, was another reason for concern by Soviet allies.[26] During the last days of their short tenure in office (March 12–April 10, 1938), Léon Blum and Joseph Paul-Boncour, his foreign minister, decided to clarify the state of the Russian alliance. On April 5, Paul-Boncour convened a conference in Paris of French ambassadors in Eastern Europe. It was decided to recommend to the Czechoslovak government—known to have particularly good relations with Moscow—to inquire in the Soviet capital about specific Soviet intentions in case of German aggression. The problem of the passage was also discussed, and it was concluded that the state of Soviet-Polish relations ruled out any possibility of a negotiated passage through Poland. As for Rumania, the only way now to secure her cooperation would be Soviet recognition of Rumanian territorial integrity, including Rumanian possession of Bessarabia.[27]

After his return to Moscow, Ambassador Coulondre told Litvinov that in the French government's view, the USSR should open talks with Prague on forms of Soviet help in case of war, and particularly on routes via which this help would be rendered.[28]

According to a report by the Czech ambassador, Fierlinger, the problem of Soviet obligations following from the pacts of 1935 was soon thereafter discussed at a meeting of Stalin, Molotov, Voroshilov, Kaganovich, Litvinov, and Alexandrovsky, the Soviet ambassador in Prague. Their conference threw no light on the passage problem—on the contrary, it simply took note that there were no routes available. The advisability of a "conciliatory disposition" of the Czechoslovak government toward the minority problems was emphasized, exactly the standpoint adopted at the Franco-British conference in London a few days later. Voroshilov was quoted to have had "no objections against envisaging the forms of assistance to Czechoslovakia . . . in agreement with the French and Czechoslovakian governments."[29] Alexandrovsky, at the same time was quoted (in the Czech version of the report only) as recommending "not to start any specific negotiations concerning the passage because it would be unacceptable for the USSR to make territorial concession to Rumania just in order to assist the French security system in Central Europe."[30] According to the Czech historian Ivan Pfaff, it was characteristic of the Soviet position after March 17 "that, instead of the defense of Czechoslovakia, [Moscow] further spoke about 'the French system in Central Europe,' i.e., in terms which sounded 'imperialistic.' "[31]

In the meantime, Blum's government in France fell and was replaced by the Daladier Cabinet with Georges Bonnet as foreign minister, a team presumably not disposed to be seriously interested in the Soviet alliance under any circumstances. Diplomatic correspondence, however, shows that the new French government, like its predecessors, was primarily interested in the most practical problem of the alliance system, that is, in the problem of Soviet access to the potential battlefields (Czechoslovakia, or German borders with Lithuania and Poland).

Even after the London Conference with Neville Chamberlain and Lord Halifax, where British preference for a conciliatory course or "appeasement" appears to have prevailed,[32] Bonnet still continued to pursue the passage problem—which did not really indicate disregard for the Soviet alliance, at least not at this point. Shortly after his return from London, Bonnet arranged for a meeting with the Rumanian foreign minister, Comnène, who confirmed that Bucharest was afraid of the Russians, *qui ont laissé un deplorable souvenir*. Asked, however, if the Rumanian position on the possibility of transfer of Soviet troops en route to Czechoslovakia would change if the Soviets gave guarantees regarding Bessarabia, Comnène replied: "Without any doubt. The Rumanian government wishes nothing else but better relations with the USSR."[33]

In Geneva, Bonnet raised the problem in a conversation with Litvinov. The commissar, however, was not of the opinion that his government could do anything to improve the prospect of a negotiated passage through Rumania. Faithful to his usual views, he replied that, "taking into account the links existing between France and Rumania, and the [French] treaty with Poland, it is up to France to obtain from these countries [their agreement] to provide the Soviet government with the facilities it needs to fulfill its obligation."[34]

What practical sense could be drawn from this answer, despite occasional Soviet statements that they still intended to fulfill their treaty obligations, is not difficult to guess. It indicated either a preference for forced passage if the situation permitted, with exactly the consequences most feared in Warsaw and Bucharest, or the intention to use the absence of negotiated settlements as an excuse to stay out of eventual conflicts. This prospect, of course, could not escape Bonnet's attention. With tensions rising at the beginning of May, he called in the Polish ambassador in Paris, J. Lukasiewicz, and asked him to urge Warsaw to avoid doing anything that would make it possible for the Germans to speculate on Polish dissidence from the French alliance.[35]

Increased French and Czechoslovak interest in the solution of the passage problem did not pass unnoticed by German diplomats.[36] Schulenburg, however, reported from Moscow that "the Russians were not making great efforts to obtain this privilege [of passage through Rumania]. . . . It is obviously no pleasant thought for the Soviet Union to have to go to war on account of Czechoslovakia."[37]

The Soviet thesis that at this juncture Moscow offered military assistance to Czechoslovakia independent of French attitudes is supported by a newspaper story published eleven years later, in 1949,[38] and by a speech by Mikhail Kalinin in April 1938 that rather surprisingly escaped the attention of interested foreign observers in Moscow, including the Czechs.[39] Accessible diplomatic correspondence contains no specific evidence in support of this assertion, except when Litvinov, in a conversation with Coulondre and Fierlinger, hinted at the possibility of an independent Soviet intervention, not against Germany, but against Poland.[40] About Soviet willingness to deal with Poland at an opportune moment, of course, there was hardly any doubt. On the other hand, Soviet behavior during the May crisis threw serious doubts on Soviet intentions to do anything against Germany, with or without France.

The first Czech crisis of 1938 was connected with municipal elections in Czechoslovakia, scheduled to take place in three rounds: May 22, May 29, and June 12. According to information obtained by the Czechoslovak government, a Nazi coup in the Sudetenland was prepared in coordination with Berlin, and was to take place before the first round of the elections. The Wehrmacht was to be called in in support of the Sudeten Germans. Czechoslovakia partially mobilized her army on May 21, and the coup was called off.

During the critical days of the crisis, both France and Great Britain publicly backed Czechoslovakia. Bonnet declared during his press conference on May 21 that in case of a German assault on Czechoslovakia, France would fulfill her treaty obligations. Herderson backed France in Berlin.[41] Moscow, however, maintained complete official silence throughout the whole critical period, showing no interest in the affair until May 26, when *Izvestiya* finally published a rather restrained commentary. A few days later, *Krasnaya Zvezda*, Voroshilov's organ, added a very significant qualification of the Soviet stand by ostensibly printing the full text of the supplement to the Soviet-Czechoslovak Treaty, which limited Soviet obligations to cases in which France acted first.[42] This official Soviet reaction to the May crisis prompted Ambassador Schulenburg to conclude:

> The Soviet government, with an eye on the internal situation in Russia and fearing a war on two fronts, must hold aloof from military enterprises for the time being, and is hardly likely to allow the Red Army, created for its own protection . . . to march in defense of a bourgeois state. It follows, therefore, the proved tactics of mobilizing other powers, particularly France, against its foes, or fomenting those conflicts which do break out—as for example in Spain and China—by delivering war material, and of extending them as much as possible by political agitation and intrigues of all kinds.[43]

Czechoslovak archival documents show that Fierlinger (whom his French counterpart found "deeply depressed") was unable to reach any [competent] member of Soviet leadership in the critical days of May; he and President Beneš's special emissary, General Husák, were finally received by Voroshilov and Litvinov on May 25, but found them evasive and their answers vague. General Husák, sent to Moscow to obtain a clarification of Soviet military actions in case of war, returned to Prague with a "puzzled impression," unable to bring any clear answers.[44]

The German ambassador also found Moscow "completely passive" during the crisis. "The Soviet government has painstakingly and systematically avoided hitherto any precise announcement on the fulfillment of its treaty obligations," he declared. "Moscow does not feel bound to synchronize its actions with Paris and . . . in a future crisis, it could well remain passive even after the realization of the French military intervention."[45] At the same time, Schulenburg speculated that Soviet diplomacy had probably been more active in London and Paris, "recommending an energetic course . . . in accordance with its well known policy";[46] but available evidence indicates no noteworthy activity of Soviet envoys either in Paris or in London, and in Prague, Alexandrovsky never showed up at the Ministry of Foreign Affairs throughout the entire crisis.

The Soviet mood was more accurately reflected in Stalin's advice, that under the current circumstances "it would be absurd and stupid to close an eye to capitalist encirclement"[47]—a concept that distinguished no difference between Germany and Czechoslovakia. Developing the theme in his "electoral" speech on June 26, Litvinov went out of his way to emphasize that the Soviet Union had had nothing to do with the settlement of the last war. He specifically singled out the Versailles Treaty, which affected Germany, and the St. Germain Treaty, which provided the international legal basis for the establishment of Czechoslovakia. "The Soviet Union had nothing whatever to do with their creation, taking no part in the struggle of imperialist interests."[48] The problem was, from the point of view of Soviet interests, that Germany "was striving not only for the restoration of her rights trampled underfoot by the Versailles Treaty, not only for the restoration of her pre-war borders"—presumably tolerable aims—but also followed the course of "unlimited aggression," including dreams of the Ukraine and the Urals. That threat need not be taken seriously, however, because "aggressors require rapid military success. They need short distances, weakly defended territories, and neither one, nor the other they would find in our country." And referring to his proposal of March 17 to call an international conference to resolve the growing problems, which had not been taken up by other powers, Litvinov added that "the Soviet government . . . relieved itself of responsibilities for the future development of events."[49]

Litvinov's speech drew appropriate attention from foreign diplomats and, first and foremost, from the German Embassy in Moscow. The Germans especially appreciated Litvinov's conciliatory tone in respect to the Reich's effort to win back lost rights and territories. Count Schulenburg's reports also stressed the fact that Moscow had repeatedly appealed to the Czechs to reach a settlement with their minorities,[50] and emphasized Litvinov's statement that Moscow felt "relieved of her responsibility."[51]

The process of Soviet-German rapprochement, which led a year later to the conclusion of the Non-Aggression Pact, actually started in summer 1938, Hilger remembers. Litvinov and Schulenburg then concluded a verbal agreement, Hilger says, according to which media of both countries would discontinue mutual recriminations of "heads of state," presumably Hitler and Stalin. This agreement was extended in November 1938 to the toning down of mutual media recriminations in general.[52]

The actual stages of this development cannot be traced in German diplomatic correspondence. With Schulenburg absent from Moscow most of the summer, the negotiations must have taken place between the ambassador's return to the Soviet capital (August 21) and Litvinov's departure for Geneva (September 4). According to archival documents, however, the two men held only one recorded conference during those days, immediately after Schulenburg's return. The ambassador's report on this conference contains no allusion to the matter described by Hilger.[53] Besides Hilger's memoirs and the archival source (*DGFP*, ser. D, vol. 2), there is no reliable way to pinpoint this affair. It was, however, entirely out of character for the methodical Schulenburg to require as many as four days to file his report on the conversation with Litvinov, and his next report is dated September 26—a whole month later.[54] Such a gap in such a stormy situation is most unusual, and there is good reason to assume that part of the correspondence of the German Embassy in Moscow is missing. Press reports can be examined only with very limited success, because moderation in mutual Soviet-German treatment characterized the whole year 1938, and may well be explained by such other factors as German concern for Central European problems, and Soviet absorption in the purges and in Far Eastern problems.

Hilger, however, who is considered an entirely reliable source, states that these negotiations were taking place both in Moscow and Berlin. In Berlin, it is hard to imagine that they could have been conducted by the newly appointed Soviet ambassador, A. Merekalov. This man, a product of the purges, was poorly qualified for his new job; he spoke no German, and was clearly unequipped to handle such a delicate affair. The fact that he was, even after a blatant "condonation" of the Yurenev episode, "very cordially" received by the Fuehrer does not necessarily contradict this assumption.[55] That might bring the Soviet Trade Delegation in Berlin in the picture again. In the accessible archives, there is no record of activities in 1938 similar to those pursued by the Trade Mission in 1936 and 1937. But the mission's new director, V. G. Davidov (who had replaced Kandelaki's successor in February 1938), was well qualified for all kinds of activity. In 1939, he took active part in the better-documented phase of Soviet-German contacts.

Even though Schulenburg's report on his conversation with Litvinov on August 22 throws no light on the affair described by Hilger, it is still interesting as a clue to the Soviet mood at the time. Litvinov, for example, told Schulenburg:

> The Soviet Union bore no responsibility for the creation and composition of the Czechoslovak state; she had not sat in Versailles; on the other hand, she must combat any increase in power of National Socialist Germany. . . .
>
> If the old democratic Germany had still existed, the Czechoslovak question would have assumed quite a different aspect for the Soviet Union. The Soviets had always been in favor of self-determination of peoples.[56]

Analyzing Litvinov's statement, Schulenburg arrived at some conclusions that he shared with his military and naval attachés. Because of the absence of common borders, he asserted, the Soviet Union would not attack Germany. In case of war following from the activation of the Franco-Soviet pact, Soviet actions would be confined to certain naval and air operations in the Baltic. As for Czechoslovakia, "sending of troops is difficult and also is not in the interest of the Soviet Union." Sending of war material and technicians was probable. The overwhelming conviction of the diplomatic corps in Moscow, Schulenburg added, including the members of the British and French embassies, was that the Soviet Union, in case of a conflict, "would do as little as possible, so that at the end of the war she would have an intact army at her disposal."[57]

However discreet the Soviet-German contacts may have been—and we may recall the ritual secrecy on which Litvinov had so insisted during his initial contacts with Paul-Boncour and Léger in 1933—rumors about a rapprochement between Germany and Soviet Russia were circulating again in European capitals at that time. Foreign correspondents in Moscow, who besieged the Press Department of the Narkomindel in an effort to obtain official Soviet opinion on that matter, finally extracted from Evgenii Gnedin, the press officer of the Commissariat, an evasive declaration that stated Soviet readiness "to receive favorably any proposal by Germany that promoted world peace."[58]

Hitler is quoted in one of the documents of the Nuremberg Trials to have observed during one of his conferences with his generals, on August 22, 1938: "On the whole, there are only three great statesmen in the world. Stalin, myself and Mussolini. Mussolini, the weakest, has not been able to break either with the power of the Crown or of the Church. Stalin and I are the only ones that see only the future."[59] The Fuehrer, it would seem, was becoming more disposed to consider favorably the possibilities that he had declined a year earlier. A basis for "disengagement" from hostile attitudes between the two powers appear to have been seen and considered both in Germany and in the Soviet Union. In this context, the extension of the provisions of the Soviet-German Trade Agreement (of March 1, 1938) "to include Austria with effect of 1st September"[60] is also not without importance, because it amounted to a tacit recognition of the Anschluss with Austria—on the eve of Munich. Councillor Tippelkirsch in Moscow observed in one of his reports in summer 1938:

The attitude of the Soviet Union to the pacts with France and Czechoslovakia has recently undergone a change. When the Soviet Union concluded the pacts with France and Czechoslovakia, she thought that by so

[155]

doing, she could protect herself from possible German attacks. In the course of the recent [May] crisis, the Soviet government has been forced to realize that the treaties no longer operate in her favor, as she originally intended, but on the contrary, impose on her embarrassing obligations.[61]

The Soviet version of the events of summer 1938 is rather grudging, from the evidence, and even relatively recent works add essentially nothing to archival items published in 1958.[62] This selection contains only the more "positive" parts of the Litvinov-Schulenburg conversation of August 22. Soviet authors particularly fail to throw any light on the views in Moscow regarding the passage problem, which is striking considering the repeated emphasis on "Soviet readiness" to fulfill treaty obligations to France and Czechoslovakia.

A close examination of available French sources shows that no other problem was in fact more crucial for Paris in the framework of the Russian alliance, and particularly in the context of the Czech crisis in the summer of 1938. Aware of their inability to provide, in time, effective assistance to their Central European ally, they continued to explore and reexplore the possibility of a Soviet intervention. Between Soviet Russia and Czechoslovakia stood no deep German territory to cross, as was the case for France. Relatively short routes to Ruthenia led through countries allied with France; and in the case of Rumania, allied even with Czechoslovakia. Hence the notion of the easier access to the presumed Czech battlefield from the east. "Pressure exerted on Warsaw and Bucharest from the French side" to yield on the question of transit of Soviet troops was reported by German diplomats as late as mid-September.[63] Daladier and Bonnet certainly had their opinions about the Soviet Union, and they were reluctant to do anything that would alienate the British; documents, however, do not justify the assumption that they were preparing the betrayal of Czechoslovakia.[64]

As the crisis was building up in August, Bonnet—still not discouraged by Litvinov's last rebuff in Geneva—called in Suritz, the Soviet ambassador in Paris. He told the Soviet representative that the general staffs of France and Czechoslovakia were discussing the problems arising from the threat of German aggression, and in that connection asked again "in what ways would the Soviet government be able to render to Czechoslovakia the assistance it had promised." At the same time, Bonnet instructed the French chargé d'affaires in Moscow, J. Payart, to make the same inquiry in the Commissariat for Foreign Affairs.[65] On September 2, Payart was received by Litvinov for a conversation that was to acquire a special importance in the history of Munich. Both this conversation with Payart and Litvinov's later (September 11) conference with Bonnet in Geneva appear to have sealed the fate of the Franco-Soviet alliance, and of Czechoslovakia as well. The question of responsibility for the failure of both governments to agree on effective measures in defense of Czechoslovakia cannot, of course, be reduced to this episode. Due account of both events must nevertheless be taken.

A short, paraphrased Soviet version of the Litvinov-Payart conversation appeared in the selection of documents published in Moscow and Prague in 1958. Minutes of the conversation certainly exist in Soviet archives, but for some reason what was published was not the authentic record, but a summary telegraphed by Litvinov to Fierlinger in Moscow. This unusual source has up to now been the only hard evidence on the case by all known Soviet works since 1958. The mystery is why at least Soviet authors have not referred to some more complete record of the conversation.[66]

The same telegraphic information on the conversation was communicated the same day (September 2, 1938) to Churchill by Ambassador I. M. Maiskiy.[67] A note of the Political Directorate of the Quai d'Orsay, obviously based on the minutes of Payart's conversations with Litvinov, was issued in September. Addressed to Bonnet, it recommends that he should continue to discuss the matter with Litvinov in Geneva; Coulondre is directed to discuss the matter in Moscow with Molotov.[68]

Bonnet went to Geneva on September 11 for the sole known purpose of seeing Litvinov; whether Coulondre went to see Molotov is not known. At all events, the assertion that it was Bonnet who "rudely falsified" Litvinov's declaration to Payart is certainly not substantiated, because the circular letter based on Payart's report was issued not by Bonnet, but by the Political Directorate.[69] What Bonnet did was to summarize this document in his memoirs, which were published immediately after the war and which became accessible much earlier than the relevant French or Soviet diplomatic documents.[70]

Litvinov's answers to Payart, according to both the Soviet and French versions, contained these points:

1. Litvinov replied by asking what the French would themselves do, because the Soviet obligation "was dependent on the action of France."

2. The foreign commissar recognized the difficulties created by the attitude of Poland and Rumania, but he thought that in the case of

Rumania these difficulties could be overcome, and that that could best be done through the agency of the League of Nations.

3. He suggested that the council of the League should be invoked under Article 11 (danger of war; this article was not mentioned in the treaties of May 1935).

4. He further suggested a common declaration of Great Britain, France, and the Soviet Union, and a convocation of a conference of general staffs.

5. The decision of the council need not be unanimous; a majority decision should be considered sufficient.[71]

The Political Directorate of the French Ministry of Foreign Affairs found Litvinov's answers "evasive and characterized by a tendency to take recourse to procedural arguments . . . failing to clarify the attitude of the USSR" toward the essential problem arising in connection with possible German aggression against Czechoslovakia. Litvinov's answers were also characterized as an "a priori exclusion of an enforced passage," but no one considered such a course of action acceptable anyway. As for the proposed recourse to the League of Nations, the probability of a timely decision of that body was almost nil. Moreover, it was very doubtful that such a decision would actually be respected in the absence of other, direct and specific Soviet guarantees. Only shortly before, Litvinov himself characterized the League of Nations as a body which "had ceased to be reckoned with, which ceased to be feared," and where member-states were "releasing themselves from the obligations which they had assumed."[72]

The French document therefore asked once more for a clarification of the Soviet political position before the start of eventual military talks, the practical value of which, in the absence of a negotiated settlement of the passage problem, was purely theoretical. As a means of encouraging Moscow in this direction, the note proposed to make it absolutely clear that France was determined to go to war against Germany in case of the latter's aggression against Czechoslovakia.[73]

The fact that Moscow proposed recourse to the League of Nations instead of a last-minute, meaningful initiative toward Poland and Rumania was visibly discouraging for the Czechs, too. Ambassador Fierlinger took the liberty of declaring, at the Narkomindel, that the Soviet proposals were too theoretical and that he would prefer to see the USSR in a more active role.[74] Shortly before Litvinov's conversation with Payart, President Beneš (as well as Hubert Ripka) had sounded out the Soviet ambassador in Prague, Alexandrovsky, on the possibility of a direct Soviet assistance to Czechoslovakia. In both cases, Alexandrovsky simply ignored the question.[75]

Ambassador Coulondre, who was absent from Moscow at the time of Payart's demarche, shared the Quai d'Orsay view of Litvinov's declaration; it can be assumed that he was acquainted with the minutes of the conversation between Litvinov and Payart. In Coulondre's opinion, "Moscow was taking shelter behind the League of Nations, whose mechanism failed in each conflict."[76] Even Fierlinger was close to this opinion. "I told Coulondre," he says in his memoirs, "that I do not rule out a certain aversion of the Soviet Union for the idea of going to war. Nor do I underestimate certain symptoms of internal difficulties of the Soviet Union. Otherwise, however, their good will and loyalty cannot be doubted."[77] Fierlinger was obviously doing his best to maintain the image of the USSR as a faithful ally, at least when talking with Coulondre. Alone with Potemkin, the Czech envoy was not so sure about Moscow's "good will and loyalty." On September 9, in another conversation with the deputy foreign commissar, he even accused the Soviets of "creating an atmosphere of general European distrust which trips up Czechoslovakia."[78] The fact that Fierlinger went so far in criticizing Soviet behavior speaks for itself.

When the General Assembly of the League of Nations convened in Geneva in September for its regular session, a number of delegates were absent, among them Beck, Halifax, Bonnet, and even the Czech foreign minister, Kamil Krofta. It was hardly necessary to recall the deplorable state of the league, but during his conference with Bonnet on September 11, Litvinov repeated his stance already communicated to Payart. At the beginning of the conversation, the commissar tried to brush aside the Czechoslovak problem by the usual formula that Moscow would "uphold its engagements." Pressed for a more specific answer, he "completely ruled out any Soviet military action against Germany" in the absence of explicit authorization by the League of Nations and without the actual observance of the council's appeal by Poland and Rumania.[79] Asked about the extent of possible Soviet help in the event that these hypothetical conditions should be met, Litvinov replied that this question would have to be discussed by experts. On the same occasion he also rejected a highly relevant British proposal to replace the unanimity principle of the league by majority principle, thereby contradicting his previous suggestion that unanimity, at least in the Czech case, would not be necessary.[80]

Bonnet objected that the delay caused by the procedure proposed by Litvinov would mean that the fate of the Czechoslovak army

[159]

would in the meantime be decided and the country occupied before the council could reach a verdict. Litvinov stuck to his position. "Under these conditions," concluded Bonnet in his circular note, "with Soviet intervention subordinated to the affirmative decision of the Council and to the consent of Rumania, it appears that the Soviet government could easily find a loophole to justify their abstention at the hour when France would already be engaged."[81]

This exchange of views, it should be noted, was still based on the assumption that Germany would invade Czechoslovakia, in spite of the fact that on September 5 Prague had accepted all demands of the Sudetendeutsche Partei for autonomy of the German-majority regions of Bohemia and Moravia. In such a case, France would have no other recourse but to uphold her treaty obligations; disregarding the offensive ability of the French Army, a French declaration of war would bind important German forces in the West. Bonnet's concern about Soviet actions at this point appears to have been sincere and understandable. By the same token, it is also worthy of note that the commissar did not inform Bonnet about the negotiations he was simultaneously conducting with the Rumanian foreign minister, Comnène (between September 9 and 13), even though these contacts, initiated by Comnène, showed clearly the prospect of Rumanian consent to the passage of Soviet troops without a verdict of the League of Nations and even without explicit Soviet concessions regarding Rumanian territorial integrity.[82]

A few days later, the situation changed abruptly when the Sudeten Germans, after Konrad Henlein's return from a conference with Hitler, maximized their demands with their new slogan *Heim ins Reich*, which amounted to a demand for the annexation of the Czech borderlands by Germany. On September 15, Chamberlain conferred with Hitler in Berchtesgaden, and two days later, Lord Runciman, back from his mission to Czechoslovakia, reported in London that anything other than a "territoral solution" of the Sudeten problem did not seem feasible. For the French, confronted with the probability of war with Germany without any immediate or effective intervention of their Soviet ally, such a solution could hardly fail to be attractive, and they needed little inducement to cosponsorship of a Munich-style variant that promised to avoid an all-out war.

On the 19th, the British and French governments urged Prague to cede to Germany border areas whose population was more than 50 percent German as a price for avoiding the onslaught on Czechoslovakia planned by Hitler for September 27. In the meantime, a Czech Socialist party deputy, J. David, brought from Moscow a message unofficially promising Soviet assistance. According to Councillor Hencke's report, the Soviets pledged "to concentrate troops about three million strong on the Polish and Rumanian borders. The Red Army was determined to extort the right of transit through Poland and Rumania, if necessary by means of an ultimatum to the governments in Warsaw and Bucharest." The message was received in Prague with skepticism.[83] Foreign Minister Krofta, in a press conference on September 16, expressed anxiety that the Soviet Union was only ready to support Czechoslovakia as it had been supporting the Republican government in Spain[84]—a concern held by President Beneš as well. The results of a visit to Moscow by the Czechoslovak air force chief, General Fajfr, were disappointing: Fajfr was well received, but his hosts avoided any discussion on the question of military cooperation.[85] The British ambassador in Moscow, Viscount Chilston, observed in his report dated September 19 that "the noncommittal attitude so far adopted by the Soviet government toward the Czechoslovak crisis has, I imagine, done much to disillusion those in France who were formally confident of Soviet assistance."[86]

Beneš still thought that a more energetic Soviet stand might affect France and eventually even England—which was altogether unlikely. Before accepting the Franco-British plan, therefore, he asked the Soviet ambassador, Alexandrovsky, to transmit to Moscow two urgent questions: What would the Soviet Union do in the event that France should fulfill her treaty obligations? and What would be the Soviet attitude in the event that France would not support Czechoslovakia, and the latter would hold to her positions?[87]

The formulation of Beneš's first question confirms that at this high point of the crisis, the Czechoslovak president was not at all certain whether Moscow would fulfill its obligations if France went to war in defense of Czechoslovakia. Equally noteworthy is the fact that Alexandrovsky—hardly on his own—changed the contents of Beneš's second question, as it appears in the selection of Soviet and Czechoslovak documents published in 1958. According to this source, Beneš asked not about the Soviet attitude to a Czechoslovak refusal of the Franco-British plan, but about the Soviet attitude in Geneva should Czechoslovakia ask for the application of articles 16 and 17 of the Covenant.[88] It may be, of course, that this "correction" is of a much later origin, simply to fit Potemkin's answer better. The Soviet answer to the first question was affirmative. As for the second question, Moscow insisted on the recourse to the League of Nations. Beneš, in his own account, told Alexandrovsky that "this would not be enough for us. . . . Knowing the situation in Geneva, where a number of states would purposefully prolong the dealings, we are afraid that the decision in Geneva would come too late. . . . It would be required that the Soviet Union act faster."[89] In his speech in Geneva on September 23, Litvinov denied that Prague had ever asked the second question. "The Czechoslovak government," he said, "had not put the question of Soviet assistance independent of French assistance."[90]

In any event, Alexandrovsky appears to have withheld the answers overnight. He brought them to the Hradčany Castle on the 21st, after the Czechoslovak government, at an emergency night meeting, decided to yield to the British and French pressures: however indirectly and inaccurately (he did not know the contents of Beneš's questions), Fierlinger had learned about Soviet answers in Moscow a day earlier. Soviet sources claim that Alexandrovsky informed Beneš about Soviet answers by telephone on the 20th, presumably before midnight. Even if the answers had been delivered before the decision was taken, however, which was obviously not the case, Soviet insistence on the League of Nations procedure would still have been discouraging. The Czech retreat made it easier for Moscow to reformulate the second answer in a way closer to Beneš expectations, but still not going as far as the president had hoped.[91] The British view was that the reluctance of the Czechoslovak government to accept the Franco-British plan "had been based on promises from the Soviet government which Prague finally decided were inadequate."[92] The American ambassador, Orme Wilson, reported from Geneva on September 22 that he had been assured by the Soviet delegation that "under no circumstances would Russia lend military assistance to Czechoslovakia except in common action with France."[93]

Beneš and the Czechoslovak government were in fact entirely uncertain about Soviet intentions. On one hand, they appreciated the Soviet support expressed in general terms, but they had no specific assurances about the practical aspects of Soviet assistance. At his press conference on September 21, Krofta declared that when deciding about the Franco-British plan, the Czechoslovak government could not themselves assume the responsibility for a war with Germany "without any possibility that any assistance would arrive."[94] That Soviet assistance was an "open problem" in September 1938, General Krejčí, Czech chief of the General Staff, confirmed as much as thirty years later.[95] In his memoirs, Beneš noted that he "was afraid that the Soviet Union . . . might get into a situation when it could only help to that extent to which it was helping the Spanish Republic."[96] In a letter in November to L. Rašín, a radical deputy in the Czechoslovak National Assembly, Beneš wrote that during the

[162]

September crisis, he had known nothing with certainty concerning an outside help, and as for Soviet Russia, "she would send only flying personnel and [then] wait the same way as the West."[97] On the other hand, according to General František Moravec, chief of the Czechoslovak Military Intelligence in September 1938, "Czechoslovakia asked the Soviet Union, in the fateful pre-Munich days, to explain what kind of concrete help it could provide. The Soviet Union answered that it could supply Czechoslovakia with 400 airplanes without flying personnel. No aid from the Red Army was mentioned."[98]

President Beneš's former secretary, Eduard Taborsky, remembers that "whenever during the long years of his exile in Great Britain the President talked to us about Munich, he invariably raised the analogy of the Soviet role in the Spanish Civil War in a way which left no doubt in his mind that this was what he feared the Soviet aid might at best amount to."[99]

The development took another turn on September 22 and 23, when Hitler, meeting once more with Chamberlain, in Bad Godesberg, put forward new territorial demands against Czechoslovakia that went substantially beyond the Franco-British formula of September 19. Part of these demands were annexations by Poland (in Moravia), and by Hungary (in Slovakia); in Bohemia and Moravia, Hitler now asked for regions with Czech majorities.

Both Paris and London informed Prague that under these new circumstances, the British and French governments could not advise against the mobilization of the Czechoslovak army. Czechoslovakia immediately mobilized, on September 23, and a day later France also ordered a partial mobilization. In Geneva, Litvinov advised Czech delegate Heidrich to present a complaint against German aggression if that occurred.[100] The British delegation in Geneva, however, reported that in the view of both de Valera, the president of the council, and Avenol, its general secretary, "it was extremely doubtful whether any such decision would be obtained from the Council. . . . We are inclined to agree with that view. In any event, action by the Council would come at a later stage."[101]

The treaties of May 1935 in fact provided for such an eventuality, stating that should the league be unable, for one reason or another, to make a recommendation, "the obligation of rendering assistance nevertheless will remain in force."[102] Soviet insistence on a formal sanction by the Council—"a condition which could not be fulfilled," according to Paul-Boncour—was therefore bound to have special meaning for both France and Czechoslovakia, especially after September 22, when the possibility of direct recourse to the Paris-

Moscow-Prague alliance system briefly resurfaced as an option. Litvinov, characteristically, still remained in Geneva, the only minister of foreign affairs in the city, a passive spectator in a crowd of second- and third-rank diplomats. In Moscow, the pressing agenda of the critical days of the crisis was handled by Potemkin.

Steps toward the revitalization of the tripartite alliance system merit noting. Upon French initiative, contacts between the general staffs were reestablished immediately after the Godesberg conference. General Gamelin informed Voroshilov about the state of French preparations, and in reply to this communication, the Soviet military attaché in Paris delivered a message from the commissar for war that stated that the Soviet High Command was readying thirty infantry divisions, motorized divisions, and air forces along the western borders of the USSR. As late as September 28, Bonnet urged Coulondre in Moscow to see Potemkin and to inform him ("for case that Marshal Voroshilov had not done so") about "useful contacts and conversations of technical nature" between the two armies.[103] The Czechs also pressed for practical steps in the same direction, and Fierlinger even imposed himself upon Potemkin during the latter's weekend stay out of Moscow. The Czechoslovak air force chief, General Fajfr, again dispatched to Moscow, managed to bring back to Prague a group of high-ranking Soviet air force officers.[104]

Since the 24th, as we now know, the Soviet government had had in their hands the Rumanian note containing the explicit consent of Bucharest to the passage of Soviet troops and to massive overflights of Rumanian territory en route to Czechoslovakia. Moscow never answered this note, however, nor did it inform Prague or Paris about it.[105] Both governments were obviously informed by Comnène about the Rumanian step and the absence of Soviet reaction could not fail to affect their subsequent behavior.[106]

Other facts deserve attention as well. A day before Godesberg, *Pravda* wrote that "the Soviet Union was indifferent to the question which imperialist brigand falls upon this or that country, this or that independent state."[107] The Soviet press continued to play down the crisis completely even after September 23, the day of the Czechoslovak mobilization, printing short summary reports under the headline "Latest Events." On September 26, halfway between Godesberg and Munich, when the prospect of the activation of the alliance system was relatively better than at any other point during the entire crisis, *Izvestia* replayed *Krasnaya Zvezda's* trick of four months earlier, and printed the text of the Soviet-Czechoslovak Treaty with a gloomy commentary emphasizing the fact that in case France abstained, the

Soviet Union would be released from all obligations toward Czecho-slovakia.[108]

During this phase of the crisis, it is easier to recognize the Soviet willingness to act eventually against Poland rather than against Germany, as it was shown in the threat to abrogate the Soviet-Polish Non-Aggression Pact of July 1932. When President Beneš initiated talks with Warsaw, immediately after Godesberg, in order to settle the Teschen problem before Germany should strike, Fierlinger reported that Moscow advised caution in these negotiations; in his expectation, the Soviet Union would attempt, in case of a "favorable development," to establish a common border with Czechoslovakia.[109] "Our negotiations with the Poles are followed with great attention here, and they [the Soviets] are resolved not to leave Warsaw's behavior toward us without punishment. They do not doubt that the hour of reckoning will arrive."[110] When commenting on Krofta's exposé during a government meeting on September 28, Beneš remarked that "Soviet assistance [against Germany] is difficult. Situation would be different if we were attacked by Poland."[111] Even that, however, was only a possibility if it did not mean a conflict with Germany; two days after Munich, when an attack on the mutilated Czechoslovak state by Poland appeared imminent and Bonnet asked Litvinov in Paris whether Moscow would act "in accordance with the promise made to Prague," Litvinov replied that "the Soviet Union will do nothing in support of Czechoslovakia."[112]

The possibility of a diplomatic settlement of the crisis, by way of an international conference, was never ruled out in September 1938, and according to Fierlinger, Beneš himself had contemplated such recourse even before he received Franklin Roosevelt's message to that effect on September 27. Beneš insisted, however, on the participation of the Soviet Union, and the idea that Czechoslovakia as the object of the negotiations could be kept out did not obviously cross his mind at all before September 28, when Mussolini started to intermediate.[113] As for the Soviet government, it had formally proposed the convocation of a conference for the same purpose as early as March 17, 1938. When Roosevelt's messages to Hitler and Beneš were published, the Soviet government immediately welcomed the initiative and specifically seconded the American proposal on September 28,[114] but always clearly with the assumption that the Soviet Union would take part in the enterprise. Speaking about a "general conference" as Moscow's preferred approach to a solution of the Czechoslovak problem, Potemkin restated this Soviet standpoint on the day of Munich, September 29. On this occasion, it must be noted, Potemkin also said that "it is really impossible to hold a conference on the fate of a country without that country being represented"[115]—a creditable principle that did not, however, play a great role in the Soviet foreign policy only eleven months later, in Poland in August 1939.

In any event, Moscow was not invited to take part in the conference, because a conclave of the format and style of Munich was Hitler's price for recalling his onslaught on Czechoslovakia, which had been rescheduled for September 28. And to speculate what the policy of the Soviet government would have been at that conference had Moscow been invited is of course fruitless. In any event, the Soviet government's last opportunity to interfere with the development appears to have been on September 30, a few hours after the signing of the Munich verdict. At seven-thirty in the morning, the desperate Czechoslovak president called Alexandrovsky and asked him more directly what he had already asked ten days earlier—namely, Is the Soviet Union willing to grant full military assistance to Czechoslovakia, independent of France and of the League of Nations, if Prague will refuse the Munich *Diktat* and defend itself?

Beneš needed an answer before noon the same day. Alexandrovsky, however, waited until 11:20 to cable his dispatch to Moscow. The delay is entirely inexplicable—the time difference between Prague and Moscow is only two hours. The Soviet answer came safely after the Wehrmacht marched into the Sudetenland—on October 2. The fact that the Soviet government answered in the affirmative was then a mockery.[116] No Soviet answer to a Czechoslovak appeal for an immediate Soviet air support, sent to Moscow on the eve of the presumed German invasion (September 27), ever arrived, despite the fact that the request was prompted by a specific offer by a high representative of the Soviet air force.[117]

The German High Command had sufficient ground to disregard the possibility of a meaningful Soviet intervention, as an examination of the diplomatic correspondence after the affair shows. German agents, sent into western border areas of the Soviet Union in early summer 1938 to report on the Red Army movements, found no trace of the concentration of those thirty divisions mentioned by Voroshilov to Gamelin. A French intelligence report obtained from German military circles stated that Soviet troops in the area were unprepared to provide assistance to the Czechoslovak army.[118] The German Embassy in Bucharest, in an evaluation of reports by diplomats and agents, reported on October 8:

Preparations of transports of war material from the USSR or any concentrations of Soviet land forces or air forces are out of question. Nothing indicates any Russian intention of passage, which proves even more completely than up to now that neither between September 19 and 30, nor in the first half of September had the Soviet Union the intention to bring into motion its war machine for the purpose of granting military assistance to Czechoslovakia.[119]

Polish intelligence sources also reported that "there had been no military preparation of any kind whatever on the Russian side of the Polish border;" and in the Polish government's view, Moscow never had the intention to do anything more than "the possible sending [of] a very few bombing planes" to Czechoslovakia.[120]

Councillor Tippelkirsch reported from Moscow on October 3 that "nothing special was observed by us here during the critical days. Whereas other governments adopted preliminary measures of mobilization, the Soviet government does not seem to have done anything of that sort."[121] A week later, Tippelkirsch filed a more comprehensive report, concluding: "The Soviet Union neglected to take such preliminary measures of mobilization as were considered necessary, for instance, in Holland, Belgium or Switzerland. Considering that the Soviet Union was under an obligation to render assistance to Czechoslovakia, this attitude must seem particularly striking."[122]

This report, it should be noted, dealt primarily with the progress of Soviet purges, especially in the Red Army and in the Commissariat for Foreign Affairs. The disappearance of V. K. Bluecher, Chief of the Protocol Barkov, and the chief of the Press Department of the Narkomindel, Gnedin, was of special interest. Tippelkirsch also observed that the isolation of the Soviet foreign policy was "fully appreciated here" (in Moscow).[123]

Litvinov did not take a train to Moscow from Geneva, where he was staying until September 30. Instead, he went to Paris to visit his friend Suritz. He even met with Bonnet on October 1 and probably also on October 2, adding a touch of credibility to the hotly disputed French assertion that even throughout the final stages of the crisis, the French government "had constantly maintained contact with the Soviet government."[124] That claim can be neither denied nor substantiated on the available evidence (and therefore cannot be translated into an indirect Soviet complicity in the Munich affair).

On the other hand, Soviet behavior during the crisis can hardly be explained by Moscow's allegiance to the League of Nations, as Paul-Boncour was inclined to believe. As an instrument of collective security, the league had been written off by no one so completely as by

Litvinov, and no one was less inclined to expect anything in Geneva in September 1938.[125] And for Josef Stalin, the real overlord of the business of the Soviet foreign policy, legalism in international affairs was certainly not a virtue to be seriously contended with.

A thorough examination of the Soviet behavior in the crises of 1938 shows that there was no departure from the direction taken in 1936, and especially in 1937. Of the complex of external problems facing the Soviet Union, only the Far Eastern theater was acknowledged as a direct security case. Even here, however, the fact that the purges did not let up even in the Maritime Province testifies to a shrewdly realistic assessment of the extent and timing of the danger.

Behind the general attitude toward external problems certainly lay a variety of reasons, some of which might well be traced back to 1928 and to the failures in China; that is, to the recognition of the fact that by none of its foreign policy instruments could the Kremlin sufficiently influence the outside world. If we do not want to explain Soviet behavior by factors that arose three years later, the more logical explanation follows from the purges. In 1937 and 1938, they were the primary concern of the Soviet leadership, and the primary factor behind its policy of withdrawal from foreign engagements. The relentless continuation of the purges in the Red Army, where in 1938 captains simply assumed the positions of division commanders,[126] is in itself a sufficient indication that a large-scale deployment of Soviet armed forces, especially in a campaign outside the USSR and eventually on two fronts, could not be seriously contemplated in the Kremlin. Once such a course was—temporarily at least—found impractical and inadmissible, the policy of withdrawal was the only acceptable one, especially as long as there still was no alternative foreign policy orientation. Ideological justifications of this policy, like the revival of the doctrine of "capitalist encirclement," mainly when canonized by Stalin, should obviously be given more weight in reading the trends of the Soviet foreign policy than Litvinov's oratorical efforts in Geneva.

This doctrine of "encirclement," combined with the doctrine of "irreconcilable contradictions between the imperialist powers," retracted the previous differentiation between democracies and totalitarian states and justified not only the withdrawal from one camp, but also the eventual association with the other.

The task of the Commissariat for Foreign Affairs was of course not only to lead Soviet foreign policy through the critical year without risk of any direct involvement of the USSR in external conflicts, but also to do so without formally sacrificing the standard accessories of the

Leninist-Stalinist doctrine, like "defense of peace" or "anti-Fascism."
According to Alexis Léger, this discretion of the Soviet foreign policy
was already recognized in Paris a year before Munich,[127] correspondingly affecting French foreign policy considerations well before
Daladier and Bonnet.

One of the most expressive traits of this course was the calculated
failure to clarify certain standpoints that were essential for France and
especially for Czechoslovakia. President Beneš consistently complained about this problem; uncertain about Soviet intentions, he
remained uncertain about the ultimate wisdom of his own decisions.[128] Considering all the facts now known, this practice was,
especially in respect to Prague, a ruthless game that cannot be justified by Stalin's explanation—five years later, in Teheran—that he
had simply ruled out any chance that Czechoslovakia would fight.
That was not possible, especially after the second mobilization on
September 23 and after September 27, when the Czechoslovak army
was fully positioned for defensive war. The evidence shows, rather,
that the Soviet Union was not willing and ready to help Czechoslovakia in any meaningful measure not only if France should abstain,
but also if she should have upheld her treaty obligation.

Conclusion

The task of drawing conclusions from the story of Soviet participation in the pre–World War II collective security system would be simpler if our examination were extended to the formal termination of the prewar period in August 1939. Post-Munich, however, a different situation existed, resulting from the abandonment and surrender of Czechoslovakia. Limiting our study to the pre-Munich era has therefore avoided the risk of applying the same criteria to two significantly different situations.

This book has established several main points on which the final conclusions are based. First, the Soviet Union did not join the collective security system after Locarno, when the international recognition of the USSR and the adherence of its principal foreign policy partner to that system provided the most suitable conditions for such a step. Until the final breakdown of its friendship with Germany, which the Soviet Union strove desperately to prevent, Soviet foreign policy attitudes were marked by a negation of the international status quo and by hostility toward its embodiment, the League of Nations. It then took several more months in 1934, and the emergence of a simultaneous potential threat to Soviet security in the east and in the west, to persuade the USSR to enter the League of Nations as the price of a realignment intended to replace the old German connection.

Second, after an initial reluctance to take part in a project—the Eastern Pact—that, especially in case of the participation of Poland, would imply explicit and direct obligations toward other powers (Poland, France, Czechoslovakia), the Soviet government took pains to contract alliances with France and Czechoslovakia, where her actual obligations, in contrast to those of her allies, were substantially weakened by the absence of common border with Germany. The basic question is whether the abrupt change after Barthou's death in Soviet attitude, from decided lack of enthusiasm for the Eastern Pact (with Poland) to ardent interest in a direct alliance with France (without Poland), can be explained otherwise than by the latter project's inherent territorial asymmetry. Sudden Soviet apprehension about a possible Franco-German collusion is an improbable motivation. Laval strove to win over Italy against Germany, but not Germany against Russia. In fact it was Moscow that threatened to make a deal with Germany; and it really tried.

Third, after concluding these pacts, the Soviet government not only made no effort to vitalize the new alliance system by decisive improvement of its relations with Poland and Rumania but, by refusing to recognize the territorial integrity of Rumania, systematically sabotaged such a solution, especially in 1935 and 1936. This last stand wrecked the possibility of complementing the alliance system by a Soviet-Rumanian treaty, which could have significantly affected the position of Poland, an ally of Rumania as well as of France.

Fourth, at variance with their alliances with France and Czechoslovakia, the Soviets made repeated secret attempts to lure Germany into a political agreement defined as a "developed form" of the earlier Treaty of Berlin. Germany's acceptance would have meant nothing less than factual debasement of the alliances of May 1935, and of the relevant obligations following from membership in the League of Nations.

Fifth, six months after the Franco-Soviet alliance entered into force, the Soviet leadership launched the Great Purges, which ruined the Soviet reputation abroad, undermined the emerging anti-Fascist blocks, weakened the Soviet Union economically as well as militarily, and undercut the entire system of alliances and collective security. Parallel Soviet foreign policy was characterized by increasing passivity and withdrawal. By the beginning of 1938, in consequence, the USSR was largely no longer counted on by other powers. Detailed examination of Soviet maneuvering between March and September 1938, which reflected their weak position, points up the soundness of this universal conclusion.

Motivations behind the Soviet external policy are usually attributed to a continuity of Russian imperial interests, the pursuit of revolutionary goals, or a combination of both. Whereas the first theory can be rather easily applied to certain Soviet activities in the 1930s, the "revolutionary theory" would have to be redefined before it could be implied with any clear meaning. Traces of the application of Marxism are discernible in the Comintern's policy of the United Front, but as has been shown, this course was largely imposed upon the Soviet leadership by the main European Communist parties; it was promulgated with reservations and as an exigency coinciding with the immediate Soviet foreign policy interests; and it was practiced for only a short period between the Seventh Congress of the Comintern and the outbreak of the Great Purges a year later.

The course of Soviet foreign policy cannot be successfully explained without taking into account the primary motivating factor behind all main Soviet decisions—that is, the essential concern of the ruling elite to maintain power. Lenin turned Marx's thesis of the dictatorship of the proletariat as a form of majority rule into his variant (fitting the Russian prerevolutionary situation) of the dictatorship of a small-minority working class, carried out by a professional organization leaning on its support. Stalin perfected this formula by a further centralization of power in the hands of the party bureaucracy. The doctrine of "socialism in one country," and the reduction of the earlier internationalism (never very consistent) to a mere trademark, were the outward incidental arrangements complementing this development. The Soviet Russian state has ever since been the property of this bureaucracy, and to view the policy of the Soviet Union in any broader and generally "Russian" or "Soviet" sense without taking into account the substance of the party bureaucracy is an entirely misleading abstraction.

The general task of Soviet foreign policy in the era examined in this book was, therefore, to secure safe external conditions for the gigantic Stalinist enterprises billed as "building of socialism" but designed primarily to consolidate the rule of the party bureaucracy in Russia. Of these enterprises, collectivization was most important politically as well as economically, because it terminated the independence of the peasantry and secured labor for industrialization. And that industrialization served no other end more thoroughly than an enormous militarization. All these projects culminated, between 1936 and 1939, in the systematic extermination of millions of real, potential, and imagined opponents of the ruling bureaucracy. The "socialist State" was thus constructed as a complex of bureaucratization and concentration of personal power, militarization, and all-comprising, generalized repression carried out by the enormous machinery of the GPU.

In striving to secure safe external conditions for undertaking the remodeling of Russia along the lines drawn by her rulers, Soviet foreign policy's primary goal was to prevent the formation of a hostile combination of foreign powers, and to keep the Soviet Union out of

[172]

international conflicts before such time as she would be strong enough to enter them without risk.

This purpose was best served, until 1934, by the "special relationship" with Germany, wherein, characteristically, the political basis of the partnership was not on the Left, but on the conservative Right and in the Reichswehr. For geographic, economic, military strategic, and also political reasons, the Soviet leadership preferred close ties with Germany to similar relations with any other country, and even after the break in 1934, they did not give up hope that the partnership with Germany could be revived, regardless of the nature of her regime.

The relationship established with France and, in a broader sense, with the West, was viewed as only an imperfect alternative, with at least three important disadvantages. First, the new partnership indirectly imposed a certain restraint upon the methods of governing the Soviet Union; as President Beneš observed, the fate of collective security, after the Soviet adherence to it, depended on "a certain adjustment of [Soviet] political conditions with the view to the concept of political freedom in Western Europe." This the Soviet leadership had no intention of carrying out, beyond such purely cosmetic measures as the "Stalin Constitution," initiated at the time when the interest in good relations with the West was most urgent.

Second, the new partnership offered no substitute for the extensive and highly satisfactory economic cooperation with Germany, which continued even after the break and in spite of the prolonged publicly displayed hostility between the Nazi and Communist regimes.

Finally, the nature of the French connection also implied the unwanted risk—which had been absent in the relationship with Germany—of possible involvement in external conflicts. This risk, of course, was outweighed by the assurance of French involvement against Germany in case of that country's aggression in the East, and was substantially minimized both by the territorial barrier separating Soviet Russia from Germany and from her nearest ally, Czechoslovakia, and by the complicated mechanism of the alliances that Soviet diplomacy managed to negotiate. Nevertheless, a certain danger was implied, as well as a risk of embarrassment in case diplomacy could find no face-saving way out of some unpredictable future situation.

It can be assumed that the Soviet Union would have energetically demanded the fulfillment of treaty obligations arising from the Covenant of the League of Nations and from the pact of May 1935, in case of German aggression against the USSR. To stay out of similar situations when the other countries would have been affected appears, however, to have been the inherent intention of the Soviet leadership. As Litvinov explained on two documented occasions, in December 1937 and June 1938, the USSR had taken no part in the organization of postwar Europe, "had won nothing in Versailles . . . and therefore nothing to give up." Its interest in opposing revisions of the status quo would be limited to cases where its own security might be directly affected.

The Soviet leadership obviously saw such a danger, especially in connection with the suspected German-Polish collusion, at the end of 1934 and in 1935. Soviet attitudes at that time were also strongly influenced by tensions with Japan, as testified to, among other things, by the Soviet effort to provide the French alliance with a universal applicability. In the course of 1936, Soviet assessment of both these dangers obviously changed, probably because of the excellent intelligence from Tokyo and hardly worse from Berlin. The Great Purges began in summer 1936, and the decision to extend them into the armed forces was probably adopted toward the end of the year, during the preparations of the Radek-Pyatakov show trial. The conclusion of the Pact against the Comintern in November apparently did not impress the Soviet leadership enough to call off the coup. Considering all the implications, they had to view this pact as a paper tiger. The question of the inevitable consequences of the purges for collective security and for the alliances contracted in May 1935 does not seem to have been a matter of great concern to the Soviet leadership. The course soon imposed upon the Comintern, in the fall of 1936, indicates a complete disregard for the fact that it was bound to undermine the government of the Popular Front in France.

The idea of enlisting the Soviet Union in the defense of collective security—which was, of course, identical with the defense of the post–World War I status quo—was obviously a fallacy in the first place. It is, however, sufficiently documented both by diplomatic correspondence and by authoritative memoirs like Paul-Boncour's, Herriot's, or Beneš's that Soviet entry into the League of Nations, and the pacts of May 1935, were perceived not merely as devices to prevent a new Soviet-German collusion, but as steps that could have the same weight as the Franco-Russian alliance before the First World War. This understanding was to a great extent based on an erroneous interpretation of the potential of the French alliance with Poland, which was not shared by some diplomatic professionals, like Alexis Léger, but surprisingly was accepted by others such as Barthou, Beneš, and Titulescu. Wishful thinking certainly played its role in these considerations, but without winning Soviet Russia over for the cause of collective security, the champions of the status quo could hardly see many chances to resist the power of Germany in the foreseeable future. Under these circumstances, the Soviet alignment with the Versailles camp could not fail to create an illusion of a safer balance of power. This conceit suffered a deadly blow in summer 1937, when the Soviet leadership decided to extend the purges into the Red Army and to bring against its leading military men the charge of collusion with Germany. Whether without this deplorable development in the USSR Germany would not have chosen a more cautious course of action, and whether the West, able to count on the support of Russia, would still have pursued the policy of appeasement, is a valid question.

It can be argued that Soviet Russia could not be expected to defend the "French order" in Europe; that she had no reason to adjust her internal behavior to suit her allies' standards; that she had no reason to recognize the territorial integrity of Rumania when the price was the "loss" of Bessarabia—all just for the sake of alliances that had meantime turned from an asset into a burden. All these questions are relevant if we choose to ignore the fact that it is not just the naked interest of the USSR that has been scrutinized, but the policy of a power allied with other powers in the defense of a cause. Whatever Soviet Russia did or did not do in the period of her association with the West inevitably had a bearing upon the family of states of which she was a member. Her share of responsibility for the outcome of the era has to be viewed as very substantial, hardly less than that of the profane policy of appeasement of Hitler. To that policy the Russia of Yezhov and Vyshinsky, after all, offered little alternative.

The War Problem of
the Soviet Union

GEORGE F. KENNAN*

I. THE POSSIBILITY OF WAR

A. From the Soviet Side

If war, as Klausewitz is said to have written, is only the projection of diplomacy, then the possibility of military complications involving Russia should be examined first and foremost in the light of Soviet diplomacy.

For this it is important to recall the fundamental peculiarity of Russia's foreign relations.

Ordinary diplomatic relations, as they have existed in modern times, have been universally regarded as the means of intercourse between *friendly* nations. Their foundation, regardless of conflicts of interest, has been at least a lip service to sentiments of friendliness and to the principle of live-and-let-live. Intercourse between open enemies, on the other hand, has generally been carried on by a different type of negotiator, under the shadow of a white flag—and has received a different name.

The peculiarity of Soviet diplomacy, insofar as it affects all nations outside Outer Mongolia and Tannu Tuva, is that it is openly regarded in Moscow as the intercourse between enemies. The masters of the

*A personal paper drafted in Moscow in spring 1935. Used with the permission of Professor Kennan. Copyright George F. Kennan.

Kremlin are revolutionary communists, whose views on government are admittedly not confined to Russia. They profess to believe that every other country in the world—(Outer Mongolia and Tannu Tuva always excepted)—is governed by unjust exploiters, and that they themselves, as leaders of a world proletariat which know no geographic boundaries, are directly concerned by this situation. They cannot view this exploitation with indifference, despite the fact that it takes place outside the boundaries of that territory where they are privileged to rule. It lies on their consciences, and they do not hesitate to express their disapproval of it, their enmity to its bearers: the bourgeois governments, their satisfaction at every defeat which these latter may suffer, their bitterness at every success which they gain, their determination at some future date to overthrow them and—as members of the world proletariat—to take their places. In theory, their political aims are not national but universal, and have nothing whatsoever to do with friendly sentiments or with the principle of live-and-let-live.

Now this is an attitude usually characterized by a state of war. But if the other great powers realized this at all, they were too tired after the war to bother about distinction of theory. After a weary gesture of protest in the form of the intervention, they recognized Russia, dismissed the Third International as an eccentricity, and determined to overlook ambiguities for the sake of practical advantage.

Not so Russia, which can tolerate ambiguities enough in practice but not in theory. It was considered in Moscow that an "armistice" had been concluded between the socialist and capitalist worlds, a "breathing period" (peredyshka), during the course of which the respective forces would glare at each other from a distance, only to renew the armed conflict at some future date; meanwhile representatives of the hostile parties, in the guise of diplomats, would hold the necessary pourparlers, properly surrounded by an atmosphere of military civility and suspicion, between the battle lines. This conception of foreign relations has had a profound effect, not only on the character of diplomatic life in Moscow, but also on the entire development of Russia's foreign relations.

In view of the failure of communist revolutions in other countries, the Soviet government had every reason to wish that this "breathing period" should be prolonged until Russia should become independent in a military sense. Its foreign policy has been built up on this motive.

In order to complete the picture of the theory underlying Soviet diplomacy, reference must be made to the conception of the "fellow

[177]

traveller." Moscow soon discovered that its own interests happened to coincide on occasions with one or the other of its capitalist enemies. It even found it possible to admit, while maintaining that the ultimate aims of all other governments are imperialistic, that a bourgeois government might be, like itself, temporarily peacefully inclined. Its way might lie, at a given moment, together with that of Moscow. In that case, though still an enemy, it would be at least a "fellow-traveller."

This conception provided the explanation for diplomatic cooperation and even the contraction of alliances with foreign powers. It did not, however, provide any adequate reason for departing from the theory of the inevitable armed conflict. On the contrary, this theory has continued to be preached to the country at large, and above all to the youth—chiefly in the form of the prediction of an early attack on Russia by some foreign power. The guiding spirit not only of Soviet foreign policy but also of domestic policy as well has become the official ghost of foreign intervention.

Under the aegis of this theory, the Soviet government has undertaken—and largely carried out—a tremendous program of militarization. All the resources of the Soviet State have been applied to the construction of a vast military machine. The entire economic and social character of the country has been changed for this purpose. For years, the energies of the people have been harnessed for the execution of an enormous program of military industrialization, masked as a five-year period of ordinary economic planning.

Simultaneously, the country has undergone a moral militarization of almost inconceivable scope. Linguistic skeletons, buried since the days of Tsarist nationalism, have been resurrected from the pages of the past to repeat their historic roles in the stimulation of mass emotion. All the clichés and gags of classic chauvinism have been revived to dominate the minds of a younger generation already none too well developed in its capacity for independent judgment. A generation has been reared whose patriotic arrogance and whose ignorance of the outside world rival the formidable traditions which the history of Tsardom can offer in this respect. The extent of the efforts of the Soviet government along the lines of militarization has been such that if a war should not come within the next two decades, the lives and works of an entire generation will have been sacrificed in vain.

Meanwhile, the Soviet foreign office has gone about its appointed task of postponing military complications. In this the main weapon, after the establishment of diplomatic relations, has been the non-aggression pact. Such treaties, in one form or another, have been concluded with several countries, including most of those along the western border, and Russia has professed readiness to conclude a number of others. The motives are obvious. Russia does not expect to attack any one by declaring war out of a blue sky and subsequently sending troops over the border. If she ever wants to attack, there will always be a communist faction in the victim country, ready to rise against the government in civil war and to request the intervention of the Red Army in the name of the whole population. Non-aggression clauses, on the other hand, may prove embarrassing to the other party, whose diplomatic technique may be less nimble, and whose greater disinterestedness in the internal affairs of other countries may deprive it of some of those advantages which Moscow enjoys. From Moscow's point of view, the non-aggression clause is a measure of security with few of the fetters of responsibility. As an impediment in the way of military conflict, particularly at a time when it suits Russia's interests to fight, it can be dismissed from serious consideration.

Of late, Russia's policy in the west has been characterized by a readiness to enter into obligations more far-going than those of the non-aggression pacts, namely, promises of military assistance to other states. An obligation of this sort, however innocuous, is contained in the Covenant of the League of Nations, to which Russia now subscribed. The proposed Eastern Pact, which Russia has supported with such fervor, is based on this principle. Finally, the alliance recently concluded with France and Czechoslovakia bind Russia to military action in Western Europe under certain definite circumstances.*

These obligations might not be dangerous if they really promoted the establishment of European peace. Unfortunately, it is difficult to believe that they serve this purpose. The policy of encirclement of Germany would appear to be motivated in Russia's case not only by a fear of German aggression but also by a determination to prevent at any cost the achievement of any real diplomatic settlement and understanding among the western European powers. Moscow considers, and has always considered, that any such settlement would threaten its own existence. For this reason it is the most unalterable opponent of any effective peace in the west. If the execution of this policy is as successful in the future as it has been in the past, there can be only one result: another European war.

It is possible to believe that Russia might keep out of such a war at

---

*The allusion to the pacts between France, Czechoslovakia, and the USSR indicates that the paper was drafted in May 1935 [J. H.].

the beginning. In view of the frank cynicism with which she views treaty obligations, it may be questioned whether she would even comply with her undertakings regarding military assistance, unless this happened to coincide with her interests at the given moment. But even this gives little ground to hope that she would not eventually be drawn into hostilities. Even supposing she did not enter a European war at the start:—later, when the other participants had weakened themselves to the point of exhaustion, when they were faced with economic collapse and social disorder, it would be too much to expect that the revolutionary appetite of a generation of fanatical young Russians could be controlled. Moscow has tasted the wine of proletarian imperialism after one world war, and though the cup was promptly snatched from her lips, the flavor has not been forgotten. She may be able to keep off the next battlefields of Europe at the start; she will hardly resist the temptation to come in at the end, if only in the capacity of a vulture.

Social fanatism, militarism, chauvinism, and a cynical policy of driving a wedge between one's neighbors: these may be means for postponing a war. They are not the same means for avoiding it.

B. From the Other Side

So much for the effects of Russia's own policy. Let us now consider the possibility of war with Russia from the other side.

No mention was made, in the above passages, of Russia's policies in the east. Here, too, it must be added, a goodly share of responsibility for the probability of hostilities lies with Russia. The encouragement of revolution in China and other parts of Asia, the establishment of armed puppet states along the Russian border, and the general rattling of the Russian sabre are all little calculated to promote confidence in the ultimate peace of the Orient. But here the war danger from the Russian side is clearly overshadowed by that which threatens from without. It is possible to suppose that a conflict between Japan and Russia can be postponed for the immediate future; it is difficult to believe that it can be avoided. The sins which Russia may have committed on the Asiatic Continent have been developed into genuine vices by Japan. There are no signs that Japan is preparing to retract from the ventures upon which she has embarked; there is indeed every sign that it would be difficult for her to do so. Thus the possibility of war in the east may be regarded as definite and immediate.

Russia's professions of anxiety over possible attack in the west show no such obvious foundation. Innumerable hints and insinuations in the various expressions of the Kremlin's attitude leave no doubt that it is, for the moment, Germany upon whom the official suspicion is centered. Insofar as the rulers of Germany are admittedly unsatisfied with their country's present borders and interested particularly in expansion toward the east, professions of nervousness from the Russian side are certainly deserving consideration. On the other hand, Hitler's policy is outstandingly one of pan-Germanism and implies the extension of the power of the Reich only to the territories now or previously controlled or inhabited by Germans. To be sure, this principle—like all other political principles—is open to very wide interpretation. It might even conceivably be interpreted to include certain states bordering on Russia. The wildest stretch of the imagination could hardly interpret it to apply to the Ukraine. There is only the possibility that the Ukraine might be "offered" by Germany to Poland, as compensation for the loss of territories in the West.

But all of these fears on Russia's part are still hypothetical. None of them has that immediate foundation that underlies the anxiety for the safety of her eastern frontiers. They are continually expressed with a histrionic vehemence which throws doubt on their sincerity, and are accompanied by a diplomatic activity better designed to aggravate than to allay the conditions to which they are attributed. Although the future is cloudy, there is little indication that a Russian government determined to tend strictly to its own business would find itself subjected to any immediate danger of aggression in the west.

There is one other factor deserving of mention in this connection. That is the temptation to foreign adventure which may at any time be presented to Soviet Russia by social disturbances abroad. The possible effect of social unrest subsequent to another major war has already been mentioned. But not only wars stimulate dissatisfaction among workers. There are other causes which can have the same effect. This is a possibility which will be lightly dismissed by those whose attentions are confined exclusively to the present. They will point to Moscow's betrayal of the workers' movements in Germany and China, to her indifference toward revolution in Spain. But our considerations refer to the less immediate future; and they cannot ignore the less immediate past. The recent Soviet indifference to the fate of the world revolution has had ample justification in the demands of a temporary situation, in the immediate interests of the Soviet State at a given moment. It has been a policy of expediency. Who can say that it will become a tradition? Who knows the minds of the present Kremlin leaders, and of those who are to be the leaders in

[181]

the future? Born in the limitlessness of the Russian plain, the principle of political universality has its roots deep in the character of the Soviet people. The early Kiev "Russ," the first Russian conception of State, knew no geographical frontiers and was a term vaguely associated with a religion of universal pretentions; for over two hundred years the Russian territory was subject to Asiatic rulers whose claims to the domination of the civilized world came only too close to realization; after the collapse of the Tatar and Byzantine Empires, the Tsars of the new Moscow state envisaged themselves as the temporal rulers of a "third Rome"; and as late as 1852, at the apex of the Imperial era, an American Minister in St. Petersbourg was compelled to report among other sad facts that: "A strange superstition prevails among the Russians that they are destined to conquer the world, and the prayers of the priests in the churches are mingled with requests to "hasten and consummate this divine mission.'" Truly, the universal pretentions of Moscow communism have their roots deep in the Eurasian past. And if they have been held in abeyance for a time through the exigencies of a period of intensive military industrialization, who shall say that they will not reappear with renewed vigor when the goal of this period—military independence—has been substantially attained?

This is not a prediction. But it is a possibility. Any major social disturbance in the outside world may, if the circumstances are favorable, bring about its realization. If it is true that quiet has descended on the Third International, at least the organization is by no means abolished. Dominated, if only sparsely financed, by Moscow, manned by foreign Communists whose naiveté must be as great as their loyalty, the International is retained as a potential weapon of Moscow's policy. It is an explosive weapon, and as long as Moscow continues to carry it, the danger of a sudden flare-up of hostilities will always be present.

C. Conclusion

Reviewing all these considerations, one does not arrive at a very comforting picture. An immediate danger of war exists in the east and shows no sign of seriously abating. In the west, Russian policy is doing little, if anything, to promote permanent peace or to avoid a conflict into which Russia would almost inevitably be drawn. In general, Moscow still clings to revolutionary political pretentions of universal scope, which may at any time become a serious source of conflict with other countries. Finally, the Soviet government has placed such tremendous stakes in the inevitability of military complications and has made such elaborate preparations for this contingency, that it is hard to envisage a future development which does not include an early outbreak of hostilities. It is one of the ironies of Russian history that while no people believes so firmly in the end as a justification for the means, no country has furnished more frequent proof that the means too often determine the end.

Ambassador Chilston's Report From Moscow, November 16, 1936

DBFP/Russia Correspondence
F.O. 371/20347, pp. 52–54,
copy No. 8.

Soviet Union   November 20, 1936
Confidential   Section 1.
N 5715/187/88

Viscount Chilston to Mr. Eden (Received November 20)
(No. 637)
                                      Moscow, November 16, 1936

Sir,

In your dispatch No. 562 of the 29th October you called for my observations on a memorandum by the British military attaché in Berlin regarding the possibility of the Reichswehr endeavouring to bring about a Soviet-German rapprochement. The task of prophecy can nowhere be more difficult than in Moscow, where the accredited foreign representative is deprived of almost all personal contact with those whose tendencies and reactions he is to estimate; and for this reason I fear that neither my military attaché nor myself can throw much light on the probable attitude of individual personalities of the Soviet government and of the Higher Command of the Red Army, to German overtures. With very rare exceptions (to one of which I shall refer later), Soviet officers and officials simply do not talk to foreigners on such subjects. Reviewing the question in the light of general principles, however, and without much assistance from local knowledge, I am inclined to believe that those who hold such a rapprochement to be a possibility of the immediate future take too little account of the changes brought about in the Soviet Union during the last few years. On the surface, indeed, some of these changes, particularly the gradual process of consolidation on national lines, seem rather to favor a rapprochement than otherwise—at any rate from German point of view; but there are others, in my opinion more important and fundamental, that strongly militate against it.

2. For the purpose of the present inquiry Soviet-German relations fall naturally under three headings: doctrinal-propagandist, economic and strategic-political. I propose to deal with the question in that order.

3. Whatever may be the weight of German doctrinal objection to an understanding with this country, I have little doubt that on the Soviet side the corresponding objections would not be found insuperable if other considerations definitely favored a rapprochement. Considerations of State policy invariably take precedence in the Soviet Union over natural political affinities—witness the excellent relations with a country so far removed from the orthodox Communist ideal as is Kemalist Turkey, and the relatively good relations which were maintained with Fascist Italy as long as the Austrian question stood in the way of an Italo-German understanding. The Soviet government undoubtedly could, if they wished, discontinue their anti-German propaganda and grasp the Nazi hand without experiencing any really uncomfortable reactions at home; nothing worthy to be called public opinion has existed in this country for a long time past. But I do not share the view of some that this could be lightly undertaken, or without a considerable period of preparation which would be unmistakably reflected in the Soviet press. The ordinary Soviet citizen may have lost long ago the faculty of independent thought, but so radical a change in the hypnotic treatment to which he is subjected would certainly require time and extreme care. He has been systematically taught to regard the National Socialist system as not something merely dangerous in matters of external policy, but inherently and ineradicably vile; and consequently no mere announcement of the public renunciation of the Rosenberg schemes, for instance, nor even the recantation of *Mein Kampf* would serve to convince him that the National Socialist leaders were suitable people for "cordial diplomatic exchanges," let alone for a closer type of union.

4. That this change of propagandist front could be brought about does not, of course, signify any means that it would be intrinsically welcome to the Soviet government; and in my opinion it would be highly unwelcome. In so far as internal propaganda is concerned, it

would, as I have indicated, be a troublesome enough change to effect; and the handling of the Soviet government's external public would clearly be a far more troublesome business still, for that public is at least theoretically accessible to other influences, and is, I believe, of enormous moral value to the Soviet government. The fact that it is so clearly despised by that government—that in the Red Dawn the sort of person who has been felicitously described as a "natural reader of the New Statesman and Nation" is obviously an early candidate for the lamp-post—has led many people to conclude that the Kremlin cares little for its intellectual and non-proletarian foreign admirers. But this, I think, is far from being the case; from the point of view of world opinion, to pose as the savior of democracy from the dark forces of fascism pays the Soviet government at least as well as it pays Herr Hitler to pose as the savior of Christendom. Meanwhile, the maintenance of the former pose costs the Soviet government absolutely nothing save printer's ink, and the regular consequential exchange of abuse enhances no whit the danger of actual hostilities, for in neither totalitarian State is the public, thus artificially incited against a foreign power, at all likely to take the bit between its teeth. In both countries the press obediently screams defiance until it is told to stop. No bones are broken and, apart from the value of the screams in creating an impression of heroism on the minds of foreign supporters, a large number of internal evils and hardships go unnoticed in the tumult. The Soviet government would, I am convinced, be loth to lose an enemy so clumsily and vociferously hostile as Nazi Germany.

5. It is chiefly in the economic sphere that misapprehensions seem to exist among those who reckon with the possibility of a Soviet-German rapprochement in the early future. In his dispatch No. 1212 on the 22nd September Sir George Clerk stated, as a comment on General Giraud's emphatic condemnation of the Franco-Soviet pact, that he had heard certain other well-qualified French military authorities defending the pact as "denying Germany the immense material resources of Russia, oil, coal, timber, and so on, which despite Herr Hitler's hatred of bolshevism, would otherwise sooner or later furnish the raison d'être of a Russo-German rapprochement." But this is surely to put the clock back to Rapallo, or thereabouts. No longer do Germany's undoubted demand for raw materials, and the Soviet Union's undoubted wealth in these materials, necessarily point to cooperations between the two countries. When Moscow and Berlin were last on speaking—as opposed to shouting—terms, the Soviet Union had bitter need of foreign help. The raw materials were there, but the Union could neither produce them efficiently without

foreign assistance nor use them itself in its almost entirely non-industrial state. The innocuous Weimar Republic supplied the need with technical assistance of high order. Now the picture is completely changed, in economic as well as political matters; not only has Germany become the most undesirable politically of all Powers, and doubly "imperialist" through her lack of an empire, but the Soviet Union has successfully reduced its foreign trade to almost negligible proportions, and is exploiting without foreign help an industry fully capable of absorbing the bulk of the country's natural resources, vast though these are. I enclose herein a copy of an interesting note by the commercial councellor to this Embassy in elaboration of the foregoing generalization;* it will be seen that there are few indeed of the Soviet Union's natural products that it has any need to export under present conditions, and that in particular the Soviet Union is most unlikely to be able to produce during the next few years more oil and coal than it requires for its own use. Probably the Union could still at the stage now reached in industrial development do better from the purely economic point of view, with a little more foreign assistance and a slightly less contained economic policy. But this would involve a painful sacrifice of prestige, and also the weakening of what is probably a very sound general principle, namely, that a State so completely sundered as is the Soviet Union from the rest of the world in political theory had best develop as independently as possible in the economic sphere also.

6. Neither, then, from the point of view of propagandist politics nor from that of international economy do I find any temptation to the Soviet government to reach a composition with the Germany of Herr Hitler, and I see definite objections, from the Soviet point of view, to any such composition. These objections would no doubt be overridden by really cogent considerations of Realpolitik, if such existed; but here again, as in the economic sphere, I am under the impression that the temptation lies almost wholly on the German side. The most obvious, and probably the most fundamental, of the differences between Germany and the Soviet Union at the present time is that the former openly craves for expansion, which can only be at some other country's expense, while the latter has almost certainly no expansionist ambitions, avowed or other. And this difference postulates, one must suppose, a corresponding difference in the attitude of each towards a partial betterment of relations with the other. Such a partial betterment, amounting perhaps to a cessation of

*Not relevant in this context; not reproduced [J. H.].

[187]

mutual abuse and the establishment of some sort of contact between the two armies, might well relieve the leaders of Germany, and in particular of the Reichswehr, of some of their anxiety as to the probable reactions of the Soviet government to German expansion at the expense of third parties. Indeed, if it did not have this effect, the Reichswehr could hardly be supposed to desire it, knowing that Germany is no longer in the slightest danger of unprovoked assault from any quarter. But the Soviet government on their side have no corresponding need to play for the chance of German neutrality while they expand; and for that matter they could scarcely be so simple-minded as to connive at a German expansion which must inevitably render their principal enemy even more formidable than before. Colonel Hotblack refers in paragraph 4 of his memorandum to an understanding which might "enable Germany to absorb the Germanic population on her eastern frontier, and even Rumania and a part of Poland." This appears to imply the absorption of the whole of Rumania, giving Germany a long frontier with the openly coveted Soviet Ukraine and supplying her at the same time with valuable resources of oil and corn. Even, however, if the process of absorption were confined to the Germanic populations of Transylvania, the general easterly trend of expansion could scarcely fail to cause the Soviet government the utmost misgiving.

7. On the other hand, as long as the map of Eastern Europe remains unchanged it is hardly too much to say that there is only one contingency which the Soviet government really fear: a combined attack by Germany and Japan, who are, indeed, the only two countries of importance that have given the slightest sign in recent years of wishing to attack the USSR. This contingency the Soviet government obviously fear very much indeed, for all their enormous recent progress in the sphere of defenses; and if they could come to an agreement with Germany which would positively ensure the neutrality of that country in the event of a Japanese attack in the Far East, they would presumably be prepared to pay highly for it. But they would be optimistic indeed to regard an agreement of this sort as a practical possibility while the two regimes last, and the situation which would arise if one or both were to collapse is almost outside the scope of useful predictions. For Germany, a serious conflict between Japan and the Soviet Union would surely afford the chance of a lifetime, whether or not any military agreement actually exists between Berlin and Tokyo: and it is reasonable to suppose from Herr Hitler's past history that he would not allow a scrap of paper to incommode him

[188]

unduly. Certainly the Soviet government, with their consuming suspicion of all other Powers, would be unlikely to credit him with a sense of treaty obligation sufficient to stand the strain of such a temptation. Germany, on her side, might be supposed equally unlikely to rate the bond of the Soviet government very highly; but for geographical and other reasons, she would be far better able to take the risk. Even a rather dubious agreement with the USSR would, in time of peace, provide a useful card for bluffing third parties into concessions: she could choose her own moment for putting the agreement to the test of war: and at the first sign of treachery on the part of the Soviet government German forces concentrated for use on another front could be detached to meet the Russian advance with a comparatively short delay, whereas Soviet communications between the Far East and White Russia or the Ukraine are notoriously such as to render a corresponding Russian maneuver very hazardous, though perhaps not impossible. If the USSR were to trust to an agreement with Germany to the extent of concentrating its forces in the Far East at the expense of its western defenses, and if the Germans were then to attack the Union, many weeks would elapse before the depleted defending forces could receive reinforcement, and the delay might well prove disastrous. If, on the other hand, the Soviet government felt unable to trust the agreement to the extent of any substantial modification of their military dispositions, then the agreement would presumably be of little practical value to them. The paper bond might, indeed, reinforce to some extent the main deterrent argument of Russian material preparedness, but the Russians themselves could hardly be expected, in such circumstances, to rate it very highly. It is no doubt true that all alliances have to overcome a certain element of mutual distrust, but Colonel Hotblack's memorandum brings up clearly the exceptionally suspect, from the point of view of the Soviet government, of any German overtures of the kind he foresees. The memorandum deals in the main with an inter-governmental rapprochement on more or less normal lines, Germany taking France's place via-à-vis Russia. But in the course of it we come upon a description of the average German officer's views: he believes, says Colonel Hotblack, "that he could supply just that organization and leadership which the Russian soldier requires." This may well be true, but I cannot see the leader of the Red Army consenting in any circumstances to relinquish that leadership to German officers. Colonel Hotblack goes on: "The fact that the Russian nation is *now* controlled, as he believes, by a gang of international Jews is a proof to the German officer that Russia might equally well be controlled by Germany." At some stage of the proceedings, therefore, and doubtless the sooner the better, the "international gang of Jews" (which, as even the average German officer must see, has a strong will of its own), is presumably to be sent packing; and I cannot believe that the gang would not be perfectly well aware of this ulterior aim of those from whom the overtures came.

8. Thus in the sphere of Realpolitik also, there seems extraordinarily little to tempt the Soviet government to come to an understanding with Germany. Such an agreement would only, I think, be acceptable to the Kremlin at a moment of real despondency and panic, and only then as a stop-gap expedient, involving important mental reservations. I see no reason to believe that the break-down of the Franco-Soviet Pact—if this should come about—would necessarily usher in such a moment. The pact certainly cannot be said to be in very flourishing health at the present time, yet from all I have heard it seems that the bigger ranks of the Red Army were never so confident as they are now of their ability to take on all comers. Abandonment of the Franco-Soviet Pact (and with it, in all probability, of the whole Litvinov policy) would, in my opinion, be more likely to usher in an era of splendid isolation than one of cooperation with Germany.

9. At the beginning of this dispatch, I referred to the extreme difficulty of estimating the individual tendencies and prejudices of Soviet officials and officers. I may, however, state for what it is worth my impression that the Red Army, influential though it undoubtedly is, has not yet attempted to take an independent line in foreign policy and is unlikely to do so, at any rate in the immediate future. One must still reckon with the interpretation of the army by the party, with its iron discipline and unswerving obedience to M. Stalin; but apart from this it is fairly clear that none of the Red Army leaders is of sufficient calibre to take political line different from that of Marshal Voroshilov—none, that is, with the possible exception of Marshal Tukhachevsky, whose training is French and whose sympathies are believed to be French rather than German. And of Marshal Voroshilov himself it may be said with a fair degree of certainty that he is trusted by M. Stalin because his loyalty is obvious, because he sticks to his last and does not interfere in matters which are outside his competence. Were that not so, the Marshal's immense popularity would surely before now have proved his undoing. That his present views on foreign policy are completely orthodox is strongly suggested in his recent interview with General Wavell, in which, as you will

recall, he held forth at length, and with that convincing appearance of sincerity which makes him such a conspicuous figure in Soviet life, on the German menace and on the desirability of accelerating the rearmament programs of Great Britain and France.

10. The foregoing paragraphs have been drafted in consultation with the military attaché of this Embassy, who concurs with them. I feel bound, in conclusion, to record the diametrically opposite opinion recently expressed to a member of my staff by the Estonian Minister, M. Traksmaa, who as an ex-Russian army officer and the representative of a border state is certainly well qualified to judge, gave it as his view that if Germans were to make an unmistakable overture to the Soviet government, the latter would fall straight into their arms. He did not, however, justify this opinion by anything more convincing than a reference to the general trend of Soviet official utterances on the subject of Soviet-German relations during the last year or so; and I, myself, have seen no report of any such utterances which indicated an unmistakable desire on the part of the Soviet government for a rapprochement with Hitlerite Germany. It is true that various Soviet speakers, e.g., M. Molotov, in the speech described in my dispatch No. 30 of the 14th January last, have stated in general terms that the Soviet government would like better relations with Germany; and this may not be altogether untrue, in spite of what I have said above about the value of a vociferous enemy from the point of view of propaganda. But such official assurances of the Soviet government's blameless intentions in regard to all foreign countries without exception are, of course, themselves part of the normal propaganda, and scarcely justify, to my mind, the special interpretation which M. Traksmaa appears to have placed upon them. Moreover, if the Soviet government were half as eager for a rapprochement as he believes, one would expect to see already some abatement of anti-Nazi propaganda in the Soviet press, of which, however, I have seen no sign. The *Izvestia,* in a recent article entitled "Goering in the Role a Hitlerite Dictator," did, indeed, attribute the General's recent accretion of influence to the concern felt by the German General Staff at Herr Hitler's Nuremberg tirades. The Reichswehr, it is explained, were still true to the traditional belief that European hegemony was only to be achieved by an attack on France. General Goering was their man, and his new appointment was "the direct result of the Nuremberg Congress, which showed the German Higher Command that the Fuehrer, by his whole behavior, might bring about the catastrophe of war before the date which they had fixed for it in an entirely different

quarter." Ludendorff, the *Izvestia* continued, had been a mere passing episode in German military history, with his attempt to reach a decisive victory in the East, and it was no accident that Goering himself had been instrumental in securing the older General's ejection from the National Socialist Party on the grounds of incorrect military-political principles. But there is nothing very new in these hopes of the Soviet newspaper that Germany will strike first in the west; nor is there anything in the article that is in the least conciliatory to the Reichswehr or to General Goering himself—on the contrary, it is even more abusive than usual. So far, therefore, the evidence of the press may be said to be entirely negative.

11. There is one contingency which, in my opinion, might possibly lead to a Soviet-German rapprochement of a thoroughly undesirable kind. Good reasons appear to exist for believing that the Reichswehr may gain control in Germany in the not far distant future; and if the Red Army were to achieve a corresponding ascendancy in this country, then a military alliance might well result. There would be no question of any such German control of the Russian military machine as is envisaged in Colonel Hotblack's memorandum for, as I have said, the Red Army leaders would never tolerate foreign influence in their own particular sphere, but an alliance as between equals would, of course, be scarcely less undesirable. This contingency, however, is really to be classed among the almost unpredictable developments resulting from a change of regime. Were the political control to pass from the Bolshevik party to the Red Army leaders, it is fairly safe to say that both the internal system and the external significance of the Soviet Union would undergo rapid and fundamental alteration. I am not convinced that even in that event the new military rulers of the country would necessarily develop that taste for foreign adventures which point the way to a German alliance; and, indeed, I suspect that, as long as Marshal Voroshilov retained control, they would not: apart, possibly, from a hankering for an ice-free Pacific port, the present Soviet rulers have almost certainly no territorial ambitions whatever. But the assimilation of the two political systems would undoubtedly have removed one of the existing obstacles to such an alliance, and the danger would be by so much greater. Meanwhile, M. Stalin is still to all appearances the undisputed master, and may have many years before him, during which, for all we can foresee, the problem of his successor may solve itself on other lines. Those who, impressed by the growing prestige of the Red Army, see no solution but a military succession, are apt, I think, to underestimate the power of the party, and also to forget that among M. Stalin's band of political

assistants to display a talent for leadership is also to display a fatal lack of discretion.

12. I am sending a copy of this dispatch to His Majesty's Ambassador at Berlin. I have, &c.,

Chilston.

Text of a Note of the Rumanian Government to the Government of the Soviet Union Dated September 24, 1938

No. 71/1938 - C./8, Vol. 3,
Archiva ministerului afacerlal
externe, Bucharest.

MINISTRE DES AFFAIRES ETRANGÈRES DU ROYAUME DE ROUMANIE
Code Secret 49/38
Ultra-Secret! Urgent!

Genève,
Bucarest, le 24 septembre 1938
Transmis par courrier personnel
le 24 september à 9 h 12

Son Excellence
M. Maxim M. Litvinov,
Commissaire du peuple aux affaires étrangères
de l'Union des républiques socialistes soviétiques
en ce jour à *Genève*

Votre Excellence!
   Le gouvernement du Royaume de Roumanie a l'honneur de présenter à Votre Excellence et au Conseil des commissaires du peuple de l'Union des républiques socialistes soviétiques l'expression de sa plus haute considération.

Après la consultation qui s'est tenue la nuit dernière entre sa Majesté le Roi, le premier ministre, le ministre de la guerre de mon gouvernement et le chef d'état-major de l'armée royale de Roumanie, j'ai été accredité, suite aux entretiens que j'ai eu à Genève avec Votre Excellence du 9 au 12 septembre et plus particulièrement à notre entente préliminaire et confidentielle du 13 septembre, pour vous communiquer à vous ainsi que par l'intermédiare de Votre Excellence au gouvernement soviétique ce que suit:

Hier soir, le président de la République tchécoslovaque a ordonné la mobilisation générale des forces armées tchécoslovaques, et ce nullement à l'insu des gouvernements britannique et français, comme je l'ai secrètement verifié. La crise tchécoslovaque est donc entrée dans sa phase ultime et culminante. Il ne fait plus aucune doute que le Reich allemande est décidé à envahir la Tchécoslovaquie, alliée de nos deux pays, en l'attaquant militairement sans avoir été provoqué, ce qui constitue indéniablement le fait d'une agression selon les articles respectifs du Pact de la Société des Nations et selon la definition internationalement obligatoire du concept d'"agresseur"; cette attaque aura lieu au plus tard dans 7–10 jours à compter du moment present, comme s'en est secrètement assuré l'état-major de mon pays.

Vu la supériorité du matériel allemande, cette agression doit avoir de conséquences catastrophiques, non seulement pour la Tchécoslovaquie, mais pour tout l'Europe du centre et du sud-est: Prague donne accès au pétrole roumain dont le contrôle ne peut revenir à l'Allemagne sans léser, comme mon gouvernement en est convaincu, les intérêts soviétiques. Cette situation menace au perspective la souverainété, l'intégrité et la liberté d'action de mon pays: la Roumanie a une frontière commune avec la Tchécoslovaquie, et la Hongrie se joindra très vraisemblement au côtés du Troisième Reich dans l'agression armée contre la Tchécoslovaquie, ce qui mettrait la Roumanie, en raison du respect des engagements de la Petite Entente pris avec la Tchécoslovaquie, en état de guerre contre l'Allemagne.

À partir de ces réflexions, le gouvernement du Royaume de Roumanie

—conscient de la portée funeste de la defaite de la Tchécoslovaquie pour la stabilité de la paix et de la securité en Europe du centre et du sud-est ainsi que de la portée negative pour le sort futur de la Roumanie elle-même s'il y a empêchement d'une aide militaire soviétique à la Tchécoslovaquie;

—lié par les multiples tentatives de ces trois dernières années pour mettre en place un nouvel aménagement contractuel de relations réciproques entre l'Union des républiques socialistes soviétiques et le Royaume de Roumanie qui permetrai le passage par voi de terre et le transport aérien des forces armées soviétiques jusqu'en Tchécoslovaquie, que ces tentatives soient issue de l'initiative de n'importe quel member du système contractuel franco-soviéto-tchécoslovaque;

—se référant expréssément aux accords préliminaires tenus secret de nos deux pays, accords engagé officieusement le 13 septembre 1938 à Genève qui concernaient le dégagement du territoire roumain pour le transit par voi de terre de 100,000 hommes de l'Armée Rouge et le dégagement de l'espace aérien pour les transports aériens illimités d'hommes et d'armes d'Union soviétique en Tchécoslovaquie, de que se fera sentir le besoin de ces fournitures défensives;

—renonçant sans réserve au conditions garanties de toutes sortes du côté soviétique pour la permission roumaine de passage, à savoir du survol aérien des forces armées soviétiques par la Roumanie jusqu'en Tchécoslovaquie et tout particulièrement: a) à tout accord ou autre garantie donnée par votre pays sur l'inviolabilité territoriale de la Bessarabie en tant que partie intégrante de la Roumanie; b) à tout garantie politique et militaire donnée par votre pays concernant la frontière roumaine avec la Hongrie, à savoir à l' engagement soviétique d'une intervention militaire contre la Hongrie en cas de violation de la frontière ouest de la Roumanie;

—mûe, dans cet esprit, par la volonté de renforcer les moyens de défense de la Tchécoslovaquie et son potentiel militaire par son allié le plus puissant, et cela, si possible, le plus tôt avant l'ouverture des hostilités, ressent fortement l'extrême necessité de soumettre à l'Ordre des commissaires du peuple de l'Union des républiques socialistes soviétiques à la direction de l'état soviétique, politique et militaire, les propositions suivantes:

I.

Le gouvernement royal de Roumanie reconnait solennellement et obligatoirement le droit de transport par chemins de fer de l'Armée Rouge, en partant de l'Union Soviétique à travers la Roumanie jusqu'en Tchécoslovaquie, à savoir le transport d'hommes, d'armes légères aussi bien que lourdes, de munitions, de carburant et d'approvisionnement de toutes sortes, à ces conditions:

a) que les premières unités soviétiques franchissent la frontière roumano-soviétique le plus tôt possible de l'ouverture de l'attaque allemande contre la Tchécoslovaquie, à savoir aprés la proclamation de l'attaque en tant que telle, si tant est que cella ait lieu univoquement avant l'ouverture de l'attaque;

[196]

b) que les forces soviétiques n'empruntent, pour traverser la Roumanie, que la voie est Mogilev (URSS)–Chotin–Cernauți–Radauți–Cimpuļung–Dorna Vatra–Bistrita–Dej–Maia Mare–Negresti–Ťačovo (Tchécoslovaquie);

c) que, dans l'esprit de la convention des ministres étrangères du 13 septembre, les unités soviétiques en transit ne depassent en aucun cas le nombre de 100,000 hommes, ce à quoi mon gouvernement complementairement demand que les armes transportées ne dépassent pas 650 canons de tous calibres (y compris les canons antiaériens) et 300 chars;

d) étant donné que les lignes des chemins de fer mentionnées traversent le territoire roumain sur un longeur de 473 km, étant donné que leur point le plus à l'est est distant des bases aériennes allemandes les plus proches (est de l'Autriche) de 850 km à vol d'oiseau, et leur point le plus à l'ouest de 430 km à vol d'oiseau, le gouvernement royal de Roumanie, se fondant sur la supposition qu' après les six premiers jours d'hostilités, l'aviation allemande ne sera pas en mesure d'utiliser les aéroports tchécoslovaques, accorde à l'Union Soviétique le droit de passage militaire pour une durée de six jours (144 heures) à compter de début de la guerre; une fois ce delai passe, les transports soviétiques doivent être interrompus et suspendues, même si les chiffres mentionnés au paragraph c)n'ont pas été entièrement atteints à ce moment par les forces soviétiques;

e) à une vitesse moyenne de 25 km/h, un train parcourt cette voie sans s'arrêter en 19 heures. Le gouvernement royal de Roumanie demande à la partie soviétique q'un train ne reste pas en territoire roumain plus que 24 heures, en comptant les arrêts nécessaires au plein de charbon et d'eau que le personnel roumain des chemins de fer effectuera sous le contrôle des gardes de l'armée roumaine;

f) en cas de panne technique durant le transport des unités soviétiques par cette ligne de chemin de fer, il est demandé que durant l'interruption de voyage pour de telle raisons, les membres des unités soviétiques ne s'eloignent pas de la voie individuellement ou en group de plus de 250 mètres, et de toute façon sans armes, et qu'ils n'entrent pas en contact avec la population civil roumaine;

g) la voie ferrée reservée aux forces soviétiques est à voie unique et techniquement modeste; s'est pourquoi il est dans l'intérêt du deroulement paisible de tout l'opération que les trains ne soient pas surchargés, notament par des chars et des canons lourds.

II.

En même temps, le gouvernement royal de Roumanie accorde solennellement, irrémédiablement, sans condition et avec une application immédiate le droit illimité a l'Union des républiques socialistes soviétiques d'établir un pont aérien entre les aéroports militaires de la sud-ouest de l'Union soviétique frontalière avec la Roumanie, et les aéroports militaires de la partie est de la Tchécoslovaquie frontalière avec la Roumanie. Le gouvernement royale de Roumanie accord ce droit à commencer par un nombre illimité de survols massifs de l'aviation militaire soviétique, transportant des machines de transport et de combat, notamment de bombardement et d'assaut, avec un chargement d'un nombre indéterminé d'hommes, d'armes lourdes et légères, y compris l'armament individuel et l'equipment des stocks necessaires en munition, des carburants et des moyens de transport (vehicules).

Pour ces traversées aériennes soviétiques, le gouvernement royal de Roumanie réserve les parties suivantes de l'espace aérien roumain: Frontière roumano-polonaise sur toute sa longeur–Cernauţi–Frontière roumano-soviétique à partir de son point le plus à l'ouest après Tiraspol–Bendery/Tighina (360 km)–Jassy–Cluj–Oradea Mare–Satu Mare—Frontière roumano-tchécoslovaque sur toute sa longeur (130 km). Dans cet espace aérien ainsi défini, le gouvernement royal de Roumanie suspendra à partir du 25 septembre à 13 heures tout trafic aérien national ou étranger, militaire, de transport, civil ou sportif. Le gouvernement royal de Roumanie accorde également le droit de ces survols pour une durrée de 6 jours (144 heures) des l'ouverture de l'attaque allemande contre la Tchécoslovaquie, les survols pouvant cependant commencer des le 25 septembre à 14 heures. Le gouvernement royal de Roumanie n'est pas disposé à risquer le danger que constitueraient des combats aériens entre l'aviation soviétique et l'aviation allemande au-dessus du territoire roumain, et encore moins les dangers que constitueraient des bombardements allemandes contre la Roumanie, ce que Votre Excellence comprendra certainement. Par ailleurs, l'état-major de mon pays et mon gouvernement supposent en outre à juste titre que, d'une part, vu les forces de l'aviation militaire tchécoslovaque et les renforts qu'elle a reçus les mois derniers de votre pays, vu, d'autre part, le difficile accès sous-mentionné de l'espace aérien roumain pour les forces aériennes allemandes à partir des bases qui ne se trouvent pas aux frontières du Reich allemand (pour parler plus precisement, vue le rayon d'action de l'aviation allemande qui, sans escales, ne dépasse un ligne de 1100–1600 km nécessaire au combat en espace aérien au-dessus du territoire roumain), il n'est pas vraisemblable qu'un assault des forces aériennes allemandes au-dessus de la Roumanie se produise avant le septième jour de guerre. La délimitation du delai de 6 jours à compter du début de la guerre est issue de ce calcul. Avant que la guerre n'éclate, aucune limitation de temps n'est, bien sûr, applicable de la part roumaine en ce qui concerne le pont aérien soviétique—à la différence des transports ferroviaires. Aussi, au cas ou les hostilités commenceraient le 1er October ou plus tardes, l'aviation soviétique disposerait d'un minimum 12 jours pour le trafic des traversées aériennes entre l'Union Soviétique et la Tchécoslovaquie.

Etant donné que la ligne aérienne entre les aéroports soviétiques les plus au sud, au nord du Dniestr, et les aéroports militaires tchécoslovaques les plus à l'est en Russie sud-carpatique et en Slovaquie de l'est décrit une distance variante entre 230 et 390 km, le gouvernement royal de Roumanie suppose que les forces aériennes soviétiques effectueront en 24 heures plusiers survols. Le nombre total des traversées aériennes, le nombre des machines pour une traversée et le nombre d'hommes, d'armes et de reserves de combustible, carburant pour un seul avion, le gouvernement royal de Roumanie le laisse entièrement au choix des authorités soviétiques compententes, à savior à un accord entre les authorités militaires soviétiques et tchécoslovaques, que seule garantirait bien entendu la capacité de réception des differents aéroports tchécoslovaques.

Afin que les traversées aériennes ne puissent être aucunement perturbées du côte hongrois, dans la region ouest de l'espace aérien reservé, mon gouvernement est disposé à détacher, sur la ligne Satu Mare–Oradea Mare à une distance de 13 km de la frontière hongroise, 3 divisions et une brigade de l'armée royale de Roumanie, renforcées par une unité de chasseurs aériens au nombre de 120 machines, y compris l'artillerie de campagne et un regiment blindé. Bien entendue, cette mesure serait appliquée uniquement à la demande expressé des gouvernements soviétique et tchécoslovaque. Le pact d'alliance avec la Pologne ne permet pas à mon pays d'appliquer une mesure semblable, preventive et defensive, sur la frontière polonoroumaine; aussi mon gouvernement demande-t-il à ce que l'aile la plus eloignée du survol se maintienne, au dessus du territoire roumain, à au moins 30 km de la frontière polonaise.

Bien que le gouvernement royal de Roumanie accorde à l'Union des républiques socialistes soviétiques le droit d'établir un pont aérien d'une manière absolue, sans conditions et immédiatement, il ne peut cependant pas ne pas respecter l'intérêt de sa propre securité, l'intérêt qu'il a de passer sous silence les survols au moins jusqu'au commencement de la guerre, et l'intérêt qu'il a d'empêcher toute sanction de droit international, politique ou même militaire, ou toute intervention de l'Allemagne contre la Roumanie. Etant convaincu de la compréhension absolue du gouvernement soviétique pour ces intérêts, mon gouvernement se voit obligé de demander avec la plus grande instance à votre pays que les survols soviétiques:

1. s'effectuent obligatoirement sans escales au-dessus du territoire roumain;

2. soient dirigé au-dessus du territoire roumain à une hauteur minimale de 3,400 metres, et si possible même à 4,000 mètres;

3. ne traversent en aucune cas au dessus du territoire roumain, la frontière sud de l'espace réservé (Bendery–Jassy–Cluj–Oradea Mare);

4. ne violent à aucune prix l'espace aérien polonais ou hongrois, notamment par quelque atterissage forcé, et en particulier se gardent absolument de raccourcir le trajet en survolant le contrefort sud-est de la Pologne. En n'import lequel de ces cas, le gouvernement royal de Roumanie serait, à son plus grand regret, obligé, pour des raisons évidentes, de suspendre et de supprimer le droit des survols soviétiques.

Le gouvernement royal de Roumanie formule le ferme espoir que sa proposition actuelle à votre pays va largement au-devant des intérêts d'existence et de securité de la République tchécoslovaque, ainsi que de ceux de l'Union des républiques socialistes soviétiques, de même que des intérêts de la securité collective, de la paix en Europe, du maintien du système international actuel et de l'inviolabilité des frontières en Europe du centre et de l'est. En ce sens, mon gouvernement croit également que la présente proposition exprimée à Votre Excellence permet à l'Union Soviétique à la fois d'envoyer en Tchécoslovaquie par une voie combinée de terre et aérienne, un corps d'elite d'une force de 250,000–350,000 hommes, ce qui diminuerait considérablement l'avantage quantitatif de l'armée allemande sur l'armée tchécoslovaque et permetrait aux forces armées tchécoslovaque une défense efficace; et lui permet à la fois de faire parvenir en Tchécoslovaquie plusiers centaines d'avions, de canons et de chars. Le gouvernement royal de Roumanie suppose en outre que la démarche de l'Union Soviétique à partir de la présente proposition, ne serait pas sans radicalement influencer l'attitude concrète de la France dans ce conflit germano-tchécoslovaque.

En vue d'une acceleration de toute l'opération et de l'obtention du but poursuivi, je prie Votre Excellence de faire remettre sans retard la response à ma note par votre gouvernement à mon gouvernement.

Je me permet également de faire savoir à votre Excellence que la teneur de ma note sera remise avant aujourd'hui minuit au courrier personnel du ministre des affaires étrangères et du president de la République tchécoslovaque, ce contre quoi votre Excellence ne peut naturellement avoir aucune objection, ne serait-ce que parce que le plan entier de ces nombreuses actions effectuées par votre pays ne peut être executé unilatéralement et exige forcément la coordination entre les autorités soviétiques et tchécoslovaques compétentes. Je prie votre Excellence de bien vouloir accepter l'assurance de mes profonds respects.

Comnen [Comnène]
Nicolae-Petrescu Comnen [Comnène]
Ministre du Royaume de Roumanie
aux affaires étrangères

Abbreviations

AMZV Prague	Archives of the Ministry of Foreign Affairs, Prague
AUD Prague	Archives of the Institute of History of the Czechoslovak Communist Party
DBFP	*Documents on British Foreign Policy*
DDF	*Documents diplomatiques français*
DGFP	*Documents on German Foreign Policy*
DSDF	Department of State Decimal File
FRUS	*Foreign Relations of the United States*
SDFP	*Soviet Documents on Foreign Policy*
SúA	State Central Archives, Prague

Notes

1. The Dissolution of the "Special Relationship"

1. V. P. Potemkin, ed., *Istoriya diplomatii* (an officially sanctioned work), 1st ed. (Moscow, 1946), p. 38, still complained that the Paris treaties had "divided Slavic nations," in spite of the fact of the creation of Yugoslavia, Poland, and Czechoslovakia, previously separated Slavic nations. The only separation the authors could have thought of was that of Poland—from Russia.

2. The "liberation" of Baltic countries, Byelorussia, the Transcaucasia, and even Turkestan is listed as the aim of the Soviet government in the immediate postwar period in *Istoriya VKP(b)* (Moscow, 1945), pp. 191, 199. Almost all the "lost provinces" of the former empire were then reintegrated into the USSR when the circumstances arose, in some cases quite early (Georgia, 1921), in other cases in 1940.

3. For the best account of this period of Soviet-German relations, see Kurt Rosenbaum, *Community of Fate: Soviet-German Relations, 1922–1928* (Syracuse, 1965): using Brockdorff-Rantzau's papers in addition to other German documents, Rosenbaum notes that the Russians (Viktor Kopp) offered the Germans a formal alliance in December 1924 in Berlin, and Rykov repeated the offer in a conversation with Brockdorff-Rantzau in February 1925 in Moscow. Coordinated Soviet-German action against Poland was specifically suggested (pp. 121–23). See also Gaines Post, Jr., *Civil-Military Fabric of Weimar Foreign Policy* (Princeton, 1973), pp. 42–43.

4. E. H. Carr, *German-Soviet Relations between the Two World Wars (1919–1939)* (Baltimore, 1951), p. 91.

5. Post, p. 112.

6. See Leonard Schapiro, *The Communist Party of the Soviet Union* (New York, 1971), p. 357.

7. Rosenbaum, p. 281.

8. *DGFP* AA 1415/2860, 560829-34, dated October 31, 1929.

9. Robert M. Slusser and Jan F. Triska, *A Calendar of Soviet Treaties 1917–1957* (Stanford, 1959), pp. 408–12.

10. John Erickson, *The Soviet High Command: A Military-Political History, 1918–1941* (London, 1962), pp. 256–57; Rosenbaum, pp. 28–29, 133–35, 217–18, 239; also see Ruth Fisher, *Stalin and German Communism: A Study in the Origin of the State Party* (Cambridge, Mass., 1948), p. 528. Known sources give no indication of disagreement between Soviet leaders on this issue. The subject never surfaced in the polemics between the warring

factions of the Bolshevik party in 1920s, it was unaffected by the purge of Trotsky from the Revvoensovet in 1924, and it was not brought up in the Moscow Trials in 1936, 1937, and 1938.

11. R. Fischer, p. 264.

12. Erickson, pp. 256–257.

13. Georges Castellan, *Le réarmement clandestine du Reich, 1930–1935, vue par le 2ᵉ Bureau de l'Etat-Major Français* (Paris, 1954). A less detailed account of the case appears in Benoist-Méchin, *Histoire de l'armée allemande* (Paris, 1938), 2:374–78.

14. Social-Democratic deputies in the Reichstag raised the question in the parliament in 1923 and 1926, but to no practical avail. The *Manchester Guardian* published its rather detailed story on Soviet-German military cooperation on December 12, 1926. The Polish press published information about the case based on disclosures of a Red Army pilot who had defected to Poland in February 1927. It was obviously all considered too fantastic to be true. According to Rosenbaum (*Community of Fate*, p. 40), Lloyd George had been told about the contacts between the Reichswehr and the Red Army as early as 1922, but he did not take the information seriously.

15. See R. Fischer, p. 533.

16. Ibid., p. 534.

17. Franz Borkenau, *European Communism* (New York, 1953), pp. 69–76. For the most detailed account of this issue and period, see Jan Valtin (Richard Krebs), *Out of the Night* (New York, 1941).

18. The idea that the Soviet leadership seriously contemplated financing of a revolution in Germany in September 1931 is not supported by sufficient evidence. According to this secret German report, a document on that question was prepared by the Soviet general consul in Hamburg, Krumin, who allegedly estimated the cost of a Communist uprising in Germany at 60 million golden marks. The Politburo is said to have refused the project on September 5, 1931; *DGFP*/AA 1417–2860, 562241-6, dated October 19, 1931.

19. R. Fischer, p. 536.

20. Alexander Baykov, *Soviet Foreign Trade* (London, 1946), p. 221; P. N. Kumykin, ed., *50 let sovetskoi vneshnei torgovli* (Moscow, 1967), p. 50; Franklyn D. Holzman, *Foreign Trade under Central Planning* (Cambridge, Mass., 1974), p. 40. The highest point in the interwar Soviet-German trade was reached in 1931, which also roughly corresponded with the highest total volume of Soviet foreign trade.

21. Baykov, p. 221; corresponding numbers for Soviet export to Germany were: 1929—23.3 percent; 1930—19.8 percent; 1931—15.9 percent; 1932—17.5 percent.

22. *DBFP*/Russia Correspondence, F.O. 371/17250, p. 4.

23. Herbert von Dirksen, *Moscow, Tokyo, London: Twenty Years of German Foreign Policy* (Norman, Okla., 1952), pp. 89, 104.

24. Collectivization of agriculture and the first Five-Year Plan so exhausted the Soviet economy that the volume of Soviet foreign trade fell between 1933 and 1936 by as much as 70 percent. Trade with Germany was correspondingly affected: Soviet imports from Germany fell from 1,798.6 million rubles in 1931 to 308.5 million rubles in 1936. Exports to Germany fell from 566.5 million rubles in 1931 to 116.6 million rubles in 1936; see Baykov, pp. 221–22.

25. Post, pp. 50–51.

26. Carr, p. 91.

27. Borkenau, p. 71.

28. J. V. Stalin, *Works* (Moscow, 1955), 13; 116–20.

29. Gustav Hilger and Alfred G. Meyer, *The Incompatible Allies: A Memoir History of German-Soviet Relations, 1918–1941* (New York, 1953), p. 255.

30. Dirksen, p. 109.

31. Walter G. Krivitsky, *In Stalin's Secret Service: An Exposé of Russia's Secret Policies* (New York, 1939), p. 8.

32. André François-Poncet, *The Fateful Years: Memoirs of a French Ambassador in Berlin, 1931–1938* (New York, 1949), p. 55.

33. *DBFP*/Russia Correspondence, F.O. 371/17250, p. 12, dated May 10, 1933.

34. Hilger and Meyer, pp. 255–56.

35. *DBFP*/Russia Correspondence, F.O. 371/17250, pp. 45–50.

36. *DGFP* ser. C, vol. 2, no. 171, pp. 318–24, Ambassador Nadolny's report dated January 9, 1934.

37. *Izvestiya*, December 30, 1933.

38. *DGFP* ser. C, vol. 2, no. 181, pp. 353–53, Ambassador Nadolny's report dated January 13, 1934.

39. *DGFP* ser. C, vol. 2, no. 171, January 9, 1934.

40. Stalin, *Works* 13:308–9: Stalin's speech sharply contrasted to that of Bukharin, whose opposition to nazism was principled and complete. See vol. XVII, *Syezd Vsesoyuznoi komunisticheskoi partii (b): Stenograficheskii otchet* (Moscow, 1934), pp. 128–29.

41. Carr, p. 102.

42. Ibid.

43. Dirksen, pp. 105–6.

44. De jure recognitions of the Soviet Union had been mostly secured before 1925, but altogether not more than 16 agreements to that effect had been contracted. Only Germany and Great Britain among the great powers had recognized the USSR de jure at that time. Agreements with France (1924) and Japan (1925) had the form of recognition de facto. See Slusser and Triska, pp. 11–48.

45. Baykov, p. 221.

46. *SDFP* 1:432–33.

47. Valtin, pp. 482–85.

48. *Istoriya diplomatii* 3:285.

49. Stalin, *Works* 11:207–8.

50. "In the course of this year, Germany and Japan announced their secession from the League of Nations. . . . It has so happened that even the League has, to a certain extent, stood in the way of the freedom of action of interventionists. In this connection the well-known restraining role played by the League of Nations in relation to forces making for war must be recognized as an established fact." *Izvestiya*, December 29, 1933.

51. J. Paul-Boncour, *Entre deux guerres: Souvenirs sur la IIIᵉ Republique*, vol. 2, *Sur les chemins de la défaite (1935–1940)* (Paris, 1946), p. 187.

52. "The intention of the sponsors of this pact has also been to turn it into an instrument of isolation and war against the USSR. Negotiations and the conclusion of the so-called Kellogg Pact have obviously been part of the encircling policy toward the USSR which directs the international relations at this time." Declaration of the commissar for foreign affairs, August 5, 1928; *Istoriya diplomatii*, 3:298.

53. Josef Korbel, *Poland between East and West* (Princeton, 1963); Roman Debicki, *Foreign Policy of Poland, 1919–1939* (New York, 1962), p. 65.

54. Maxim Litvinov, *Vneshnaya politika SSSR: Rechi i zayavleniya, 1927–1937* (Moscow, 1937), p. 57.

55. Louis Fischer, *Men and Politics: An Autobiography* (New York, 1941), p. 127.

56. Henry L. Roberts, "Maxim Litvinov," in Gordon A. Craig and Felix Gilbert, eds., *The Diplomats, 1919–1939* (Princeton, 1955), pp. 364, 370.

57. Max Beloff, *The Foreign Policy of Soviet Russia, 1929–1941* (London, 1949), 1, p. 90.

58. I. M. Maiskiy, *Vospominaniya sovetskogo diplomata, 1925–1945 gg.* (Moscow, 1971).

59. Maxim Litvinov, *Notes for a Journal* (London, 1955). E. H. Carr thought that the first half of the diary was probably genuine. In later years, Carr's doubts about the authenticity of the diary were growing, but he believed that it contained "a substratum of genuine material emanating in some form or another from Litvinov himself." According to family sources, parts of the diary were probably forged by one of Litvinov's secretaries, which may explain the touch of authenticity in many entries. In this study, the diary is referred to only for illustrative purposes.

60. Arthur Upham Pope, *Maxim Litvinov* (New York, 1943), p. 261.

61. Ibid.

62. Dirksen, p. 81.

63. Theodor von Laue, "Soviet Diplomacy: G. V. Chicherin, People's Commissar for Foreign Affairs, 1918–1930," in Craig and Gilbert, eds., *The Diplomats*, p. 278.

64. Litvinov, *Vneshnaya politika*, pp. 60–62.

65. Stalin, *Works*, 12:263.

66. Xenia Eudin-Joukoff and Robert M. Slusser, eds., *Soviet Foreign Policy, 1928–1934: Documents and Materials* (University Park, 1966–1967), 2:342.

67. Yu. V. Borisov, *Sovetsko-frantsuskie otnoshenia i bezopasnost Evropy* (Moscow, 1960), p. 163; Borisov quotes from the Archives of the Foreign Ministry of the USSR, Fund 0136, 13/131, 487/17, 15/149, 668/132.

68. Korbel, 250; Debicki, p. 65.

69. Dirksen, pp. 103–6; *League of Nations Treaty Series*, vol. 136-1933, nos. 1–4, pp. 41–53.

70. Litvinov presented this proposition of the Definition of Aggression in Geneva on February 6, 1933. It is impossible to say whether the Definition had been prepared earlier or, if it had been, then how long the Soviet delegation waited with its presentation. The fact is that it was tabled not before but after Hitler's accession to power, and that it represented a substantial change of mind on the part of the Soviet government. Earlier it had been the official Soviet standpoint that an effective definition of aggression could not be adopted. Chicherin himself declared in the name of the Soviet government that "it is absolutely impossible to adopt the system of deciding which state is the aggressor . . . and to make definite consequences depend upon such decisions" (*SDFP*, 1:432–33). The Soviet draft of February 1933 represented an abrupt departure from this previous standpoint. The definition proposed by the Soviets in 1933, especially in its version complemented by the Committee of the Assembly of the League, was in fact so thorough that twenty years later Moscow had to replace the old text with a new one better fitting the new realities of Eastern Europe after World War II. This version was tabled by Soviet delegate Morozov in the Sixth Committee of the General Assembly of the United Nations on January 5, 1952. What was especially missing in the new draft was the old Article 3 of the original proposal, which had decreed that "no political, military, economic or other considerations may serve as an excuse or justification for the aggression referred to in Article 2," i.e., military invasion with or without a declaration of war. *Istoriya diplomatii*, p. 337; see also Marina S. Finkelstein and Lawrence Finkelstein, eds., *Collective Security* (San Francisco, 1967), pp. 123–31.

2. *The French Connection*

1. *DBFP*/Russia Correspondence, F.O. 371/17256, p. 222, Ambassador Strang's report on a conversation with Alphand, August 12, 1933.

2. *DDF* 1st ser., vol. 4, nos. 20, 228, dated July 19 and September 19, 1933.

3. Available information indicates that the French Deuxième Bureau did not learn the full extent of the secret rearmamament of Germany until late 1930. All intelligence gathered before that time had been fragmentary and incomplete. For example, the Deuxième Bureau knew of the temporary disappearances of dozens of active officers of the Reichswehr, but was unable to account for the reasons. In October 1930 a document clearing up this mystery was obtained from the Polish Intelligence Service. The Polish report contained a detailed description of the collusion between the Reichswehr and the Red Army, including the development and production of armaments, prohibited by the Versailles Treaty, in jointly operated facilities on the territory of the USSR. Georges Castellan explains the achievement of the Polish Intelligence by the fact that in 1930 the Polish service had more than 200 active officers, the Deuxième Bureau only 60.

French experts examined the Polish document with great skepticism until their own military attaché in Berlin was able, in the course of 1931, to supply his superiors with independent information confirming it. It took another year before all the facts were thoroughly verified.

French diplomatic correspondence shows that the French Embassy in Moscow was urged to authenticate information on Soviet-German military cooperation as late as October 1932 and February 1933. Ambassador Dejean reported, in November 1932, that his staff had been unable to "find direct indications" of the existence of the Hammerstein-Tukhachevsky convention of 1929, which had presumably regularized the military cooperation between the Reichswehr and the Red Army. "No informer has been able to provide the Embassy with accurate information on this subject," wrote Dejean, but, according to corroborative indications, "everything is done as if the said convention existed." In February 1933 the Quai d'Orsay instructed Dejean to seek verification of certain information about the cooperation between the Soviet and German air forces. According to his qualified informer, Dejean replied, this information "should be accepted only with reservations," but he confirmed the existence of two jointly operated Soviet-German aviation schools in Russia.

It therefore follows that the Deuxième Bureau was still not quite in the clear when it finally produced its report for the French General Staff in November 1932. The General Staff needed another six months to inform the French government about the state of secret German rearmament with Soviet help. According to General Weygand, the document, endorsed by all members of the Supreme Council of War, stated that "the French Army, in its existing strength, is not capable of facing the German Army, going through its rebuilding." Georges Castellan, *Le réarmement clandestin du Reich, 1930–1935, vue par le 2e Bureau de l'Etat-Major français* (Paris, 1954), pp. 9–10, 185–86; *DDF* 1st ser., vol. 2, nos. 15 and 307, pp. 18–19 and 637–38, dated October 8 and November 19, 1932, and February 6 and 15, 1933.

4. *DDF* 1st ser., vol. 4, no. 308, pp. 570–72, Pierre Cot's report for Foreign Minister Paul-Boncour, dated October 4, 1933.

5. Elisabeth E. Cameron, "Alexis Saint-Léger," in Gordon A. Craig and Felix Gilbert, eds., *The Diplomats, 1919–1939* (Princeton, 1955), p. 381.

6. Maurice Gustave Gamelin, . . . *Servir* . . . , vol. 2, *Le prologue du drame, 1930–août 1939* (Paris, 1946), p. 56.

7. An analysis of Franco-Soviet relations prepared by the Political Directorate of the Quai d'Orsay in April 1934 separated the preliminary negotiations between Philip Berthelot and Soviet ambassador Dovgalevsky in 1931 as the first stage of the rapprochement, the most characteristic trait of which was French concern about the improvement of relations between the USSR and her western neighbors, Poland and Rumania. *DDF* 1st ser., vol. 6, no. 100, pp. 258–62, dated April 16, 1934.

8. *SDFP*, 3:30–31.

9. *DDF* 1st ser., vol. 3, no. 358, pp. 645–46, Pierre Cot's letter to Daladier, dated June 4, 1933.

10. In Léon Blum's view, Herriot's "purely private" visit of Russia was "an extension of, and a complement of his [Herriot's] official mission to America. He had to plead with Soviet leaders, as he had done with Roosevelt, for the case of peaceful security. . . . Not more than the United States is the Soviet Union officially affiliated with the League of Nations. At the same time, however, neither one nor the other can be left out of the supreme effort which still can block the route toward a future too similar to the past." Léon Blum, in *Le Populaire*, September 30, 1933, quoted from Léon Blum, *L'ouvre du Léon Blum* (Paris, 1963–72), 3-2:531; for more information on Herriot's visit in the USSR, see E. Herriot, *Jadis, d'une guerre à l'autre, 1914–1936* (Paris, 1952), 2:130; see also Michel Soulier, *La vie politique d'Edouard Herriot* (Paris, 1962), p. 432, and Geneviève Tabouis, *They Called Me Cassandra* (New York, 1942), pp. 174–76.

11. Tabouis, pp. 174–76; André Geraud (Pertinax), "France, Russia and the Pact of Mutual Assistance," *Foreign Affairs* (January 1935):227.

12. *DDF* 1st ser., vol. 4, no. 308, pp. 570–72, dated October 14, 1933; for Soviet sources, see Yu. V. Borisov, *Sovetsko-frantsuskie otnosheniya i bezopasnost Evropy* (Moscow, 1960), pp. 192–93; V. G. Trukhanovsky, *Istoriya mezhdunarodnykh otnoshenii i vneshnei politiki SSSR, 1917–1939* (Moscow, 1967), 1:304.

13. *DDF* 1st ser., vol. 4, no. 20, pp. 32–33, "Note de la Direction politique," dated July 19, 1933; the same information appears in Ambassador Alphand's report on the results of Herriot's visit. Alphand terms the proposed agreements "une convention de consultation." *DDF* 1st ser., vol. 4, no. 195, p. 331, dated September 10, 1933; see also no. 252, pp. 432–33, dated September 28, 1933.

14. *Annales de la Chambre des Deputés: Session ordinaire de 1933* 1:627; Pierre Cot's report before the Chamber of Deputies, October 31, 1933.

15. *DDF* 1st ser., vol. 4, no. 308, pp. 570–72, dated October 14, 1933.

16. Ibid.

17. *DDF* 1st ser., vol. 4, no. 252, pp. 432–33, dated September 28, 1933.

18. FRUS/The Soviet Union 1933–1939, pp. 53–54, Ambassador Bullitt's report from Moscow, dated December 24, 1933.

19. *DDF* 1st ser., vol. 3, no. 115, pp. 206–7, Ambassador Dejean's report, dated April 4, 1933; ibid., vol. 5, no. 77, p. 156, Ambassador Alphand's report, dated December 4, 1933.

20. J. Paul-Boncour, *Entre deux guerres: Souvenirs sur la IIIᵉ République*, vol. 1, *Les lendemens de la victoire (1919–1934)* (Paris, 1946), p. 363.

21. This version is supported by three sources: It appears in a note of the Political Directorate of the Quai d'Orsay which recapitulates *The Origins of Franco-Soviet Rapprochement* (*DDF*, 1st ser., vol. 4, no. 100, pp. 258–62, dated April 16, 1934); it is confirmed by Paul-Boncour in his memoirs (pp. 363–64); and it is also supported by Borisov, who quotes from the Archives of the Ministry of Foreign Affairs of the USSR, folliant 0136, no. 17, p. 159 (p. 202).

22. In Léger's version, as recorded by E. Cameron, it was France "who had been

approached by the Soviet Union." Léger characterized the alleged Soviet project as "the most cynical of all projects, a top secret plan for bilateral agreement with France outside the League, devised as a shield for Soviet imperialism in Asia." Léger seems to have been the obvious source for both G. Tabouis and "Pertinax." Cameron, p. 385; Tabouis, pp. 202–3; Pertinax, pp. 226–35.

23. Paul-Boncour, p. 363.

24. Ibid.

25. Borisov, pp. 202–3.

26. Ibid.

27. *DDF* 1st ser., vol. 4, no. 100, pp. 258–62, dated April 16, 1934.

28. Ibid.

29. *Istoriya Komunisticheskoi partii Sovetskogo Soyuza* (Moscow, 1962), p. 474. It seems much more probable that the decision was made by the Politburo, and not the Central Committee, which is rather mentioned in the official history of the CPSU for the sake of "democratic centralism."

30. Borisov, p. 204.

31. *DDF* 1st ser., vol. 5, no. 193, "Note du Departement, Conversations franco-russes," dated January 4, 1934.

32. Ibid.

33. Borisov, p. 211.

34. Cameron, p. 385.

35. Tabouis, p. 202.

36. Borisov, p. 217.

37. *DDF* 1st ser., vol. 6, no. 221, pp. 496–502, dated May 18, 1934.

38. André François-Poncet, *The Fateful Years: Memoirs of a French Ambassador in Berlin, 1931–1938* (New York, 1949), p. 124.

39. Borisov, pp. 218–19.

40. *DDF* 1st ser., vol. 6, no. 221, pp. 496–502, dated May 18, 1934.

41. *DDF* 1st ser., vol. 7, no. 103, pp. 198–201, Ambassador François-Poncet's report, dated August 20, 1934.

42. See W. E. Scott, *Alliance against Hitler: The Origins of the Franco-Soviet Pact* (Durham, N.C., 1962), p. 183.

43. FRUS, 1934, 6:889, dated July 20, 1934.

44. *DGFP*, ser. C, vol. 2, no. 504, Memorandum of the Foreign Minister, dated June 13, 1934.

45. Ibid.

46. *DGFP*, ser. C, vol. 3, no. 106, Memorandum of the State Secretary (Buelow), dated July 21, 1934.

47. French efforts to win Polish consent to the plan are recorded in a number of documents; e.g., *DDF*, 1st ser., vol. 7, nos. 137, 138, 160, 236, 247, 284, 379; in vol. 8, no. 134.

48. *DDF* 1st ser., vol. 7, no. 127, pp. 202–05, dated August 20, 1934.

49. *DGFP* ser. C, vol. 3, no. 74, Councillor Twardowski's report on a conversation with the Italian ambassador in Moscow, Attolico, dated July 9, 1934.

50. *DGFP* ser. C, vol. 3, no. 156, pp. 311–14, dated August 11, 1934.

51. *DDF* 1st ser., vol. 7, no. 3, p. 5, Payart's report for Barthou, dated July 27, 1934.

52. The Soviets sought in fact a new German credit of 200–300 million marks, which the Germans were not prepared to provide, especially not in the form of a normal financial credit instead of the *Wahrenkredit*, which had been more usual in Soviet-German trade. See *DBFP*/Russia Correspondence, F.O. 371/18315, p. 126 and p. 151,

dated May 1 and August 15, 1934; see also *DGFP* ser. C, vol. 4, no. 181, pp. 366–67, dated August 29, 1934; as for the doubts about the durability of the Soviet-German feud, see, for example, *DBFP* 2d ser., vol. 6, no. 558, dated August 2, 1934.

53. Alfred Mallet, *Pierre Laval: Des années obscures à la disgrace du 13 decembre 1940* (Paris, 1955), p. 61.

54. *DDF* 1st ser., vol. 7, no. 379, pp. 590, 592, dated September 27, 1934. It is interesting to note that in refusing the membership of Czechoslovakia in the project, the Poles used a geographical argument similarly to Barthou's reasons for refusing Rumania. According to the Poles, Czechoslovakia, as "a Danubian country," did not belong to the Northeastern region of Europe. Rumania, in Barthou's view, was more interested in the Balkans. The fact is that Rumania, during Titulescu's tenure in the office of foreign minister, was strongly interested in the Eastern Pact.

55. Gamelin, p. 131.

56. Sir Anthony Eden, *Facing the Dictators: The Memoirs of Anthony Eden, Earl of Avon* (Boston, 1962), pp. 132–33.

57. AMZV Prague, Incoming 1934/No. 451.

58. *Peregovory o Vostochnom pakte 1933–1935 gg.: Podbordka dokumentov* (*Mezhdunarodnaya zhizn*), (Moscow 1963/7), p. 159.

59. Eduard Beneš, *Paměti* (Memoirs) (Prague, 1947), p. 41.

60. "When, in 1934, Soviet Russia returned to an active role in international politics," observed Franz Borkenau, "the first thing she was obliged to do was to hide her attitude toward democracy," because, in the previous period, the USSR "had become a totalitarian country . . . which joined the ranks of the totalitarian, or fascist powers." Franz Borkenau, *European Communism* (New York, 1953), p. 72.

61. DSDF 751.61/165, U.S. Chargé d'Affaires John C. Willey's report from Moscow, dated October 31, 1934.

62. Borisov, p. 233.

63. Mallet, pp. 83–84; Herriot, p. 488; Borisov, p. 233.

64. Robert Kvaček, *Nad Evropou zataženo* (Clouds over Europe) (Prague, 1966), p. 97.

65. *DDF* 1st ser., vol. 8, no. 250, p. 378, Laval to Laroche, December 14, 1934. The explanation of the reasons for Czechoslovakia's accession to the Protocol is quoted from Beneš's exposé in the Czechoslovak government on December 12, 1934. SÚA Prague, PMR-II/4392.

66. Mallet claims that Marchandeau found out during his talks in Moscow that the Soviets were informing Berlin, every day, about the progress of the talks (p. 83).

67. Borisov, p. 244; relevant French documents are not available.

68. Eden, p. 164.

69. Borisov, p. 248.

70. *Pravda*, March 31, 1935, p. 2.

71. Herriot, p. 530.

72. Borisov, pp. 248–49; Herriot, p. 530. Laval preferred two bilateral treaties, between the USSR on one side and France and Czechoslovakia on the other, because, as Borisov claims, he hoped to complement the system by a treaty with Italy, which would not, considering her close ties with Hungary, join a grouping whose members included Czechoslovakia.

73. AMZV Prague, Incoming 1935, Ambassador Osuský's report from Paris, dated April 9, 1935; quoted from Věra Olivová, "Čs.-sovetská smlouva z r. 1935" (Czechoslovak-Soviet Treaty of 1935), *Czechoslovak Historical Review* 13 (April, 1965):490.

74. AMZV Prague, 6. KR. 309, no. 67037-35; ibid. Incoming Paris, April 21, 1935, Osuský to Beneš; quoted from Ivan Pfaff, "Jak tomu opravdu bylo se sovětskou pomocí

v mnichovské krizi" (How it really was with the Soviet assistance in the Munich crisis), Svědectví-Temoignage 56 (Paris 1978):571.

75. Pfaff, 56:572.

76. John Wheeler-Bennett, ed., *Documents on International Affairs,* vol. 1 (London, 1935), p. 139.

77. Ibid., p. 117.

78. *Istoriya diplomatii* 3:387.

79. *Zahraniční politika* (Foreign policy) (Prague 1935), pp. 324–26; *DBFP*/Russia Correspondence, F.O. 371/19461, p. 55.

80. *Istoriya diplomatti* 3:389.

81. Trukhanovsky, p. 316.

82. All that the pact was expected to achieve in relation to Poland was to neutralize the latter country, which had been recently waging an anti-Czechoslovak campaign. The topic of the summer war games of the Polish Army was the invasion of Slovakia. Kvaček, p. 126.

83. AMZV Prague, IV-KR. 309, no. 67037-35, quoted from Pfaff, 56:573–74.

84. Zdeněk Fierlinger, *Ve službách ČSR* (In the service of the Czechoslovak Republic) (Prague 1947), 1:27–28.

85. Articles 2 and 3 of the Franco-Russian Military Convention, August 5–17, 1892, George B. Manhart, *Alliance and Entente, 1871–1914* (New York, 1932), pp. 29–30.

86. According to Léger, as recorded by Cameron, Laval was playing politics when going hastily to Moscow without further trying to realize the broader initial concept of the Eastern Pact. Léger did not explain what steps Laval might have taken in this direction, but he accused his former boss of lack of patience for the cautious methods of the permanent establishment of the Quai d'Orsay. According to this testimony, Laval bypassed Léger in spring 1935 and negotiated directly with Potemkin, who quickly grasped the rift between the amateurish Laval and the professionals in the French foreign service, and played Laval's game. Laval's trip to Moscow extended the life of his cabinet. Léger called Laval's journey to Moscow "un voyage de cabotin" (a trip of a ham-actor). Cameron, p. 386.

87. *DBFP*/Russia Correspondence, F.O. 371/19456, pp. 62–63, dated March 9, 1935.

88. George F. Kennan, *Memoirs, 1925–1950* (Boston, 1967), pp. 70–71.

3. On the Access to Battlefields

1. AÚD KSČ, President Beneš's Archives, 105/1936, quoted from Věra Olivová, "Čs.-sovětská smlouva z roku 1935" (Czechoslovak-Soviet Treaty of 1935), *Czechoslovak Historical Review* 13 (April 1965):477–500. On April 11, the Soviet ambassador to Bucharest, Ostrovsky, had a conversation with the Czechoslovak envoy, Jan Šeba, and, talking about the passage problem, "emphasized that the USSR would stand by her obligations toward Czechoslovakia even without a formal agreement with Rumania." AMZV Prague, Bucharest-Incoming 1936/206, April 11, 1936.

2. *DBFP*/Russia Correspondence, F.O. 371/20349, pp. 79–80.

3. Roman Debicki, *Foreign Policy of Poland, 1919–1939* (New York, 1962), p. 83.

4. Maurice Gustave Gamelin, . . . *Servir* . . . , vol. 2, *Le prologue du drame (1930–août 1939)* (Paris, 1946), p. 213.

5. Laval's conclusions resulting from his conversation with the Poles; Alfred Mallet, *Pierre Laval: Des anneés obscures à la disgrace de 13 décembre 1940* (Paris, 1955), pp. 83–84.

6. Gamelin, p. 213.

7. *DBFP*/Russia Correspondence, F.O. 371/19460, pp. 209/11.

8. See appendix C, "Archiva Ministerului afacerlal externe" (Archives of the Rumanian Ministry of Foreign Affairs), Bucharest, no. 71/1938-C/18, vol. 3, dated September 24, 1938. General Krejčí was interviewed by the editors of the Czech liberal weekly *REPORTÉR* in September 1938; see *REPORTÉR*, Prague, 1968/38, pp. i–iv.

9. *DDF* 2d ser., vol. 2, no. 304, pp. 460–61; Robert Coulondre, *De Stalin à Hitler; Souvenirs de deux ambassades, 1936–1939* (Paris, 1950), p. 136; Winston S. Churchill, *The Second World War: The Gathering Storm* (Boston, 1948), p. 312; assessments differ from 6 divisions to 30 transferable within 30 days. Also see Borisov, p. 314; *Svĕdectví/Temoignage* (Paris), 1978/56, p. 563.

10. *Archiva ministerului*, p. 12.

11. Alexandry V. Boldur, *La Bessarabie et les relations rousso-roumanienes* (Paris, 1927); Antony Babel, *La Bessarabie: Etude historique, ethnographique et economique* (Paris, 1926).

12. I. M. Oprea, *Nicolae Titulescu's Diplomatic Activity*, Bibliotheca Historica Romaniae, vol. 22 (Bucharest, 1968), pp. 76–77.

13. Max Beloff, *The Foreign Policy of Soviet Russia, 1929–1941* (London, 1949), 1:22.

14. Louis Fischer, *Men and Politics: An Autobiography* (New York, 1941), pp. 130–34.

15. *SDFP* 2:136–37.

16. Grigory Bessedovsky, *Revelations of a Soviet Diplomat* (Westport, Conn., 1931), pp. 190–91.

17. Arthur Upham Pope, *Maxim Litvinov* (New York, 1943), p. 276.

18. Oprea, p. 60.

19. Ibid., p. 61.

20. *DBFP*/Russia Correspondence, F.O. 371/15624, Ambassador Palairet's report dated December 28, 1931.

21. Oprea, p. 61.

22. W. E. Scott, *Alliance against Hitler: The Origins of the Franco-Soviet Pact* (Durham, N.C., 1962), p. 65.

23. Ibid.

24. Oprea, pp. 61–62.

25. AMZV Prague, Dr. Krofta notes, quoted from Robert Kvaček, *Nad Evropou zataženo* (Clouds over Europe) (Prague, 1966), p. 67.

26. *Istoriya diplomatii* 3:337.

27. Oprea, p. 71.

28. *DBFP*/Russia Correspondence, F.O. 371/17277, p. 135, dated April 12, 1933.

29. Ibid.

30. Oprea, p. 75.

31. Ibid.

32. Litvinov himself sounded out Barthou on the possible interest of Rumania in the Eastern Pact; Barthou, to Litvinov's obvious relief, replied that Rumania did not have to be included in a regional pact of northeastern Europe. *DDF* 1st ser., vol. 4, no. 221, pp. 496–502; see also Edouard Herriot, *Jadis, d'une guerre à l'autre, 1914–1936* (Paris, 1952), p. 437.

33. AMZV Prague, III/2, no. 78645-34, Cabinet 1934. See also Ivan Pfaff, *Svĕdectví-Temoignage* 56 (Paris, 1978:569; Oprea, p. 78.

34. Oprea, pp. 97–98.

35. Paul Reynaud, *Memoires: Envers et contre tous, 7 Mars 1936–16 Juin 1940* (Paris, 1963), p. 155. Potemkin may not have been very effective in selling his idea. Fabry, the French minister of war, quotes him making the following statement: "Why are we not

afraid of war? Soviet Russia was the result of the last war; Soviet Europe will result from the next one."

36. Czechoslovak government intervened several times in Paris through diplomatic channels as well as through the French Military Mission in Prague (General Faucher) between August 1935 and November 1936 to persuade the French government to conclude a military convention with the Soviets. In August 1936, Prague offered the Soviets to conclude a military convention between the USSR and Czechoslovakia, but this offer was declined. *Les evénements survenues en France de 1933–1945*, 1:128, Paris 1947; ibid., 5:1199, Paris 1949; *DDF* 2d ser., vol. 3, no. 396; AÚD KSČ Prague, Beneš's Archives, France 1937, 1:21–39, Ripka's report for Beneš dated September 30, 1936; *REPORTÉR* 38 (Prague, 1968):i–iv; Borisov, pp. 339–56; *Voprosy istorii* 8 (Moscow, 1961):166. The background of the French attitude toward the military convention with the USSR deserves due attention. The Franco-Soviet pact was ratified by France on February 11, 1936, in the midst of a political crisis that in June brought to power the government of the Popular Front. As we know from diplomatic sources, as well as from Coulondre and from Léon Blum, the Popular Front government did not take up the Soviet proposal concerning the military convention until mid-October 1936, in connection with General Schweisguth's report, composed after his return from the USSR (the report is dated October 5, 1936). On the whole, Schweisguth's report was negative. It characterized the Red Army as "insufficiently prepared for a conflict with a major European power," and offered the opinion that Moscow was making an effort to channel German aggression toward France. Recent activities of the Comintern's agents indicated unfriendly Soviet attitude toward France. According to General Schweisguth, in case of a German onslaught on France, the Red Army would stay out of the conflict because of the lack of common border between the USSR and Germany, making it possible for Moscow to play the role of an arbiter similar to that of the USA in 1918 (*DDF* 2d ser., vol. 3, no. 343, pp. 510–14). The basis for discussion on the problem of the Franco-Soviet military convention in the fall of 1936 was therefore rather discouraging and all but blocked in December, upon the receipt of the first information on the Tukhachevsky affair, which Léon Blum's son brought in confidence from President Beneš. The first of the Moscow show trials had taken place in August, the purges in the Soviet Union were in full swing, and on top of everything else, the French-Soviet diplomatic agenda from October to December 1936 was filled with incessant French protests against Soviet (Comintern) interference into French internal affairs. DSDF 751.55/29, dated October 16, 1936; ibid. 852.00/3922, dated November 1, 1936; Coulondre, pp. 13, 18, 31–32, 44–45; DSDF 751.61/202; see also Victor Serge, *Memoires d'un révolutionaire, 1901–1941* (Paris, 1951), p. 375.

A detailed breakdown of the whole story of the Franco-Soviet military convention is therefore much more complex than a simple overview of diplomatic exchanges on the subject would indicate, and the time when there was any chance at all to act on the Soviet proposal was actually limited to about eight weeks. Similar interstate issues are rarely negotiated in such a short period. Even a military convention could in itself solve nothing regarding the passage problem, because France could never agree to a forceful entry of Soviet troops into either Poland or Rumania.

37. AMZV Prague, Ambassador Šeba's report to Beneš dated June 3, 1935; quoted from Pfaff, 56:576.

38. Oprea, p. 98.

39. *DBFP*/Russia Correspondence, F.O. 371/19461, p. 182, Ambassador Hoare's dispatch from Geneva, July 16, 1935.

40. J. Paul-Boncour, *Entre deux guerres: Souvenirs sur la IIIe République* (Paris, 1946), 2:60.

41. AMZV Prague, II/SN-19035, no. 158, Ambassador Heidrich's report from Geneva, quoted in Pfaff, 56:578.

42. AMZV Prague, Bucharest 1935/80, dated October 19, 1935, quoted ibid.

43. Ibid. AMZV Prague, II/SN no. 158190/35. Oprea understandably avoids specifics when describing the course of these negotiations, and claims that the talks never extended "beyond the stage of exchange of views" (Oprea, p. 99). Borisov, who quotes liberally from *l'Humanité* as a documentary source, limits himself to a passing remark that "Soviet-Rumanian negotiations broke down because of the active struggle of the Polish diplomacy and the Rumanian reaction against the policy of Titulescu" (Borisov, p. 263).

44. Oprea, p. 102.

45. AMZV Prague, Bucharest 1936/20, Ambassador Šeba's report for Beneš, dated February 17, 1936.

46. Pfaff, 56:579/80; AMZV Prague, Bucharest 1936/21, dated February 28, 1936.

47. *DDF*, 2d ser., vol. 2, no. 84, pp. 139–41, Ambassador De Lacroix's report from Prague, dated April 16, 1936.

48. Zdeněk Fierlinger, *Ve službách ČSR; paměti z druhého zahraničního odboje* (In the service of the Czechoslovak Republic), vol. 1 (Prague, 1947), p. 65.

49. Edvard Beneš, *Paměti* (Memoirs) (Prague, 1947), p. 49.

50. *DDF* 2d ser., vol. 2, no. 295, pp. 452–53, De Lacroix to Delbos, dated June 13, 1936.

51. Ibid., no. 303, pp. 458–60, Ambassador d'Ormesson's report from Bucharest, dated June 15, 1936.

52. Ibid., p. 460.

53. Oprea, pp. 103–4.

54. Ibid.

55. Paul-Boncour, 2:60.

56. Ibid., p. 64.

57. AÚD KSČ Prague, Beneš's Archives, SSSR (May, 1936), 5 Krofta's Papers, quoted from Kvaček, p. 273.

58. The legal basis for the project had been established in March 1933 by the adoption of the Organizational Pact by the three Allies. It provided for an extension of sphere of action of the Little Entente (against Italy and Germany). This scheme was then to be complemented by a general trilateral alliance, which would then sign a collective treaty of mutual assistance with France. This new system would presumably have given Rumania the guarantees she had been vainly seeking in her negotiations with the Soviet Union. Texts of both proposed treaties were drafted in Prague after the Bratislava conference of the Little Entente in September, and sent to Bucharest, Belgrade, and Paris in November. On November 10, 1936, Delbos instructed French ambassadors in the capitals of the Little Entente to communicate to the governments with which they were accredited the readiness of Paris to open negotiations on the project. The plan failed because of Yugoslavia's ultimate refusal to take part in it. *DDF* 2d ser., vol. 3, no. 207, pp. 288–89; ibid. no. 468, pp. 737–38; ibid. no. 453, p. 702; see also *FRUS 1936*, 1:308–10; Beneš, pp. 38–39, 49.

59. Oprea, p. 105.

60. Ibid.

61. *Izvestiya*, September 2, 1936, p. 1.

62. Oprea, p. 105.

63. Pfaff, 56:584.

64. Pope, p. 276; Oprea, p. 107. See also *DDF* 2d ser., no. 71, pp. 113–16, Chargé d'Affaires Jean Paul-Boncour's report from Bucharest for Massigli, dated June 14, 1937. In a conversation with Fierlinger, Litvinov falsely pretended that his "gentlemen's agreement" with Titulescu was still valid. On top of that, he claimed that part of this agreement was a Soviet promise to withdraw the Red Army beyond the Dniester, in case of passage, after the cessation of hostilities. This created the false impression that Moscow had settled the problem of the Rumanian passage directly with Bucharest. In reality, this issue was not a part of the Litvinov-Titulescu verbal agreement, and Litvinov simply lied to Fierlinger. See Fierlinger, 1:108.

65. AMZV Prague, Krofta/Cabinet 1937, no. 2732.

66. Borisov, p. 352; Gamelin, pp. 285–86. It is interesting that Borisov does not refer to Soviet sources in case of Potemkin's presentation. On the other hand, he footnotes an unspecified Soviet source when dealing with the military convention. He also leaves out the question of the possibility of passage through Lithuania via East Prussia. Soviet *History of Diplomacy* does not mention this important episode at all.

67. Gamelin, pp. 285–86.

68. Borisov, pp. 353–54.

69. *DDF* 2d ser., vol. 9, no. 306, pp. 671–72.

70. September 11, 1938, the Rumanian foreign minister Comnène informed Georges Bonnet that there would be no difficulty in letting the Red Army go through Rumania once the war started. The fact that Beneš was also informed at that time is verified by Hubert Ripka, among others. The Czechoslovak government was also informed about the Rumanian note to Moscow on September 24. Both Prague and Paris were therefore also aware of the lack of Soviet response. See Alexander Werth, *France and Munich, Before and After the Surrender* (London, 1939), pp. 334–35; Hubert Ripka, *Munich, Before and After* (London, 1939), pp. 338–39.

71. *DBFP*/Russia Correspondence, F.O. 371/22287, pp. 13–15.

72. Georges Bonnet, *Defense de la Paix, de Washington au Quai d'Orsay* (Paris, 1946), pp. 163–65.

73. During his visit of Warsaw in June–July 1937, King Carol stated that the entry of the Red Army into Rumania did not come into question. Two months later, however, he assured General Gamelin during the latter's attendance of Rumanian war games that "he would permit the Russians to go through the northern part of his territory to get into Czechoslovakia." AMZV Prague, Warsaw 1937/50, Ambassador Slávik's report dated July 4, 1937; Gamelin, p. 279.

74. Paul-Boncour, 2:112.

75. *Archiva ministerului.*

76. AMZV Prague, Moscow-Incoming 1938/937; see also Coulondre, p. 159; N. P. Comnène, *Preludi del grande drama* (Rome, 1947), p. 86; Pfaff, 57:63.

77. AMZV Prague, Moscow-Incoming 1938/862, 903; see also DSDF 740.00/493, dated October 10, 1938; *DGFP* ser. C, vol. 4, p. 606, dated October 8, 1938; Ripka, p. 338; Borisov, pp. 387–89; Pfaff, 57:64. See also František Lukeš, *Poznámky k čs.-sovětským vztahům v září 1938* (Notes on Czechoslovak-Soviet relations in September 1938), *Czechoslovak Historical Review* 5 (1968):703–31.

4. The Comintern and the Short Life of the United Front

1. Point 8 of the statutes of the Communist International gave the CPSU five seats on the Executive Committee, which was composed of 15 to 18 members. See *Quatre*

premiers congrès mondiaux de l'Internationale Communiste, 1919–1923, Textes complets (Paris, 1934), pp. 39–41.

2. Jacques Rupnik, *Histoire du Parti Communiste Tchécoslovaque, des origines à la prise du pouvoir* (Paris, 1981), pp. 94–97.

3. *The Communist International* X-16(1933):551–56.

4. Maurice Thorez, *Oeuvres* (Paris, 1950–51), 5:246, 249.

5. *XIII Plenum Ispolnitelnogo Komiteta Komunisticheskogo Internatsionala: Stenograficheskii otchet* (Moscow, 1934), pp. 589–90.

6. Franz Borkenau, *European Communism* (New York, 1953), pp. 107–8; see also Georges Lefranc, *Histoire du Front Populaire, 1934–1938* (Paris, 1965), pp. 44–46.

7. Miloš Hájek, *Jednotná fronta: K politicke orientaci Komunistické Internacionály letech, 1921–1925* (The United Front) (Prague, 1969), pp. 208–9; see also Ernst Fischer, *Le grande rêve socialiste: Souvenírs et réflexions* (Paris, 1974), pp. 280–81.

8. *Tridtsat let zhizni i borby Italianskoi Komunisticheskoi partii: Sbornik statei i dokumentov* (Moscow, 1953), pp. 360–62.

9. Arthur Koestler, *The Invisible Writing: An Autobiography* (Boston, 1954), p. 23.

10. *XIII Plenum ECCI*, pp. 589–95.

11. Borkenau, pp. 110–11; see also Boris Moiseyevich Leibzon and K. K. Shirinia, *Povorot v politike Kominterna* (Moscow, 1965), pp. 76–77.

12. *The Communist International*, November 20, 1934, p. 751, editorial entitled "For Soviet Power."

13. Leibzon and Shirinia, p. 81.

14. André Philip, *Les Socialistes* (Paris, 1967), p. 83.

15. *L'Humanité*, Paris, July 13, 1935.

16. Leibzon and Shirina, p. 77.

17. *The Communist International*, November 20, 1934, pp. 760, 762.

18. Wilhelm Pieck, *Der neue Weg zum Gemeinsamen Kampf fuer der Sturz der Hitler Diktatur* (Berlin, 1955), pp. 40–41.

19. Koestler, pp. 269–270.

20. Artur London, *Španělsko, Španělsko* (Spain, Spain) (Prague, 1963), p. 96.

21. It took two years to draw conclusions from the blatant failure of the old course in Germany, the principal ground of its application.

22. See chapter 5. It deserves noting in this context that in December 1935, five months after its Seventh Congress, the Comintern—certainly not without the Soviet Politburo's consent—severely criticized the leadership of the Czechoslovak Communist party for supporting the candidacy of Dr. Eduard Beneš in presidential elections in Czechoslovakia. It had been Beneš, of course, who had worked tirelessly for a rapprochement between France (as well as Czechoslovakia) with the Soviet Union; he signed the Soviet-Czechoslovak alliance treaty in May 1935 and he remained the principal advocate of cooperation with the Soviet Union in Czechoslovakia. The Comintern's opposition to his election as president of Czechoslovakia in December 1935 is a flagrant example of the double standard of Soviet foreign policy in the era. (A detailed account of the events of 1935 in relations between the Comintern and the CzCP is part of the unpublished memoirs of the late Stanislav Budín, then member of the Central Committee of the CzCP and chief editor of *Rudé právo*; Stanislav Budín, "Paměti" (Memoirs) (unpublished), 1:197–200, 202–08.

23. *Seventh Congress of the Communist International: Resolutions and Decisions* (Moscow, 1935), p. 3.

24. Ibid., p. 6.

25. Ibid., p. 10.

26. Ibid., p. 11.

27. Jane Degras, ed., *The Communist International, 1919–1943, Documents* (London, 1965), 3:412–13.

28. Ibid., p. 358; a realistic analysis of the documents of the Seventh Congress is largely missing in existing works on the interwar Soviet foreign policy. Even Franz Borkenau was inclined to view the Seventh Congress as "a wholesale overthrow of the basic principles of communism," something that the Congress certainly had not performed. See Borkenau, *European Communism*, p. 387.

29. *Seventh Congress of the Communist International: Stenographic Record of Proceedings* (Moscow, 1939); see also Leibzon and Shirinia, pp. 307–9, for comments on the postponement of the publication of the protocol.

30. *SDFP* 3:222; see also *For the President, Personal and Secret: Correspondence between Franklin D. Roosevelt and William C. Bullitt* (Boston, 1972), p. 655, and *DSDF* 862.20/883, July–August 1935.

31. Koestler, *Invisible Writing*, pp. 275–76; it deserves noting that both main organizers of the whole enterprise, Willy Muenzenberg and Otto Katz (André Simone), became victims of the GPU, Muenzenberg in 1939, Katz in 1952.

32. This uncritical view of the "Stalin Constitution" is still echoed by some authors even forty years later. For example, Adam B. Ulam, in *Stalin, the Man and His Era* (New York, 1973), had this to say about the Soviet constitution of 1936: "No doubt about it, the document was as advertised, 'the most democratic constitution in the world.' Elections were to be free, equal and secret. To the list of individual rights found elsewhere, the Soviet documents proudly added the right of every individual to demand that his government provide him with employment. Neither J. S. Mill nor Thomas Jefferson could have objected to single provision" (p. 403). The author did not mention the complete absence of any constitutional guarantees.

33. London, pp. 169–70.

34. David T. Cattell, *Communism and the Spanish Civil War* (Berkeley, 1955), pp. 71–73. First Soviet arms shipments arrived in October.

35. Walter Krivitsky, *In Stalin's Secret Service: An Exposé of Russia's Secret Police* (New York, 1939), p. 2; see also Alexander Orlov, *The Secret History of Stalin's Crimes* (New York, 1953), pp. 230–45.

36. Cattell, pp. 71–73.

37. Krivitsky, pp. 11–12.

38. Koestler, p. 276.

39. *The Communist International*, no. 11/1936, article by M. Ercoli (Palmiro Togliatti), "The Lessons of the Trial of the Trotsky-Zinoviev Terrorist Center," pp. 1439–57; quotations from pp. 1442–43.

40. Ibid., p. 1442.

41. *Communist International*, 3:412–13.

42. Ibid., p. 408.

43. *Communist International*, no. 11(1936):1439.

44. Enrique Castro-Delgado, *J'ai perdu la foi à Moscou* (Paris, 1950), pp. 33, 115, 133.

45. The process of the transformation of the Comintern from an agency of the world revolution into a department of the Soviet government has been attested to by a number of witnesses. The accounts of Jan Valtin (Richard Krebs), *Out of the Night* (New York, 1951), and of Koestler, *Invisible Writing*, are probably the best. Castro-Delgado's story is more intimate because of the author's high position in the apparatus of the ECCI as José Diaz's secretary, but he describes the era when Soviet control over the Comintern was already firmly established. Best-documented secondary works on the

subject are Borkenau's *European Communism* and Guenther Nollau's *International Communism and World Revolution History and Methods* (London 1961).

46. Krivitsky, pp. 81 and 128; Nollau, pp. 177–78. For a detailed description of the GPU network in the KPD, seen Valtin, p. 199; the author, Richard Krebs, refers to the Comintern as the "Moskauer Fremdenlegion" (p. 139).

47. Louis Fischer, *Men and Politics: An Autobiography* (New York, 1941), p. 380.

48. Nollau, pp. 190–91.

49. Numbers of victims are impossible to be established with any degree of accuracy. Tuominen, the alternate member of the ECCI until 1939, claimed that as many as 20,000 Finnish Communists living in the USSR at the time of the purges were sent to concentration camps, and many of them never came back. Almost all members of the prewar Polish Communist Party's Central Committee and many other activists were shot. A similar fate met the Yugoslavs, the Germans, the Hungarians, and even the Italians. For best account of this case, see Milorad Drachkovich and Branko Lazitch, eds., *The Comintern: Historical Highlights* (New York, 1966).

50. Nollau, p. 173.

51. For the fate of the Interbrigadists, see Orlov, pp. 230–45. See also Krivitsky, p. 2. The Interbrigadists were in fact purged until the 1950s, most thoroughly in Hungary and Czechoslovakia.

52. E. Fischer, p. 382.

53. Borkenau, p. 170.

54. Philip, pp. 88–89.

55. Borkenau, pp. 194–95.

56. Hájek, pp. 255–56. Manuilsky's speech appears in D. Manuilsky, *Die Ergebnise des VII. Kongresses der Kommunistischen Internationale* (Strassbourg, 1936), p. 11. J. V. Stalin's theory is in his *Works* (Moscow, 1955) 6:260.

57. Valtin, pp. 199 and 482–85; Orlov and Krivitsky give the same testimony.

5. *Germany and Russia, 1934–1937*

1. Together with the Soviet debts Hitler agreed to refinance in March 1933, Germany supplied the USSR with credits amounting to over 1.8 billion marks in this period; see Gustav Hilger and Alfred G. Meyer, *The Incompatible Allies: A Memoir-History of German-Soviet Relations, 1918–1941* (New York, 1953), pp. 283–87.

2. E. H. Carr, in *German-Soviet Relations between The Two World Wars, 1919–1939* (Baltimore, 1951), did not take the role of Soviet-German economic cooperation into consideration.

3. Diplomatic and military sources, especially those originating in Berlin, predicted the imminence of a Soviet-German political agreement as a by-product of the economic cooperation quite often after the spring of 1935.

4. Hermann Rauschning, *The Voice of Destruction* (New York, 1940), pp. 130–31. Rauschning, probably the keenest interpreter of the Nazi doctrine and of Hitler's personality, belonged to the Fuerher's inner circle in the Nazi party until 1934. In 1935, he broke with the regime and was exiled to the United States.

5. *DGFP* ser. C, vol. 2, no. 176, pp. 338–39, dated January 11, 1934; ibid., no. 181, pp. 352–53, dated January 13, 1934.

6. *DGFP* ser. C, vol. 2, no. 364, p. 686, Ambassador Nadolny's report dated March 29, 1934.

7. *DBFP* 2d ser., vol. 6, no. 537, pp. 875–77, dated July 26, 1934.

8. Ibid. L. Schapiro claims that according to the same document "the Russians were sounding out the possibility of a pact with Germany." The report contains no such information. See Leonard Schapiro, *The Communist Party of the Soviet Union* (New York, 1971), p. 490.

9. *DBFP*/Russia Correspondence, F.O. 371/18315, p. 151, Mr. Newton from Berlin, dated August 15, 1934. See also ibid., p. 126, Sir Eric Phipps's "Private and Most Secret Report from Berlin," dated May 1, 1934; see also *DGFP*, ser. C, vol. 3, no. 250, pp. 482–85, dated October 15, 1934. Alexander Barmine's claim that the Germans were already at that point anxious to provide the Soviet Union with another long-term loan of 300–400 million marks is not supported by archival documents; see Alexander Barmine, *Vingt ans au service de l'URSS: Souvenirs d'un diplomat soviétique* (Paris, 1939), p. 270. Sources indicate rather that the organizational grounds for the German credit policy that distinguished the German-Soviet economic cooperation in the 1934–38 period were only laid in September 1934 in Schacht's Foreign Trade Program, part of a broader program launched by the Nazi *Wehrwirtschaft*. See *Office of the United States for the Prosecution of Axis Criminality, Nazi Conspiracy and Aggression*, vols. 1–8 (Washington, D.C., 1946), 7:306–9; see also Hjalmar Schacht, *Confessions of "the Old Wizard": The Autobiography of Hjalmar Horace Greeley Schacht* (Boston, 1956), p. 302.

10. Walter G. Krivitsky, *In Stalin's Secret Service: An Exposé of Russia's Secret Policies* (New York, 1939), pp. 2–3.

11. *Izvestiya*, July 16, 1934, p. 1.

12. *DDF* 1st ser., vol. 4, no. 221, pp. 496–502, dated May 18, 1934.

13. François-Poncet's definition used at the Wilhelmstrasse; *DGFP* ser. C, vol. 3, pp. 349–51, dated August 20, 1934.

14. *DDF* 1st ser., vol. 4, no. 221, pp. 496–502.

15. *DBFP* 2d ser., vol. 6, no. 459, pp. 753–54, Foreign Office minute dated June 16, 1934.

16. *DGFP* ser. C, vol. 3, no. 92, pp. 176–82, circular of the foreign minister, dated July 17, 1934.

17. *DGFP* ser. C, vol. 3, no. 106, pp. 209–10, memorandum of the state secretary (Buelow), dated July 21, 1934.

18. Hilger and Meyer, p. 267.

19. *DBFP* 2d ser., vol. 6, no. 558, pp. 892–93, Sir G. Clerk from Paris, dated August 2, 1934.

20. Computed from statistical tables in Alexander Baykov, *Soviet Foreign Trade* (London, 1946), pp. 221–22.

21. It is very difficult to compare the German credit policy toward Russia, especially after September 1934, when the centralized system of *Wehrwirtschaft* was put into effect, with that of the Western countries whose governments' role in foreign trade was quite unimportant. Soviet trade representatives had to negotiate—in France, England, or the United States—all business deals and payment arrangements directly with private banks and enterprises.

22. Barmine, p. 270.

23. Hilger and Meyer, pp. 283–287.

24. *DBFP*/Russia Correspondence, F.O. 371/19459, p. 234, dated January 1935.

25. *DGFP* ser. C, vol. 3, no. 181, pp. 366–67, Foreign Ministry to Moscow Embassy, dated August 29, 1934.

26. *DBFP*/Russia Correspondence, F.O. 371/19459, pp. 260–65.

27. Schacht, p. 302.

28. *DGFP* ser. C, vol. 4, no. 154, pp. 975–76, dated March 2, 1935.

29. *DBFP*/Russia Correspondence, F. O. 371/19460, p. 38, dated April 10, 1935.

30. The Soviet ambassador to London, Maiskiy, mentioned even a billion-mark German loan being negotiated between the Germans and the Soviets in January 1936, "to finance a program of orders spread over the next ten years," *DBFP*/Russia Correspondence, F.O. 371/20646, pp. 143–45, Foreign Office minute dated January 27, 1936. Ibid., p. 135, Sir Phipps's report from Berlin, dated January 8, 1936.

31. *DGFP* ser. C, vol. 4, no. 483, pp. 967–70, Foreign Ministry memorandum dated January 6, 1936.

32. Ibid. The interest in the cooperation with the Carl Zeiss optical complex in Jena was especially connected with the Soviet need of submarine periscopes.

33. *DGFP* ser. C, vol. 4, no. 518, p. 1033, dated January 24, 1936.

34. *DGFP* ser. C, vol. 5, no. 619, pp. 512–15, memorandum of the German-Russian economic negotiations, dated February 21, 1938.

35. *DGFP* ser. C, vol. 5, nos. 20, 21, 302, pp. 28–30, 488–94; Hilger and Meyer, p. 284. In 1936, the German share in Soviet imports was 22.8 percent. Corresponding figures for England, the United States, and France were 15.1, 15.5, and 3.1 respectively.

36. German assistance preceded the formal recognition of General Franco's government in November 1936. Soviet aid to the loyalists was limited, at the beginning, to foodstuffs. Moscow acceded to the Non-Intervention Pact in August 1936, but first Soviet ships with armaments reached the port of Alicante in October. See Krivitsky, p. 202; David T. Cattell, *Communism and the Spanish Civil War* (Berkeley, 1955), p. 73; Artur London, *Španělsko, Španělsko* (Spain, Spain) (Prague, 1963), p. 156.

37. Robert Coulondre, *De Staline à Hitler: Souvenirs de deux ambassades, 1936–1939* (Paris, 1950), p. 34.

38. *DBFP*/Russia Correspondence, F.O. 371/21102, dated June 28, 1937.

39. *DGFP* ser. C, vol. 5, no. 619, pp. 912–15, dated February 21, 1938.

40. *DBFP*/Russia Correspondence, F.O. 371/22289, dated January 8, 1938.

41. *DGFP* ser. C, vol. 5, no. 619, pp. 914–15.

42. *DBFP*/Russia Correspondence, F.O. 371/19460, pp. 177–78, Sir R. Vansittart's memorandum on the international position of Russia, dated February 21, 1935.

43. Ibid., p. 18, Mr. Nixon's report from Berlin, dated March 20, 1935.

44. Edouard Herriot, *Jadis, d'une guerre à l'autre, 1914–1936* (Paris, 1952), p. 530.

45. *DGFP* ser. C, vol. 4, no. 70, pp. 128–30, Ambassador Schulenburg's report from Moscow, dated May 6, 1935.

46. Georges Castellan, *Le réarmement clandestin du Reich, 1930–1935, vue par le 2ᵉ Bureau de l'Etat-Major Français* (Paris, 1954), p. 196. For Kandelaki's statement, see note 92. Earlier Soviet approaches bypassing the Narkomindel also deserve to be noted. Since at least October 1933, the German Embassy in Moscow (Twardowski) maintained regular contacts with an anonymous Soviet person who claimed to be acting on behalf of Stalin and Molotov and who repeatedly suggested that the latter "did not necessarily" share the standpoints on Germany then being expressed by the Soviet foreign policy. According to Evgenii Gnedin, this anonymous person was Karl Radek, who, after his return from banishment, headed a subdepartment in Stalin's personal secretariat (he was also member of the editorial board of *Izvestiya*). See E. Gnedin, *Iz istorii otnoshenii mezhdu SSSR i fashistskoi Germaniei: Dokumenty i sovremennye komentarii* (New York, 1977), pp. 22–23. As for German documents, see two reports by Twardowski, dated October 2 and 24, 1933, in *DGFP* ser. C, vol. 1, no. 477, pp. 884–85, and ibid., vol. 2, no. 24, p. 40.

47. *DGFP* ser. C, vol. 4, no. 211, Dr. Schacht's minute of a conversation with the Russian Trade Delegate, dated July 15, 1935. See also Hilger and Meyer, p. 269.

48. Schacht, p. 379.

49. *DGFP* ser. C, vol. 4, no. 383, pp. 778–79, Ambassador Schulenburg's report, dated October 28, 1935.

50. *Pravda*, March 31, 1935. For the German report on this case, see *DGFP* ser. C, vol. 3, no. 15, pp. 18–20, dated April 5, 1935.

51. *DBFP*/Russia Correspondence, F.O. 371/19460, p. 126, Wing Commander Collier's report, dated October 17, 1935.

52. *DGFP* ser. C, vol. 4, no. 407, pp. 811–13, dated November 7, 1935.

53. *DGFP* ser. C, vol. 4, no. 439, pp. 870–72, memorandum of the deputy director of Department II (Roediger), dated December 2, 1935. According to Gnedin, who was also assigned to the Soviet Embassy in Berlin at that time, Bessonov probably acted in tandem with Kandelaki, and in any case reported directly to Molotov. In March 1938, Bessonov was a key witness in (and a victim of) the last show trial. See Gnedin, p. 35.

54. *DGFP* ser. C, vol. 4, no. 453, memorandum of the deputy director of Department IV(Twardowski), dated December 10, 1935.

55. Ibid.

56. Ibid.

57. *DGFP* ser. C, vol. 4, no. 472, pp. 931–33, memorandum of the deputy director of Department II (Roediger), dated December 21, 1935.

58. No record of the conversation to which Bessonov was alluding was found.

59. John Erickson, *The Soviet High Command: A Military Political History, 1918–1941* (London, 1962), pp. 411–12.

60. Geneviève Tabouis, *They Called Me Cassandra* (New York, 1942), p. 257.

61. William E. Dodd and Martha Dodd, eds., *Ambassador Dodd's Diary, 1933–1938* (New York, 1941), p. 297.

62. *Izvestiya*, January 12, 1936.

63. Ibid.

64. *DBFP*/Russia Correspondence, F.P. 371/19460, pp. 142–48, dated December 7, 1935.

65. Ibid., 371/20346, pp. 150–52, Foreign Office minute (secret), dated January 29, 1936.

66. Ibid., pp. 132–35, Viscount Chilston to Collier, dated February 11, 1936.

67. Ibid.

68. Ibid., 371/20347, pp. 52–54, Viscount Chilston to Eden, dated November 26, 1936.

69. *SDFP* 3:173–74.

70. James E. McSherry, *Stalin, Hitler and Europe* (Cleveland, 1968), 1:51.

71. *DGFP* ser. C, vol. 5, nos. 312, 341, pp. 512, 571–73.

72. Ibid., no. 312, p. 512, memorandum by an official of Department II (Hencke), dated May 6, 1936. Gnedin himself has nothing to say about his role in these dealings. "On Kandelaki's contacts with the Germans I had only general knowledge," he says (p. 35). In another context, he nevertheless notes: "I can confirm German informations about the special role played by Kandelaki" (p. 34). Gnedin's theory is that the Narkomindel—i.e., Litvinov and also Suritz—were not engaged in the efforts to arrive at a deal with Nazi Germany. Documents show otherwise.

73. *DGFP* ser. C, vol. 5, no. 341, pp. 571–73, Herbert L. W. Goering to Ambassador Schulenburg, dated May 20, 1936.

74. Ibid., p. 573.

75. *DGFP* ser. C, vol. 5, no. 615, pp. 1115–18, memorandum by the head of Economic Policy Division IV (Schnure), dated October 19, 1936.

76. Ibid.

77. Herbert von Dirksen, *Moscow, Tokyo, London: Twenty Years of German Foreign Policy* (Norman, Okla., 1952), p. 153.

78. Peter Kleist, *Zwischen Hitler und Stalin, 1939–1945, Aufzeichnungen* (Bonn, 1950).

79. Rauschning, pp. 127–29.

80. *DGFP* ser. C, vol. 5, no. 590, Ambassador Schulenburg's report dated October 12, 1936.

81. *DDF* 2d ser., vol. 4, no. 343, pp. 510–14, Daladier to Delbos, October 13, 1936; General Schweisguth's report was dated October 5, 1936.

82. *DBFP*/Russia Correspondence, F.O. 371/21105, Ambassador Alphand's disclosure after his transfer from Moscow to Bern, dated December 18, 1936.

83. DSDF 751.55/29, Ambassador Bullitt's report, dated October 16, 1936; see also Coulondre, pp. 31–32.

84. Alexander Orlov, *The Secret History of Stalin's Crimes* (New York, 1953), pp. 169–78.

85. Ibid.

86. Litvinov's speech on November 29, 1936 (*Izvestiya*, November 29, 1936) was marked by bitter criticism of France and England, and can be interpreted as a signal of retreat from previous Soviet stands in Geneva.

87. Krivitsky, pp. 21–22, 216.

88. Litvinov, *Notes for a Journal* (London, 1955), p. 217.

89. Krivitsky, p. 21.

90. Litvinov, pp. 209–14. The letter was allegedly photographed by Soviet agents in Vienna after the murder of Dollfuss. Mussolini characterized Hitler as a liar, a madman, and a sexual pervert.

91. *Akten zur Deutschen Auswertigen Politik, 1918–1945*, ser. C, vol. 6, no. 183, pp. 401–2, dated February 6, 1937.

92. Ibid., p. 402.

93. The Wilhelmstrasse, according to Neurath, had no knowledge of the Soviet proposal alluded to by Kandelaki. It is possible that the Soviets, acting on the incorrect assumption that the German bureaucratic machine was as thoroughly centralized as their own, had addressed their offer to an agency or a person who did not pass it on. It is also possible that they contacted the Nazi party Foreign Bureau, the records of which have not been found. RG 242, Records of the National Archives, Collection of Foreign Records Seized 1945——, Microcopy T-120, roll 282, serial 393, frames 212210–15; see also roll 1057, serial 1907, frames 429293–300, where the contents of the correspondence between Schacht and Neurath were communicated to Ambassador Schulenburg.

94. Ibid.

95. Krivitsky, p. 226.

96. Litvinov, pp. 217–19.

97. Walter Schellenberg, *The Labyrinth: Memoirs of Walter Schellenberg* (New York, 1956), pp. 25–28. No evidence has been found about any illegal contacts of Tukhachevsky with the German General Staff. Fritz Thyssen's assertion that General Fritsch had established contact with Tukhachevsky has so far been supported by no known evidence. Fritz Thyssen, *I Paid Hitler* (London, 1941), pp. 194–95.

98. Ambassador Bullitt told Coulondre some time later that "they had proofs in Washington that Moscow and Berlin did not cease to communicate in the years preceding the war," but there is no evidence that this knowledge extended to the secret negotiations conducted, for example, by Kandelaki. See Coulondre, p. 125.

99. *DDF* 2d ser., vol. 5, nos. 38, 285, pp. 58–60, 526. Ambassador François-Poncet

thought that the thaw in Soviet-German relations was motivated by economic interests on both sides.

100. *DDF* 2d ser., vol. 5, nos. 192, 229, pp. 311–12, 363–65, dated March 30, April 8, 1937.

101. Ibid., p. 311.

102. Orlov, p. 238; Cattell, pp. 76–79.

103. *DDF* 2d ser., vol. 5, no. 356, p. 599, dated April 28, 1937.

104. Litvinov, pp. 231–32.

105. *DGFP* ser. D, vol. 2, no. 613, pp. 902–3, dated January 10, 1938.

106. *DDF* 2d ser., vol. 6, no. 259, pp. 437–38, dated July 22, 1937.

107. *DBFP*/Russia Correspondence, F.O. 371/22288, p. 129 (1–8), Viscount Chilston's confidential report dated January 24, 1938.

108. Rauschning, pp. 128–29.

109. *DBFP*/Russia Correspondence, F.O. 371/22288, p. 129.

110. Ibid.

111. *DDF* 2d ser., vol. 7, no. 390, pp. 785–88, dated December 25, 1937.

112. Robert M. Slusser and Jan F. Triska, *A Calendar of Soviet Treaties 1917–1957* (Stanford, 1959), pp. 56, 78.

113. B. N. Ponomarov, A. A. Gromyko, B. M. Khvostova, eds., *Istoria vneshnei politiki SSSR, chast pervaya, 1917–1945* (Moscow, 1966). All Soviet history textbooks of the period are based on this volume, which contains a number of corrections in regards to, for example, the early postwar *History of Diplomacy*.

114. For the most thoughtful analysis of this problem, see Robert C. Tucker, "*Stalin, Bukharin and History as Conspiracy*," an introduction to R. C. Tucker and Stephen F. Cohen, eds., *The Great Purge Trial* (New York, 1965), pp. xxxiii–xxxviii. More on this subject in chap. 6.

115. *DBFP*/Russia Correspondence, F.O. 371/19460, pp. 146–47.

6. *The Great Purges and Collective Security*

1. André Gide in Richard Crossman, ed., *The God That Failed* (New York, 1950), p. 169.

2. Louis Fischer, *Men and Politics: An Autobiography* (New York, 1941), p. 333.

3. Louis Fischer in Crossman, ed., p. 216.

4. James Billington, *The Icon and the Axe* (New York, 1970), p. 540.

5. *DDF* 2d ser., vol. 6, no. 183, pp. 296–97, Ambassador De Lacroix's report to Delbos on his conversation with President Beneš on July 3, 1937.

6. Georges Etienne Bonnet, *Vingt ans de vie politique, 1918–1938, de Clemenceau à Daladier* (Paris, 1962), p. 207.

7. George F. Kennan, *Memoirs, 1925–1950* (Boston, 1967), pp. 55–56.

8. Ibid.

9. Maxim Litvinov, *Notes for a Journal* (London, 1955), p. 146. See also Alexander Barmine, *Vingt ans au service de l'URSS: Souvenirs d'un diplomat soviétique* (Paris, 1939), p. 53.

10. Zdeněk Fierlinger, *Ve službách ČSR, paměti a druhého zahraničního odboje* (In the service of the Czechoslovak Republic; Memoirs of the second external resistance) (Prague, 1947), 1:49.

11. *DDF* 2d ser., vol. 5, no. 398, pp. 673–76, Coulondre to Delbos, May 4, 1937.

12. *DDF* 2d ser., vol. 6, no. 144, pp. 225–28, Coulondre to Delbos, dated June 28,

1937. The German ambassador to Moscow, Schulenburg, also complained several times about the difficulties resulting from the purges of the Soviet diplomatic personnel, which also affected the Commissariat for Foreign Trade. German-Soviet commercial negotiations in January 1938, for example, were substantially paralyzed by the fact that the chief Soviet delegate in Berlin, Smolensky, was so horrified by his responsibility that he was unable to express any opinion on the issues discussed. He did not get much advice from Moscow, either, where "the personnel situation" at the Commissariat for Foreign Trade was, in the German view, "completely unsettled." *DGFP* ser. C, vol. 6, no. 609, pp. 902–3, memorandum on the status of German-Russian commercial negotiations, dated January 10, 1938.

13. Bonnet, p. 57.

14. Arthur U. Pope, *Maxim Litvinov* (New York, 1943), p. 419. See also Barmine, p. 53.

15. *DDF* 2d ser., vol. 7, no. 170, p. 297, dated October 31, 1937.

16. The French Embassy in Moscow formally protested against repated wholesale attacks by the Soviet press and Soviet officials against "capitalist countries," because such attacks made no exception of at least the allies of the USSR, i.e., of France and Czechoslovakia. *DDF* 2d ser., vol. 8, no. 419, pp. 772–74, dated March 11, 1938.

17. On top of that, the Soviets flatly refused to compensate Prague for the "not inconsiderable funds" that the Czechs had spent in improving the building. *DGFP*, ser. C, vol. 6, nos. 614 and 615, pp. 903–9.

18. Arthur Koestler in Crossman, ed., p. 66.

19. "As far as Catalonia is concerned, the purge of the Trotskyist and anarcho-syndicalist elements already started and will be carried out with the same energy as in the Soviet Union." *Pravda*, December 17, 1936, p. 1. The murderous assault on the POUM Party in Barcelona occurred in May 1937. See, for example, Victor Serge, Memoirs d'un revolutionaire, 1901–1941 (Paris, 1951), pp. 366–368.

20. Max Beloff, *The Foreign Policy of Soviet Russia, 1929–1941* (London, 1949), 1:31.

21. André Gide, *Retour de l'URSS* (Paris, 1936), p. 34; *Retouches à mon retour de l'URSS* (Paris, 1937), p. 61. Both pamphlets were quickly published in several editions and translated into a number of foreign languages.

22. Idem, Retour, p. 61.

23. *DDF* 2d ser., vol. 4, no. 372, pp. 641–42, Coulondre to Delbos, January 30, 1937. Coulondre alludes to the trial with Pyatakov, Sokolnikov, Radek, and other defendants in January 1937.

24. *DDF* 2d ser., vol. 4, no. 353, pp. 607–11, Coulondre to Delbos, dated January 26, 1937.

25. Ibid., p. 610.

26. DSDF 861.00/11786, Ambassador Davies's final summary and report, dated June 6, 1938.

27. František Lukeš, "Poznámky k čs.-sovětským vztahům v září 1938" (Notes on Czechoslovak-Soviet relations in September 1938), *Czechoslovak Historical Review* (May 1968):705. See also Eduard Beneš, *Paměti* (Memoirs) (Prague, 1947), pp. 33–34, 231–32. Whereas the first stage of Beneš's role in the transaction between Heydrich and Yezhov in late 1936 is not clearly documented, he recalls that in January 1937 he had informed the Soviet ambassador in Prague, Alexandrovsky, about German expectations of a political change in Moscow. He mentioned specifically the case of German contacts with "Soviet anti-Stalinist conspirators, Marshal Tukhachevsky, Rykov and others," as they were allegedly revealed to the Czechoslovak ambassador in Berlin, Dr. Mastny, by "a slip of the tongue" of Ribbentrop's contact man, Trautmannsdorf. Walter Schellen-

berg's account sounds entirely probable, in spite of the fact that the author himself is a rather obscure source. See Walter Schellenberg, *The Labyrinth: Memoirs of Walter Schellenberg* (New York, 1956).

28. Isaac Deutscher, *Stalin: A Political Biography* (London, 1949), p. 425.

29. *DBFP*/Russia Correspondence, F.O. 371/21101, pp. 180–81, Mac Killop from Moscow, dated October 4, 1937.

30. Ibid., p. 216, Moscow Chancery to the Northern Department of the Foreign Office, October 19, 1937. A later dispatch, dated November 2 (ibid., p. 237), corrected the number of October executions to 500. A surprisingly great number of executions was reported from the Pacific provinces, where the purge reached its peak nine months later, in summer 1938.

31. Nadejda Mandelstam, *Contre tout espoir* (Paris, 1970), p. 111. Yagoda was dismissed as head of the NKVD in September 1936, shortly after the trial with Zinoviev, Kamenev, and other defendants, and was replaced by Yezhov. The reason for Stalin's displeasure with Yagoda appears to have been the exoneration of Bukharin and Rykov. Yagoda was criticized for his lack of ability "to unmask the Trotskyists" and for allegedly turning the concentration camps into "nursing houses for class enemies." Osip Mandelstam commented on the news by saying, "I did not know we had been in the hands of humanists." Ibid., p. 41. For an account of the trials see, for example, Leonard Schapiro, *The Communist Party of the Soviet Union* (London, 1960).

32. B. H. Liddel-Hart, ed., *The Red Army* (New York, 1956), pp. 68–69; see also John Erickson, *The Soviet High Command: A Military-Political History, 1918–1941* (London, 1962).

33. Sir Denis William Brogan, *The Development of Modern France, 1870–1939* (New York, 1966), p. 720.

34. DSDF 861.00/11713, Ambassador Bullitt's report from Paris, dated July 30, 1937.

35. *DDF* 2d ser., vol. 4, no. 144, pp. 225–28, Coulondre to Delbos, dated June 28, 1937.

36. Ibid. An interesting piece of information in this document is Coulondre's remark, "As your Excellency knows, indications about the relations between the German and Soviet general staffs came from London and from the Baltic states." This suggests that Blum did not inform Delbos, or at least Delbos did not inform Coulondre about the communication the prime minister received in December 1936; but he probably informed General Gamelin, because Coulondre alludes to the fact that the French General Staff had been informed before the affair broke out. In his memoirs, Coulondre adds another detail to the story: in June 1937, he learned from Potemkin that the information about the collusion between the German and Soviet general staffs allegedly came from Daladier, through Potemkin (then still in Paris), in February 1937. See Robert Coulondre, *De Staline à Hitler: Souvenirs de deux ambassades, 1936–1939* (Paris, 1950), p. 83. The French ambassador to London, Corbin, reported to Delbos on June 22, 1937 that the British government had acquired information from a certain source confirming the secret transactions between the German General Staff and some Soviet military leaders. *DDF* 2d ser., vol. 6, no. 123, pp. 123–24.

37. *DDF* 2d ser., vol. 5, no. 285, pp. 448–49, dated April 15, 1937; ibid., no. 480, pp. 825–28, dated May 3, 1937. Both documents emphasize the importance of the passage problem for any practical consideration of a French-Soviet military convention.

38. Ibid., vol. 6, no. 35, pp. 50–52, "Note de l'Etat-Major de l'Armée sur l'éventualité d'une contact militaire franco-soviétique," dated June 9, 1937.

39. František Moravec, *Špion, jemuž nevěřili* (The spy whom they did not believe) (Toronto, 1977), pp. 155, 158.

40. Ibid., pp. 159–60.

41. *DGFP* ser. D, vol. 2, no. 81, pp. 165–66, dated March 14, 1938.

42. DSDF 851.00/1684, Ambassador Bullitt's report dated June 17, 1937. German diplomatic sources claim that the French still believed, in 1938, in the substantiation of the Soviet accusation that Tukhachevsky and the other executed military leaders had been German agents. A French diplomat in Moscow is quoted to have asserted that very seriously at the Commissariat for Foreign Affairs. This fact annoyed Schulenburg so much that he found it necessary to reassure the Wilhelmstrasse that his office found "no grounds for such an assumption," and he even speculated that the documents on the basis of which the Soviet generals had been shot might have been falsified—by the French. *DGFP* ser. D, vol. 2, no. 64, pp. 150–51, dated February 28, 1938.

43. *DDF* 2d ser., vol. 4, no. 457, and ibid., vol. V, no. 285.

44. Georges Castellan, *Le réarmement clandestin du Reich, 1930–1935, vue par le 2ᵉ Bureau de l'Etat-Major Français* (Paris, 1954), pp. 192, 193, 196.

45. See, for example, *DDF* 2d ser., vol. 4, no. 73, pp. 116–20, report of the French military attaché in Moscow, Lt.-Col. Simon, dated June 14, 1937; ibid., vol. 7, no. 52, p. 100, dated October 11, 1937; ibid., no. 185, pp. 314–19, dated November 3, 1937; ibid., vol. 9, no. 192, pp. 390–94, report of the French military attaché in Moscow, Col. Pallasse, dated April 18, 1938. See also DSDF 861.60/305, dated June 3, 1938.

46. Uninterrupted in the western military sectors, the purge was further extended to the Far East, disregarding the danger involved in view of the Japanese threat. The purge of the Far Eastern Red Army appears to have culminated in September 1938. Marshal Bluecher was reported to have been shot during the Munich crisis. An editorial in the *Tikhookeanskaya Zvezda* (the organ of the Soviet government in the Far East, published in Vladivostok) stated on July 16, 1938: "During recent years, masked enemies of the people held the leading positions in the Vladivostok and Provincial Party organizations as well as in the Pacific Fleet." On Marshal Bluecher's execution, see DSDF 751.61/128, dated October 2, 1938. For the purge of the Far Eastern Red Army, see Petro G. Grigorenko, *Memoirs* (New York, 1982), pp. 111–12. When the purge actually finished is still a valid question. According to Grigorenko, General Stern was shot in June 1941.

47. *DDF* 2d ser., vol. 9, no. 450, pp. 399–401, "Note du 2ᵉ Bureau de l'Etat-Major de l'Air sur l'aviation soviétique," dated May 25, 1938. The document, the most comprehensive of similar reports available in diplomatic archives, gives the number of Soviet aircraft immediately deployable as 3,200. Doubts are expressed regarding the quality of command. Principal technical weakness is seen in the lack of a heavy bomber with action radius of over 2,000 km. Production capacity of the aircraft industry is reported to be 5,000 machines per year, and 15,000 engines in the European part of the USSR.

48. Erickson, p. 501.

49. *For the President, Personal and Secret: Correspondence between Franklin D. Roosevelt and William C. Bullitt* (Boston, 1972), pp. 109–10.

50. *DBFP*/Russia Correspondence, F.O. 371/22287, pp. 122–24. The dispatch reported the disappearance of six members of the Council of People's Commissars and the dismissal of five others, adding casually that "at least fifteen Deputy Commissars of the USSR have been liquidated since the 1st January [1938]." After an enumeration of further casualties among government rank officials in ten Soviet republics, the report concluded: "Out of a total of approximately 175, close to 150 People's Commissars . . . have been liquidated in the first half of 1938."

51. *DBFP*/Russia Correspondence, F.O. 371/22287, pp. 10 and 41. The most important Soviet deserter in Manchuria was General (NKVD) G. Lushkov, the only surviving

member of the main group of the GPU interrogators who had organized the first and second show trials. Lushkov was spared in the purge of his colleagues after Yagoda's downfall and was assigned to Manchuria as the head of the NKVD in the Pacific provinces. He escaped to the Japanese in summer 1938 when his arrest was imminent. See Alexander Orlov, *The Secret History of Stalin's Crimes* (New York, 1953), p. 219.

52. Coulondre, p. 83.

53. Sir Samuel Hoare, Viscount Templewood, *Nine Troubled Years* (London, 1954), p. 342. Hoare recalls that he was host to Admiral Orlov in May 1937 during the coronation of King George V when the Soviet admiral—during a dinner on the Admiralty yacht, *Enchantress*—received a telephone message ordering him to return immediately to Moscow. Whether Orlov was one of the "judges" of Tukhachevsky is entirely uncertain. The admiral himself was shot, probably in February 1938.

54. DSDF 760F.62/191, p. 3, Ambassador Biddle's report, dated April 2, 1938.

55. Ibid., 740.00/369, dated Warsaw April 25, 1938.

56. *DDF* 2d ser., vol. 8, no. 419, pp. 772–74, dated March 11, 1938. Allusion is made to Stalin's "Letter to Comrade Ivanov" in February 1938, where the theme of "capitalist encirclement" reappeared together with the idea of the so-called united front from below. *Pravda*, February 16, 1938, p. 1.

57. Joseph Davies, *Mission to Moscow* (New York, 1941), p. 221.

58. *DDF* 2d ser., vol. 7, no. 185, pp. 314–19.

59. *DBFP*/Russia Correspondence, F.O. 371/22287, p. 125, dated September 19, 1938.

60. Alexander Werth, *France and Munich, Before and After the Surrender* (London, 1939), p. 333.

61. DSDF 861.00/11713, Ambassador Bullitt's report dated July 17, 1937, p. 4.

62. Ibid., Bullitt's report dated July 30, 1937.

63. Coulondre, p. 147.

64. Davies, p. 130.

65. Winston S. Churchill, *The Second World War: The Gathering Storm* (Boston, 1948), p. 289.

66. For the Comintern's activities, see chap. 4. For the attitudes of the French Communist Party toward the French state, see Coulondre, p. 105. In the view of many observers, the PCF was, from at least summer 1937, under instructions to assist in bringing down the government of the Popular Front. See, for example, *DSDF* 851.00/1684, dated June 17, 1937.

67. Hermann Rauschning, *The Voice of Destruction* (New York, 1940), pp. 130–31.

68. *Trial of the Major War Criminals before the International Military Tribunal, Nuremberg 14 November 1945–1 October 1946*, vol. 12, *The Ministries Case*, pp. 430–39.

69. According to Walter Schellenberg, Heydrich's file on Tukhachevsky was delivered to Yezhov's emissary in Berlin in mid-May 1937—for 3 million golden rubles. See Schellenberg, p. 28.

70. *DDF* 2d ser., vol. 5, no. 229, pp. 363–64.

71. DSDF 800.51 W/89, report of the under secretary on his conversation with the Czechoslovak ambassador, dated June 12, 1937.

72. *DGFP* ser. C, vol. 6, no. 609, pp. 898–900 (extracts from Ambassador Schulenburg's lecture before the Wehrmacht Academy, November 25, 1937).

73. Ibid., ser. D, vol. 1, pp. 917–18, Schulenburg's report dated May 16, 1938.

74. Ibid., ser. C, vol. 2, no. 235, pp. 379–83. Shortly following "Strategic Directive of the OKW" dated June 18, 1938 marginally admits that the Russians might send reinforcements (for the Czech air force) and armaments. Ibid., no. 282, pp. 473–77.

75. Ibid., ser. D, vol. 2, no. 448, pp. 727–28.

76. Ibid., no. 437, pp. 710–11, Chargé d'Affaires in Prague Hencke's report, dated September 6, 1938. The Rumanian consent to Soviet overflights of Bukovina was confirmed by another German source from Bucharest on the day when the Nuremberg Conference started, September 9, 1938. *DGFP* ser. D, vol. 2, no. 445, p. 724.

77. *DDF* 2d ser., vol. 11, no. 23, p. 36. The same expectation appears in Hitler's speech to his generals in August 1939; see U.S. Chief Counsel for the Prosecution of Axis Criminality, Nazi Conspiracy and Aggression (Washington, 1946), vol. 7, p. 753.

78. Gustav Hilger and Alfred G. Meyer, *The Incompatible Allies: A Memoir-History of German-Soviet Relations 1918–1941* (New York, 1953), p. 288.

79. *DDF* 2d ser., vol. 7, no. 355, p. 715. Trotsky's views exposed before the Congress of the Fourth International in December 1937 on the question of the possibility of Stalin's rapprochement with Hitler differ from his views expressed in *The Revolution Betrayed* (London, 1936).

80. Robert C. Tucker, "Stalin, Bukharin and History as Conspiracy," introduction to *The Great Purge Trial*, R. C. Tucker and Stephen F. Cohen, eds. (New York, 1963), p. xxxvi.

81. See Stephen F. Cohen, *Bukharin and the Bolshevik Revolution* (New York, 1973).

82. Tucker and Cohen, pp. xxxv, xxxvii.

83. *The Times*, London, September 29, 1937, p. 6.

7. The Soviet Union and the Crises of 1938

1. The appeasement policy of England and France has been the centerpiece of these works, whereas Soviet actions have been given, as a rule, only marginal attention. Of the early works, J. Wheeler-Bennett's *Munich: Prologue to Tragedy* (London, 1948) still represents the best presentation of the case against the appeasers, and Charles A. Micaud's *The French Right and Nazi Germany* (New York, 1943) the best analysis of its French variant. Keith Eubank's *Munich* (New York, 1943) and Arthur H. Furnia's *The Diplomacy of Appeasement: Anglo-French Relations and the Prelude to World War II, 1931–1938* (Washington, D.C., 1960) are less critical of the British and French policies, especially in 1938, but the role of the Soviet Union is still given no systematic attention in the context. Keith Robbins's *Munich 1938* (London, 1968) is primarily a reexamination of the British foreign policy in 1938. Max Beloff's *Foreign Policy of Soviet Russia, 1929–1941* (London, 1949), in spite of its limited use of primary sources, can still serve as a starting point of each study of the issue. Adam B. Ulam's work on Soviet foreign policy, *Expansion and Coexistence: The History of Soviet Foreign Policy, 1917–1967* (New York, 1968), could devote only a few pages to Soviet actions in 1938, and the author is more concerned with Soviet reactions to the policies of the West (which cannot, after all, be properly verified) than the way how Soviet behavior was affecting the West and Germany. Ulam also gives undeserved credit to certain Soviet diplomatic gestures (like the declaration of March 17, 1938) that appear, in the light of Soviet behavior in its totality, to have been of rather limited importance. In Telford Taylor's *Munich: The Price for Peace* (New York, 1979), Soviet actions and behavior are not in the focus of attention. The author's version of Ambassador Alexandrovky's telegram to Moscow (pp. 55–56) is inaccurate. So is his assumption that Moscow had joined, in 1934, in Barthou's efforts to establish an Eastern Locarno (p. 179). *The Greatest Treason: The Untold Story of Munich* (New York, 1968), by Lawrence Thompson, suffers from a very narrow documentary basis, contains many errors both of fact and judgment, and deals with the role of the

Soviet Union only marginally. Lenient assessment of Soviet actions in 1938 also prevails in such textbooks as R. R. Palmer and Joel Colton, *A History of the Modern World since 1815* (New York, 1978), Richard F. Roser, *An Introduction to Soviet Foreign Policy* (Englewood Cliffs, N.J., 1969), or Crane Brinton, John B. Christopher, and R. L. Wolff, *Civilization in the West* (Englewood Cliffs, N.J., 1973), vol. 2, 3d ed. For Soviet and Czech works on the subject, see note 3.

2. *DDF* 2d ser., vol. 9, no. 144, pp. 292–302, "Note du Conseil supérieur de la défense nationale," Daladier to Paul-Boncour, April 8, 1938.

3. V. P. Potemkin, ed., *Istoriya diplomatii, 1919–1939*, vol. 3 (Moscow, 1945), represented the first installment on this theory. In the 1950s and 1960s, it was furthered by several less interesting Soviet works, of which only two were important: S. S. Stegar's *Miunkhenskaya politika frantsuskogo imperializma v Evrope i yei proval* (Moscow, 1964) and Yu. V. Borisov's *Sovetsko-frantsuskie otnosheniya i bezopasnost Evropy* (Moscow, 1960). Two histories of Soviet foreign policy appeared in Moscow in quick succession in 1966 and 1967: *Istoriya vneshnei politiki SSSR, chast pervaya, 1917–1945* (Moscow, 1966), ed. B. N. Ponomarov, A. A. Gromyko, and B. M. Khvostova, and *Istoriya mezhdunarodnykh otnoshenii i vneshnei politiki SSSR 1917–1939*, vol. 1(Moscow, 1967), ed. V. G. Trukhanovsky. Both works—of which the first is especially authoritative, because of the official standing of its editors—add further emphasis to the theory of Soviet readiness to march alone to defend Czechoslovakia in 1938; the only extension of the documentary basis of both works had, however, been provided by a selection of Soviet and Czechoslovak documents published in Prague and Moscow in 1958 *(New Documents on the History of Munich)*. This selection relied mostly on largely inconclusive Czechoslovak documents, a practice already questioned by a Czech historian, František Lukeš, in 1968. Lukeš demanded the publication of relevant Soviet documents to clarify the case (F. Lukeś, "Poznámky k čs.-sovětským vztahům v září 1938" (Notes on Czechoslovak-Soviet relations in September 1938). *Czechoslovak Historical Review* [May 1968]:703–31). The second edition of the third volume of Potemkin's *Istoriya diplomatii*, also deserves noting. The part dealing with the Czech crises was somewhat extended compared to the first edition, but the documentary basis is essentially the same as in the two works mentioned above. It is, of course, rather difficult to imagine that Ponomarov or Gromyko had no access to authentic Soviet sources to support their theses. Several Czech works on the subject appeared in Czechoslovakia in the postwar period, and after 1968, exiled Czech historians have continued to examine the problem in the West. Aside from works that are concerned with propaganda and not with historical truth, the problem has gradually, since 1965, come under the critical scrutiny of younger historians (Gajanová, Kvaček, Lukeš, Olivová, and others). Cautious as they had to be even in the relatively relaxed atmosphere of the 1960s, they produced at least two especially noteworthy works: Robert Kvaček's *Nad Evropou zataženo* (Clouds over Europe) (Prague, 1966) and A. Gajanová's *ČSR a středoevropská politika velmoci, 1918–1938* (Czechoslovakia and the Central-European policies of great powers) (Prague, 1967). In 1968 the examination of the problem was significantly advanced by František Lukeš both in his above-mentioned article and in his book *Podivný mír* (The strange peace) (Prague, 1968). For several months in the spring and summer of 1968, some of the archival funds closed to historians since 1948 were made accessible, a real breakthrough in the research of the events. Among the Czech studies produced in exile, the following are most interesting: M. Hauner, "Září 1938: Kapitulovat či bojovat?" (September 1938: To surrender, or to fight?), *Svědectví/Témoignage* 49 (Paris 1975):151–57; Edvard Taborsky, *President Edvard Beneš between East and West, 1938–1948* (Stanford, 1981) and idem, *President Edvard Beneš and the Crises of 1938 and 1948*, vol. 5,

East Central Europe, (Tempe, Ariz., 1978), pt. 2, pp. 203–14). So far the most comprehensive work on the subject has been Ivan Pfaff's "Jak tomu opravdu bylo se sovětskou pomocí v mnichovské krizi" (How it really was with the Soviet assistance in the Munich crisis), *Svědectví/Temoignage* 56 (Paris 1978):566–85 and 57 (Paris, 1978):51–68. Pfaff's study is primarily based on German archival documents as well as on a selection of new Czechoslovak diplomatic documents.

4. DDF 2d ser., vol. 8, no. 419, pp. 772–74, Coulondre to Delbos, dated March 11, 1938.

5. DGFP ser. C, vol. 5, no. 127, pp. 237–38, dated March 28, 1938.

6. DBFP/Russia Correspondence, F.O. 371/22288, p. 176, dated March 19, 1938.

7. AMZV Prague, Central State Archives Sofia, December 27, 1937, February 7, 1938; quoted from Pfaff, 57:52.

8. *SDFP* 3:167. Zhdanov's speech before the Supreme Soviet, January 17, 1938. This speech is also remarkable for its complete lack of any opinion on Germany, side by side with a diatribe against France.

9. *Les evénements survenues en France de 1933–1945,* 1:95.

10. *DDF* 2d ser., vol. 8, no. 19, pp. 37–39.

11. Ministries of Foreign Affairs, Czechoslovak Republic, USSR, *New Documents on the History of Munich* (hereafter *New Documents*), no. 2, pp. 19–20. Potemkin made it clear that "the position of France herself was decisive in the question raised by Coulondre." The background of the ethnic problems in Bohemia and Moravia, including the Czech share of responsibility for the polarization of the relations between the Czechs and the Bohemian Germans, cannot be discussed here in any substantial detail. It can be briefly noted, however, that these relations did not in fact acquire the quality of an international problem before March–April 1938, when the Sudetendeutsche Partei (the SDP) submitted itself completely to Berlin and adopted the so-called Carlsbad Program. This program, nevertheless, still demanded a solution within the Czechoslovak state, and the Reichsdeutsche variant embodied in the slogan *Heim ins Reich* was declared publicly only in September 1938. The Carlsbad Program in itself was not immediately understood as a preparatory step toward the annexation of the Czech borderlands by Germany, and it certainly did not implicate any justifiable changes in the European system of states, of which Czechoslovakia was as much a part as any other internationally recognized country. No part of Bohemia or Moravia had ever before been included in the territory of Prussia or Germany. On the contrary, a part of Germany (Silesia) had been, until the eighteenth century, one of the crown lands of the Kingdom of Bohemia.

12. The timing shows the weight of the purges in the Soviet agenda: proceedings of this show trial took place from March 3 to March 12. The verdict was passed on the 13th, and the next three days occupied the well-organized "public approval of the trial." The Germans marched into Austria on March 12, but the Politburo was not ready to adopt any attitude on it before Bukharin was shot and his execution properly celebrated. *Izvestiya*'s editorial on March 16 (the first editorial published since the opening of the trial) bore the title "The People's Will Was Fulfilled." Only after the "people's will" was satisfied was Litvinov instructed to make his statement on the Anschluss.

13. *Vneshnaya politika SSSR: Sbornik dokumentov* (Moscow, 1946), 4:344.

14. Borisov, p. 374. In a conversation with Schulenburg on August 22, 1938, Litvinov said bluntly that without Hitler "the Czech question would have a quite different aspect for the Soviet Union." *DGFP* ser. D, vol. 1, no. 924, dated August 22, 1938.

15. George F. Kennan, *Memoirs, 1925–1950* (Boston, 1967), p. 209.

16. Most of the leading Czechoslovak military men with whom the Soviets had to

relate, including the chief of the General Staff, General Krejčí, and the inspector-general of the Czechoslovak army, General Syrový, were former Czech legionnaires in Russia. The Soviet view of the legion has been that its revolt in 1918 served as a signal for a general White uprising in the whole Volga River Basin and in Siberia. See, for example, *Istoriya VKPb* (Moscow, 1938), p. 188.

17. Eduard Beneš, *Paměti* (Memoirs) (Prague, 1947), p. 9.

18. Jan Šeba, *Rusko a Malá dohoda v politice světové* (Russia and Little Entente in world politics) (Prague, 1936).

19. *DBFP*/Russia Correspondence, F.O. 371/19461, pp. 140–42, Sir J. Addison's report from Prague, dated June 24, 1935.

20. Ibid., dated May 13, 1935.

21. Neither Masaryk nor Beneš was opposed to socialization per se. What they deplored was the lack of freedom in the Bolshevik type of socialism.

22. Beneš, pp. 33–34.

23. DSDF 760F.62/191, p. 3, Ambassador Biddle's report, dated April 2, 1938. See also *DDF* 2d ser., vol. 9, no. 228, pp. 477–88 ("At this time, our [French] interest is to let ourselves believe, as do the Czechoslovaks, without self-illusions, that the Soviet Army is strong").

24. Deliveries for the Red Army from the Škoda Works in Pilsen continued even after Munich, and were only interrupted after March 15, 1939, when the Protectorate of Bohemia and Moravia was established. Renegotiated between Berlin and Moscow, Czech armament deliveries continued until 1941—through the Russo-Finnish War, when deliveries of war material for the Finnish Army from Pilsen and also from the Brno Armament Works (Zbrojovka) in Moravia were stopped on German orders. Soviet business with Škoda appears to have been the main reason why the Germans permitted the maintenance of a Soviet Consulate in Prague until June 1941. On the Soviet side, this in fact amounted to another act of a de facto recognition of the breakup of Czechoslovakia—the other being the de jure recognition of the Slovak *Ersatz* state and the closure of the Czechoslovak Embassy in Moscow in 1939. The French government let the Czechoslovak Embassy in Paris function until June 1940. *DDF* 2d ser., vol. 9, no. 225, dated April 24, 1938; ibid., no. 362, pp. 768–69, dated May 17, 1938; Zdenék Fierlinger, *Ve službách ČSR, paměti z druhého zahraničního odboje* (In the service of the Czechoslovak Republic: Memoirs of the second resistance) (Prague, 1947), pp. 67, 291–92, 313–14; A. Rossi, *Le Pact germano-soviétique, l'histoire et le myth* (Paris, 1954), p. 53; U.S. Department of State, *Nazi-Soviet Relations 1939–1941* (Washington, D.C., 1948), W-IV, 1493, Foreign Office memorandum, Berlin, May 5, 1939, p. 3. Soviet purchases of armament in the United States in the same period are documented in *FRUS*/*Soviet Union 1933–1939*, pp. 457–90, 670–707.

25. *DDF* 2d ser., vol. 10, no. 198, pp. 362–63, Coulondre to Bonnet, dated July 12, 1938.

26. *DBFP*/Russia Correspondence, F.O. 371/22288, p. 18 (1-8), and ibid., F.O. 371/22289, p. 134, Viscount Chilston's reports from Moscow dated January 22 and 24, 1938. See also *DGFP* ser. D, vol. 1, no. 613, dated January 21, 1938.

27. *DDF* 2d ser., vol. 9, no. 306, pp. 671–72, dated May 9, 1938.

28. AMZV Prague, II/2, no. 59692/38, Ambassador Fierlinger's report dated April 16, 1938, quoted from Pfaff, 57:54.

29. All information about this conference is based on three versions of a secret report of Fierlinger. One was his own, sent to Prague; one was Ambassador Coulondre's report, based on Fierlinger's account; lastly, there is a Russian version of the same report that is quoted by Borisov. There are important differences among the three

versions. It is surprising that even Soviet authors are unable to quote from authentic Soviet documents and have to refer to foreign sources when dealing with important issues of Soviet foreign policy like this one. *DDF* 2d ser., vol. 9, no. 225, pp. 471–72, dated April 24, 1938; AMZV Prague, Moscow-Incoming, II/2, no. 380, April 24, 1938; Borisov, p. 375; Ponomarov et al., eds., p. 313.

30. *AMZV* Prague, II/2, no. 59692/38. Fierlinger's Report dated April 16, 1938.

31. Pfaff, 57:54.

32. *DBFP* 3d ser., vol. 1, pp. 231–32.

33. *DDF* 2d ser., vol. 10, no. 511, pp. 899–900.

34. *DDF* 2d ser., vol. 9, no. 306, pp. 671–72, dated May 9, 1938. The French interest in this problem had also been shown in a General Staff document in April, when the military advised the French government to ask the Soviets to open negotiations with Poland and Rumania and to offer guarantees of noninterference in case of a transfer of troops. *DDF* 2d ser., vol. 9, no. 144, pp. 202–3, April 8, 1938.

35. Ibid., no. 302, pp. 667–70, dated May 9, 1938.

36. *DGFP* ser. D, vol. 2, no. 122, p. 180, dated April 8, 1938.

37. Ibid., no. 213, p. 348, dated May 27, 1938.

38. *Pravda*, December 28, 1949, p. 3. See also Borisov, p. 379. According to this version, Klement Gottwald, the leader of the Czechoslovak CP, delivered to President Beneš a proposal to that effect in mid-May 1938. Using the agency of the local Communist party to communicate with foreign "bourgeois" governments was otherwise not the practice of the Soviet government.

39. Ponomarov et al., eds., p. 313.

40. *DDF* 2d ser., vol. 10, no. 5, p. 6, Coulondre to Bonnet, dated June 10, 1938.

41. *DBFP* 3d ser., vol. 1, pp. 332, 340.

42. *Izvestiya*, May 26, 1938; *Krasnaya Zvezda*, May 30, 1938.

43. *DGFP* ser. D, vol. 2, no. 261, pp. 423–26, dated June 22, 1938.

44. AÚD KSČ Prague, Beneš Archives, Moscow 1938/I, file 39, Fierlinger's report to Beneš, dated May 26, 1938; ibid., Beneš's conversation with General Husák, June 1, 1938; see Pfaff, 57:56. Fierlinger appears not to have been the only person in Moscow to be depressed on these days. Louis Fischer, who interviewed Litvinov also at that time, found the commissar "empty inside" because almost all his appointees, with the exception of Maiskiy and Suritz, had already been arrested or shot and "the Soviet diplomatic service was dominated by the secret police." L. Fischer, *Men and Politics*, p. 496.

45. *DGFP* ser. D, vol. 2, nos. 213 and 262, pp. 348 and 426, dated May 23, and June 23, 1938.

46. Ibid., no. 261, dated June 22, 1938.

47. *SDFP* 3:276.

48. *Izvestiya*, June 24, 1938. Litvinov gave his "pre-electroral" speech in Leningrad on June 23, 1938.

49. Ibid.

50. *DGFP* ser. D, vol. 2, no. 254, pp. 413–14, Councillor Tippelkirsch's report dated June 13, 1938.

51. Ibid., vol. 1, no. 627, pp. 921–24, June 27, 1938.

52. Gustav Hilger and Alfred G. Meyer, *The Incompatible Allies: A Memoir-History of German-Soviet Relations, 1918–1941* (New York, 1953), p. 288.

53. *DGFP* ser. D, vol. 2, no. 396, pp. 629–31, dated August 26, 1938.

54. Ibid., no. 620, pp. 946–49, dated September 26, 1938.

55. Ibid., vol. 1, no. 629, pp. 926–27, dated July 5, 1938. Merekalov is characterized

in Schulenburg's report, ibid. no. 624, pp. 918–19, dated June 18, 1938. Merekalov told the German ambassador that he was happy to have been assigned "to such a great country as Germany," and that "he hoped that German-Soviet relations would be expanded and strengthened."

56. Ibid., vol. 2, no. 396, p. 630. For the Soviet Trade Mission in Berlin in 1938, see *DBFP*/Russia Correspondence, F.O. 371/22288, pp. 18, 163.

57. Ibid., p. 631.

58. Ibid., vol. 1, no. 626, pp. 920–21.

59. Office of the U.S. Chief Counsel for the Prosecution of Axis Criminality, *Nazi Conspiracy and Aggression*, 7:753.

60. *DBFP*/Russia Correspondence, F.O. 371/22289, p. 173, dated September 8, 1938.

61. *DGFP* ser. D, vol. 2, no. 280, pp. 467–69, dated July 5, 1938.

62. *New Documents*. The Soviet account of summer 1938 can be found, for example, in Potemkin, *Istoriya diplomatii* 3:734 (2d ed.), and in Ponomarov, et al., eds., p. 314, and in Borisov, pp. 383–85.

63. *DGFP* ser. D, vol. 2, no. 478, Councillor Hencke's report from Prague, dated September 14, 1938.

64. The Czech crisis, after all, was not nearly as simple as it may look in postwar hindsight. The fact that there was a 3-million German minority living in Bohemia and Moravia, and that it was demanding "the right of self-determination," could not be ignored; and as for the British, they had had a rather consistent opinion on these problems since the Paris Peace Conference. Henlein, who traveled twice to London, in 1935 and 1937, to seek British support for the demands of the SDP (before the adoption of its Carlsbad Program), was not considered an agent of Berlin, and in fact did not follow Hitler's orders before the Anschluss. For an intimate look at the SPD and Henlein, see Wilhelm Hoettl, *The Secret Front* (New York, 1954), pp. 101–22.

65. *DDF* 2d ser., vol. 10, no. 511, pp. 899–900, dated August 31, 1938. See also Georges Bonnet, *Défense de la paix, de Washington au Quai d'Orsay* (Paris, 1946), pp. 197–98; Ponomarov et al., eds., p. 314; Borisov, p. 387.

66. *New Documents*, pp. 62–63.

67. Winston Churchill, *The Second World War: The Gathering Storm* (Boston, 1948), pp. 294–95.

68. *DDF* 2d ser., vol. 11, no. 29, pp. 43–45, "Note de la direction politique (pour le ministre), mis en oeuvre eventuelle du pact sovieto-tchecoslovaque" (Paris, September 6, 1938). According to the Soviet-Czechoslovak selection of documents, Payart visited Potemkin on September 5 and asked for a clarification of Soviet standpoints, because in the version sent to Fierlinger (which Payart had, in the meantime, seen at the Czecho-slovak Embassy in Moscow), the latter obviously found certain discrepancies (*New Documents*, pp. 64–65). The note of the Political Directorate of the Quai d'Orsay is probably based on Payart's reports of September 2 and 5, which, however, have not been found.

69. Borisov, p. 387.

70. Bonnet, p. 199.

71. Based on document no. 26, pp. 62–63 of *New Documents*, and on *DDF* 2d ser., vol. 11, no. 29, pp. 43–45. In the version repeated by Potemkin on September 5, Litvinov made these points: (1) In case of Germany attacking Czechoslovakia, the people's commissar pointed to the desirability of immediately calling the Council of the League of Nations, as provided by article 11 of the Covenant. (2) The Soviet Union also proposed to call a conference of the USSR, France, and England "to prevent an armed conflict." (3) "On the question of concrete forms of the aid for Czechoslovakia, the

Soviet government's reply proposed calling a conference of representatives of General Staffs of France, the USSR, and Czechoslovakia." (4) Should Czechoslovakia be attacked by Poland, the Soviet Union had no obligations, but would reserve for itself the right to take one or another decision. *New Documents,* pp. 64–66.

72. *SDFP* 3:285–86.

73. *DDF* 2d ser., vol. 11, no. 29, pp. 43–45.

74. AMZV Prague, Incoming No. 725/1938, quoted from Lukeš, *Czechoslovak Historical Review* (May 1968):707.

75. AÚD KSČ, Beneš's Archives, Moscow 1938, file 39, conversation Ripka-Alexandrovsky on August 11, 1938; conversation Beneš-Alexandrovsky on August 15, 1938; quoted from Pfaff, 57:57.

76. Fierlinger, 1:143.

77. Ibid.

78. AMZV Prague, Incoming 726/1938, Fierlinger to Krofta, September 9, 1938.

79. *DDF* 2d ser., vol. 11, no. 95, pp. 159–60, dated September 11, 1938. See also Robert Coulondre, p. 156.

80. Ibid.

81. Robert Coulondre, *De Staline à Hitler: Souvenirs de deux ambassades, 1936–1939* (Paris, 1950), p. 160. Soviet versions either leave the Bonnet-Litvinov conversation completely out (*Istoriya diplomatii,* pp. 735–36; *Istoriya vneshnei politiki SSSR,* pp. 314–15) or (Borisov, pp. 388–89) refer to it by secondary sources like Pertinax.

82. Rumanian initiative seems to be obvious. Before his departure for Geneva, Litvinov received the Rumanian ambassador to Moscow, Dianou, but avoided any discussion on the subject of passage. Comnène himself, who remained discreet in his memoirs concerning his talks with Litvinov in Geneva, nevertheless indicated that the commissar was showing little interest in the problem. Comnène, *Preludi del grande drama* (Rome, 1947), pp. 83, 86, 90. See also Coulondre, p. 159.

83. *DGFP* ser. D, vol. 2, no. 478, dated September 14, 1938.

84. Ibid., no. 516, pp. 824–25, dated September 17, 1938.

85. *DDF* 2d ser., vol. 11, no. 267, p. 413, Coulondre to Bonnet, dated September 21, 1938.

86. *DBFP*/Russia Correspondence, F.O. 371/22287, p. 125, dated September 19, 1938.

87. Eduard Beneš, *Mnichovské dny* (The days of Munich), (Prague, 1968), p. 316.

88. *New Documents,* pp. 86–88.

89. Beneš, *Mnichovské dny,* p. 317. French version in *DDF* 2d ser., vol. 11, no. 266, p. 412, dated September 21, 1938. For Soviet version, see *New Documents,* pp. 86–88, 90. The formulation of Beneš's first question clearly indicates his doubt about Soviet intentions.

90. *New Documents,* pp. 114–116; *Izvestiya,* September 24, 1938. In his conversation with Arthur Pope in Washington a few years later, Litvinov changed the Soviet version once more, claiming that Alexandrovsky had assured Beneš, on September 21, that "Soviet Russia would help even if France would not help at all." Arthur Upham Pope, *Maxim Litvinov* (New York, 1943), p. 25.

91. Beneš, *Mnichovské dny,* p. 317.

92. DSDF 760F.62/946, dated September 21, 1938.

93. Ibid. 751.6111/215, dated September 22, 1938.

94. AMZV Prague, Krofta, September 21, 1938.

95. REPORTÉR, Prague, no. 1968/38, September 2–9, 1968, interview with General Ludvík Krejčí, pp. i–iv.

Notes

96. Beneš, *Mnichovské dny*, p. 322.

97. AUD KSC Prague, Fund 39/1938, quoted from Lukeš, *Czechoslovak Historical Review* (May 1968):712.

98. Moravec, František, *Spion, jemuž nevěřili* (The spy whom they did not believe) (Toronto, 1977), pp. 199–200.

99. Edvard Taborsky, "President Beneš and the Crises of 1938 and 1948," in *East Central Europe*, 2:206; see also Taborsky's *President Edvard Beneš between East and West*, pp. 59, 61. According to Taborsky, Beneš "suspected that the Soviets were bluffing and that their aid could boil down to fiery protests in the League of Nations and on Comintern's waves" (p. 61).

100. AMZV Prague, Incoming no. 899/1938, quoted from Lukeš, *Czechoslovak Historical Review* (May 1968):716.

101. *DBFP* 3d ser., vol. 2, no. 1175, pp. 594–95, United Kingdom Delegation in Geneva to Viscount Halifax, dated September 28, 1938.

102. John Wheeler-Bennett, *Documents on International Affairs* (London, 1930–38), 1:117–39.

103. *DDF* 2d ser., vol. 11, no. 380, p. 589, "Note du directeur politique," Paris, September 26, 1938; ibid., no. 416, p. 632, Bonnet to Coulondre, dated September 28, 1938.

104. AMZV Prague, PZ-Moscow 17/1938, Fierlinger to Krofta, dated September 24, 1938.

105. *Archiva ministerului afacerlal externe* (Archives of the Rumanian Ministry of Foreign Affairs), Bucharest, C18, col. 3, no. 71 (1938).

106. *DDF* 2d ser., vol. 11, no. 457, pp. 684–85, report of the French military attaché in Bucharest, Colonel Delmas, dated September 28, 1938. See also Bonnet, *Defense de la Paix*, p. 304. According to Ripka, Beneš was informed about the preliminary arrangement between Comnène and Litvinov in Geneva. From the note of September 24 we know that the Czechoslovak government received a copy. Hubert Ripka, *Munich, Before and After* (London, 1939), pp. 338–39.

107. *Pravda*, September 21, 1938.

108. *Izvestiya*, September 26, 1938.

109. AMZV Prague, Incoming 328 and 961/1938, Fierlinger to Krofta, September 23 and 25, 1938.

110. Ibid., PZ Moscow 17/1938, Fierlinger to Krofta, September 24, 1938.

111. SÚA Prague, PMP/1938, 9–10, I/4142.

112. DSDF 740.00/484, Ambassador Bullitt's report, dated October 3, 1938.

113. Fierlinger, 1:164–65. According to Taborsky, Beneš was "deeply aggrieved" by FDR's action, and "particularly resented Roosevelt's failure to differentiate between the aggressor and the victim and to consider the origin of the conflict." He saw it as "the last heavy blow of the September conflict." Taborsky, *Beneš between East and West*, p. 44.

114. *Istoriya diplomatii* (2d ed.) 3:738.

115. *DGFP* ser. D, vol. 4, no. 667, pp. 998–99, dated September 29, 1938.

116. Archives of the Office of the President of the Republic, Prague, T/1589/38, minutes of Chancillor Šámal; AMZV Prague, Moscow Incoming, nos. 104 and 1049, October 2 and 3, 1938; quoted from Pfaff, 57:64.

117. AMZV Prague, Incoming no. 961, Fierlinger to Krofta, dated September 27, 1938. Testimonies of generals Fajfr and Nosál before the trial of traitors in Prague February 19–20, 1947, quoted from Pfaff, 57:64.

118. *DDF* 2d ser., vol. 12, no. 14, p. 206, dated in Munich, October 14, 1938.

119. Pol. Abt. 4, Pol. 3, Rumaenien-Russland, Bd. 2, PAAA Bonn, dated Bucharest, October 8, 1938; courtesy of Dr. Pfaff.

120. DSDF 740.00/493, dated October 10, 1938.

121. *DGFP* ser. D, vol. 4, no. 476, dated October 3, 1938.

122. Ibid., no. 477, dated October 10, 1938.

123. Ibid.

124. *DDF* 2d ser., vol. 12, no. 58, p. 387, dated October 10, 1938.

125. Paul-Boncour, 2:112–13. Paul-Boncour admits that Litvinov's only condition for a Soviet action to help Czechoslovakia "was the same which could not be fulfilled: a decision of the League of Nations." Coulondre also thought that sticking to the Geneva procedure was the reason for Soviet passivity. In case of an action against Poland, however, the League would not matter so much. *DDF* 2d ser., vol. 13, no. 20, Coulondre to Bonnet, dated October 4, 1938.

126. DSDF 760F.62/191, p. 2, Ambassador Biddle's report dated April 2, 1938. For the most comprehensive contemporary reports on the state of the Red Army, see *DDF* 2d ser., vol. 9, no. 192, dated April 15, 1938, and DSDF 760F.62/1108, dated September 27, 1938.

127. Elisabeth E. Cameron, "Alexis Saint-Léger," in Gordon A. Craig and Felix Gilbert, eds., *The Diplomats, 1919–1939* (Princeton, 1955), p. 394.

128. On September 21: "At that moment, the next practical course of action [of the Soviet Union] was still not quite clear to me" (Beneš, *Mnichovské dny*, p. 264). On September 30: "Which exactly and surely was the Soviet government's standpoint I did not know at that time, and the Soviet Minister in Prague did not, or could not, give me any clarifications on this matter" (*Ou vont les Slaves?* p. 212). General Krejčí's and Syrový's report to Beneš at the moment of decision: "What the Soviets will do in practical military terms is impossible to say" (*Mnichovské dny*, p. 264).

Bibliography

Documentary Collections and Other Primary Sources

Czechoslovakia

Archiv kanceláře presidenta republiky (Archives of the Office of the President of the Republic). Prague.

Archiv ministerstva zahraničních věcí (Archives of the Ministry of Foreign Affairs). Prague.

Archiv Ústavu dějin KSČ (Archives of the Institute of History of the Czechoslovak Communist Party). Prague.

Czechoslovak Sources of Documents. Vols. 1–4. New York: The Czechoslovak Information Service, 1942–43.

Ministry of Foreign Affairs of the Czechoslovak Republic; Ministry of Foreign Affairs of the USSR. *New Documents on the History of Munich.* Prague: Orbis, 1958.

Státní ústřední archiv (State Central Archives). Prague.

France

Documents diplomatiques, 1938–1939: Pièces relatives aux evénéments et aux négotiations qui ont précédé l'ouverture des hostilités entre l'Allemagne d'une part, la Pologne, la Grande Bretagne et la France d'autre part. Paris: Imprimerie nationale, 1939.

Documents diplomatiques français, 1932–1939. Commission de publication de documents relatifs aux origin de la guerre 1939–1945. 1st ser., vols. 6, 9; 2d ser., vols. 1–12. Paris: Imprimerie nationale, 1972–78.

Les événéments survenue en France de 1933–1945, Témoignages. Vols. 4–5. Paris: Imprimerie nationale, 1945.

Germany

Akten zur deutschen auswertigen Politik, 1918–1945, ser. C, vol. 6. Bonn, 1981.

Documents on German Foreign Policy, 1918–1945, ser. C, vols. 2–5; ser. D, vols. 1, 2, 4, and 5. Washington, D.C.: U.S. Government Printing Office, 1953–59.

Records of the German Foreign Ministry, Collection of Foreign Records Seized 1945–. Washington, D.C.: National Archives.

Bibliography

Great Britain

British Foreign Office Records of General Political Correspondence with Russia (Documents of British Foreign Policy/Russia Correspondence), F.O. 371, film rolls 17250-22287, 1934–38. Wilmington, Del.: Scholarly Resources, 1976.

Documents on British Foreign Policy, 2d ser., vols. 12–18 (1972–80); 3d ser., vols. 1–3 (1949–50). London: Her Majesty's Stationery Office.

Poland

Polish White Book: Documents Concerning Polish-German and Polish-Soviet Relations, 1933–1939. London: Hutchinson, 1939.

The United States

Department of State Decimal File, 1910–44. Washington, D.C.: National Archives.

Department of State. Foreign Relations of the United States. Vols. 2/1935, 2/1937, 2/1939, Soviet Union 1933–1939. Washington, D.C.

Department of State. *Nazi-Soviet Relations 1939–1941*. Washington, D.C., 1948.

For the President, Personal and Secret: Correspondence between Franklin D. Roosevelt and William C. Bullitt. Boston: Houghton Mifflin, 1972.

Office of the United States Chief Counsel for the Prosecution of Axis Criminality. *Nazi Conspiracy and Aggression.* Vols. 1–8. Washington, D.C.: U.S. Government Printing Office, 1946.

USSR

Communist International 1919–1943. Documents selected by Jane Degras. London: Oxford University Press, 1956.

The Communist International, organ of the Executive Committee of the Communist International. Vols. 13–15. New York: Workers' Library Publishers, 1935–38.

Dokumenty vneshnei politiki SSSR. Moscow: Gosudarstvennoe izdatelstvo politicheskoi literatury, 1946.

Izvestiya. Moscow, 1930–1938.

Litvinov, Maxim. *Vneshnaya politika SSSR: Rechi i zayavleniya, 1927–1937.* Moscow: Gosudarstvennoe sotsialno-ekonomicheskoe izdatelstvo, 1937.

Molotov, V. M. *Rechi.* Moscow: Izdatelstvo Pravda, 1955.

Pravda. Moscow, 1930–1938.

Seventh Congress of the Communist International, Stenographic Record of Proceedings. Moscow: Foreign Languages Publishing House, 1939.

Soviet Documents on Foreign Policy. Vols. 2 and 3. Compiled by Jane Degras. London: Oxford University Press, 1954.

Soviet Foreign Policy, 1928–1934: Documents and Materials. Ed. Xenia Eudin-Joukoff and Robert M. Slusser. University Park: Pennsylvania State University Press, 1966–67.

Stalin, J. V. *Works.* Vols. 10–13. Moscow: Foreign Languages Publishing House, 1955.

Vneshnaya politika SSSR: Sbornik dokumentov. Vols. 1–3 (1935–41); vol. 4 (1946). Moscow: Gosudarstvennoe izdatelstvo politicheskoi literatury.

Other

Documents on International Affairs. Ed. John W. Wheeler-Bennett. London: Oxford University Press, 1930–38.

International Military Tribunal. Trial of Major War Criminals before the International Military Tribunal, Nuremberg, 1945–46. Proceedings and Documents in Evidence. Nuremberg: International Military Tribunal, 1947–49.

League of Nations Treaty Series. International Engagements Registered with the Secretariat of the League of Nations. Vols. 56–149. Geneva, 1926–39.

MEMOIRS

Barmine, Alexander. *Vingt ans au service de l'URSS: Souvenirs d'un diplomat soviétique.* Paris: Albin Michel, 1939.

Beck, Joseph. *Dernier Rapport: Politique polonaise 1926–1939.* Neuchatel: Editions de la Baconnière, 1951.

Beneš, Eduard. *Mnichovské dny* (The days of Munich). Prague: Svoboda 1968.

———. *Paměti* (Memoirs). Prague: Orbis 1947.

———. *Šest let exilu a druhé světové války* (Six years of exile and of the Second World War). Prague: Orbis, 1947.

Bessedovsky, Grigory. *Revelations of a Soviet Diplomat.* Westport, Conn.: Hyperion Press, 1931.

Blum, Léon. *L'oeuvre de Léon Blum.* Vols. 3–2, 4–1, 4–2. Paris: Editions Albin Michel, 1963–1972.

———. *L'histoire jugera.* Montreal: Editions de l'Arbre, 1943.

Bonnet, Georges Etienne. *Défense de la paix, de Washington au Quai d'Orsay.* Paris: Les éditions du cheval ailé 1946.

———. *Vingt ans de vie politique, 1918–1938, de Clémenceau à Daladier.* Paris: Fayard, 1962.

Buber-Neumann, Margaret. *La revolution mondiale: L'histoire du Komintern, 1919–1943.* Brussels: Casterman, 1971.

Budín, Stanislav. "Paměti" (Memoirs). Vol. 2. Unpublished manuscript.

Castro-Delgado, Enrique. *J'ai perdu la fois à Moscou.* Paris, Gallimard 1950.

Churchill, Sir Winston Leonard Spencer. *Step by Step, 1936–1939.* London: T. Butterworth, 1939.

———. *The Second World War: The Gathering Storm.* Boston: Houghton Mifflin, 1948.

———. *Memoirs of the Second World War,* vols. 1–5. Boston: Houghton Mifflin, 1959.

Comnène, N. P. *Preludi del grande dramma.* Rome: Edizioni Leonardo, 1947.

Cot, Pierre. *Le procéss de la République.* New York: Editions de la Maison française, 1944.

Coulondre, Robert. *De Stalin à Hitler: Souvenirs de deux ambassades, 1936–1939.* Paris, Hachette, 1950.

Davies, Joseph. *Mission to Moscow.* New York: Simon & Schuster, 1941.

Dirksen, Herbert von. *Moscow, Tokyo, London: Twenty Years of German Foreign Policy.* Norman, Okla.: University of Oklahoma Press, 1952.

Dodd, William E., and Martha Dodd, eds. *Ambassador Dodd's Diary, 1933–1938.* New York: Harcourt Brace, 1941.

Eden, Sir Anthony. *Facing the Dictators: The Memoirs of Anthony Eden, Earl of Avon.* Boston: Houghton Mifflin, 1962.

Feierabend, Ladislav. *Paměti* (Memoirs), vols. 1 and 2. New York: Universum Press, 1964.

Fierlinger, Zdeněk. *Ve službách ČSR, paměti z druhého zahraničního odboje* (In the service of the Czechoslovak Republic: Memoirs of the second external resistance). 2 vols. Prague: Dělnicke nakladatelství, 1947.

Fischer, Ernst. *Le grande rêve socialiste: Souvenirs et réflexions.* Paris: Denoel, 1974.

Fischer, Louis. *Men and Politics: An Autobiography.* New York: Duell, Sloane and Pearce, 1941.

Fischer, Ruth. *Stalin and German Communism: A Study in the Origins of the State Party.* Cambridge: Harvard University Press, 1948.

Flandin, Pierre-Etienne. *Politique français, 1919–1940.* Paris: Les Editions nouvelles, 1947.

François-Poncet, André. *The Fateful Years: Memoirs of a French Ambassador in Berlin, 1931–1938.* New York: Harcourt Brace, 1949.

Gafencu, Grigore. *The Last Days of Europe: A Diplomatic Journey in 1939.* London: Frederick Muller, 1947.

Gamelin, Maurice Gustave. . . . *Servir* . . . , vol. 2, *Le prologue du drame (1930–août 1939).* Paris: Librarie Plon, 1946.

Gauché, Général. *Le deuxième bureau au travail, 1935–1940.* Paris, Amiot-Dumont, 1956.

Gnedin, Evgenii. *Katastrofa in vtoroye rozhdenie.* Amsterdam: Fond imeni Gercena, 1977.

Grigorenko, Petro G. *Memoirs.* New York: Norton, 1982.

Henderson, Sir Neville. *Failure of a Mission: Berlin 1937–1939.* New York: Putnam's, 1940.

Herriot, Edouard. *Jadis, d'une guerre à l'autre, 1914–1936.* Paris, Flammarion, 1952.

Hilger, Gustav, and Alfred G. Meyer. *The Incompatible Allies: A Memoir-History of German-Soviet Relations 1918–1941.* New York: Macmillan, 1953.

Hoare, Sir Samuel, Viscount Templewood. *Nine Troubled Years.* London: Collins, 1954.

Hoettl, Wilhelm. *The Secret Front: The Story of Nazi Political Espionage.* New York: Praeger, 1954.

Hull, Cordell. *The Memoirs of Cordell Hull.* Vol. 1. New York: Macmillan, 1948.

Hyde, Douglas. *I Believed: The Autobiography of a Former British Communist.* London: Heineman, 1951.

Kennan, George Frost. *Memoirs, 1925–1950.* Boston: Little, Brown, 1967.

Khrushchev, Nikita. *Khrushchev Remembers.* Ed. Strobe Tallbot. Boston: Little, Brown, 1970.

Kleist, Peter. *Zwischen Hitler und Stalin, 1939–1945, Aufzeichnungen.* Bonn: Athenaeum Verlag, 1950.

Koestler, Arthur. *The Invisible Writing: An Autobiography.* Boston: Beacon Press, 1954.

Kopecký, Václav. *KSČ a ČSR* (The CzCP and the Czechoslovak Republic): *A Memoir History.* Prague: Svoboda, 1959.

Krivitsky, Walter G. *In Stalin's Secret Service: An Exposé of Russia's Secret Police.* New York: Harper, 1939.

Laroche, Jules Alfred. *La Pologne de Pilsudski: Souvenirs d'une ambassade, 1926–1935.* Paris: Flammarion, 1953.

Lebrun, Albert François. *Témoignage.* Paris: Plon, 1945.

Litvinov, Maxim. *Notes for a Journal.* London: André Deutsch, 1955.

Lockhart, Robert Hamilton Bruce. *Diaries of Sir Robert Bruce Lockhart, 1915–1938.* London: Macmillan, 1973.

Maiskiy, I. M. *Vospominaniya sovetskogo diplomata, 1925–1945 gg.* Moscow: Izdatelstvo Nauka, 1971.

Mandelstam, Nadejda. *Contre tout espoir.* Paris: Gallimard, 1970. Published in English as *Hope against Hope.* New York: Atheneum, 1976.

Moravec, František. *Špion, jemuž nevěřili* (The spy whom they did not believe). Toronto: Sixty-Eight Publishers, 1977.

Bibliography

Noel, Léon. *L'aggression allemande contre la Pologne: Une ambassade à Varsovie, 1935–1939.* Paris: Flammarion, 1946.

Orlov, Alexander. *The Secret History of Stalin's Crimes.* New York: Random House, 1953.

Paul-Boncour, J. *Entre deux guerres: Souvenirs sur la IIIe République.* Vol. 1: *Les lendemens de la victoire (1919–1934).* Vol. 2: *Sur les chemins de la défaite (1935–1940).* Paris: Plon, 1946.

Pilsudski, Józef. *L'année 1920.* Paris: La Renaissance du livre, 1929.

Rauschning, Hermann. *The Voice of Destruction.* New York: Putnam's, 1940.

Reynaud, Paul. *Memoires: Envers et contre tous, 7 Mars 1936–16 Juin 1940.* Paris: Flammarion, 1963.

Schacht, Hjalmar. *Confessions of "the Old Wizard": The Autobiography of Hjalmar Horace Greeley Schacht.* Boston: Houghton Mifflin, 1956.

Schellenberg, Walter. *The Labyrinth: Memoirs of Walter Schellenberg.* New York: Harper, 1956.

Serge, Victor. *Memoires d'un revolutionaire, 1901–1941.* Paris: Editions du Seuil, 1951.

Simon, John Allsebrook, Viscount Simon. *Retrospect: The Memoirs of the Rt. Hon. Viscount Simon, G.S.S.I., G.C.V.O.* London: Hutchinson, 1945.

Szembek, Count Jean. Journal 1933–1939. Paris: Plon, 1952.

Tabouis, Geneviève. *They Called Me Cassandra.* New York: Scribner's, 1942.

Valtin, Jan (Richard Krebs). *Out of the Night.* New York: Alliance Book Corporation, 1941.

Zhukov, G. K. *Vospominaniya i razmyshleniya.* Moscow: Novosti, 1969.

SELECTED SECONDARY LITERATURE

Babel, Anthony. *La Bessarabie: Etude historique, ethnographique et economique.* Paris: F. Aloan, 1926.

Baykov, Alexander. *Soviet Foreign Trade.* London: Oxford University Press, 1946.

Beloff, Max. *The Foreign Policy of Soviet Russia, 1929–1941.* London: Oxford University Press, 1949.

Beneš, Eduard. *Ou vont les Slaves? Essais sur Slavism.* Paris: Editions de notre temps, 1947.

Benoist-Méchin. *Histoire de l'armée allemagne.* Vol. 2, *La discorde (1919–1925).* Vol. 3, *L'essor (1925–1937).* Paris: Albin Michel, 1938.

Boldur, Alexandry. *La Bessarabie et les relations rousso-roumanienes.* Paris: Gamber, 1927.

Borisov, Yu. V. *Sovetsko-frantsuskie otnosheniya i bezopasnost Evropy.* Moscow: IMO, 1960.

Borkenau, Franz. *European Communism.* New York: Harper, 1953.

Brogan, Sir Denis William. *The Development of Modern France, 1870–1939.* New York: Harper, 1966.

Brzezinski, Zbygniew. *The Permanent Purge: Politics in Soviet Totalitarianism.* Cambridge: Harvard University Press, 1956.

Budish, J. M. *Soviet Foreign Trade: Menace or Promise.* New York: Liveright, 1931.

Carr, Edward Hallet. *International Relations between the Two World Wars (1919–1939).* London: Macmillan, 1947.

———. *German-Soviet Relations between the Two World Wars (1919–1939).* Baltimore: Johns Hopkins Press, 1951.

Castellan, Georges. *Le réarmement clandestin du Reich, 1930–1935, vue par le 2e Bureau de l'Etat-Major français.* Paris: Plon, 1954.

[243]

Cattell, David T. *Communism and the Spanish Civil War*. Berkeley: University of California Press, 1955.

Chaney, Otto Preston, Jr. *Zhukov*. Norman, Okla.: University of Oklahoma Press, 1971.

Clubb, O. Edmund. *China and Russia, the Great Game*. New York: Columbia University Press, 1971.

Cohen, Stephen F. *Bukharin and the Bolshevik Revolution*. New York: Knopf, 1973.

Craig, Gordon A., and Felix Gilbert, eds. *The Diplomats, 1919–1939*. Princeton: Princeton University Press, 1955.

Dallin, David J. *Soviet Russia's Foreign Policy, 1939–1942*. New Haven: Yale University Press, 1942.

Debicki, Roman. *Foreign Policy of Poland, 1919–1939*. New York: Praeger, 1962.

Degras, Jane, ed. *Calendar of Soviet Documents of Foreign Policy*. London: Royal Institute of International Affairs, 1948.

Deutscher, Isaac. *Stalin: A Political Biography*. London: Oxford University Press, 1949.

Dreifort, John E. "The Popular Front and the Franco-Soviet Pact," *Journal of Contemporary History* (September 1976):217–36.

———. *Yvon Delbos at the Quai d'Orsay: French Foreign Policy during the Popular Front, 1936–1938*. University Press of Kansas, 1973.

Erickson, John. *The Soviet High Command: A Military-Political History, 1918–1941*. London: Macmillan, 1962.

Finkelstein, Marina S., and Lawrence S. Finkelstein, eds., *Collective Security*. San Francisco: Chandler, 1967.

Fischer, Louis. *The Soviets in World Affairs: A History of Relations between the Soviet Union and the Rest of the World, 1917–1929*. New York: Vintage Books, 1960.

———. *The Life and Death of Stalin*. New York: Harper, 1962.

Gajanová, A. *ČSR a středoevropská politika velmocí, 1918–1938* (Czechoslovakia and the Central-European policies of great powers, 1918–1938). Prague: Svoboda, 1967.

Géraud, André (Pertinax). "France, Russia and the Pact of Mutual Assistance," *Foreign Affairs* (January 1935):226–35.

Gide, André. *Retour de l'URSS: Retouches à mon retour de l'URSS*. Paris: Gallimard, 1936 and 1937.

Gnedin, E. *Iz istorii otnoshenii mezhdu SSSR i fashistskoi Germaniei: Dokumenty i sovremennye komentarii*. New York: Izdatelstvo Kronika, 1977.

Hájek, Miloš. *Jednotná fronta: k politické orientaci Komunistické Internacionály v letech 1921–1935* (United Front: On the political orientation of the Communist International 1921–1935). Prague: Academia, 1969.

Hauner, Milan. "Září 1938: Kapitulovat, či bojovat?" (September 1938: To surrender, or to fight?) Paris: *Svědectví/Témoignage* 49 (1975):151–63.

Holzman, Franklyn D. *Foreign Trade under Central Planning*. Cambridge: Harvard University Press, 1974.

Jendrzejewicz, Waclaw, ed. *Diplomat in Berlin: "The Lipski Papers," 1933–1939*. New York: Columbia University Press, 1968.

Kennan, George F. *Soviet Foreign Policy, 1917–1941*. Princeton: Van Nostrand 1960.

———. *Russia and the West under Lenin and Stalin*. Boston: Little, Brown, 1960.

Kiszling, Richard. *Die militaerische Vereinbarungen der kleinen Entente, 1929–1937*. Munich: Fischer, 1959.

Komjathy, Anthony Tihamer. *The Crises of France's East Central European Diplomacy 1933–1938*. Boulder: East European Quarterly, 1976.

Kopecký, Václav. *Třicet let KSČ* (Thirty years of CzCP). Prague: Sboboda, 1951.

Korbel, Josef. *Poland between East and West*. Princeton: Princeton University Press, 1963.

Bibliography

Kumykin, P. N., ed. *50 let sovetskoi vneshnei torgovli*. Moscow: IMO, 1967.

Kvaček, Robert. *Nad Evropou zataženo* (Clouds over Europe). Prague: Svoboda, 1966.

Lefranc, Georges. *Histoire du Front Populaire, 1934–1938*. Paris: Payot, 1965.

Leibzon, Boris Moiseyevich, and K. K. Shirinia. *Povorot v politike Kominterna*. Moscow: Mysl, 1965.

Liddel-Hart, B. H., ed. *The Red Army*. New York: Harcourt Brace, 1956.

Lukeš, František. *Podivný mír* (The strange peace). Prague: Academia, 1968.

————. "Poznámky k čs.-sovětským vztahům v září 1938" (Notes on Czechoslovak-Soviet relations in September 1938), *Czechoslovak Historical Review* (May 1968):703–31.

McKenzie, Kermit E. *Comintern and the World Revolution, 1928–1943: The Shaping of a Doctrine*. New York: Columbia University Press, 1964.

McSherry, James E. *Stalin, Hitler and Europe*. Vol. 1, *The Origins of World War II, 1933–1939*. Cleveland: World, 1968.

Mallet, Alfred. *Pierre Laval: Des années obscures à la disgrace de 13 décembre 1940*. Paris: Amiot Dumont, Archives d'histoire contemporaine, 1955.

Meiskins, Gregory. *The Baltic Riddle*. New York: Fischer, 1943.

Miliukov, Pavel. *La politique extérieure des Soviets*. Paris: M. Giard, 1934.

Moulis, V. "Ke vzniku čs.-sovětské spojenecké smlouvy z r, 1935" (On the origins of the Czechoslovak-Soviet Alliance Treaty of 1935). Prague: *Slovanský přehled* (March 1965):21–37.

Nollau, Guenther. *International Communism and World Revolution: History and Methods*. London: Hollis and Carter, 1961.

Olivová, Věra. "Čs.-sovětská smlouva z r ohu 1935" (Czechoslovak-Soviet Treaty of 1935), *Czechoslovak Historical Review* 13 (April 1965):477–500.

Oprea, I. M. *Nicolae Titulescu's Diplomatic Activity*. Bibliotheca Historica Romaniae, Vol. 22. Bucharest: Publishing House of the Academy of the Socialist Republic of Romania, 1968.

Pertinax. *See* Geraud, André.

Pfaff, Ivan. "Jak tomu opravdu bylo se sovětskou pomocí v mnichovské krizi" (How it really was with the Soviet assistance in the Munich crisis). Paris: *Svědectví/Temoignage* 56 (1978) and 57 (1978): 566–85 and 51–68.

Ponomarov, B. N., A. A. Gromyko, and B. M. Khvostova, eds. *Istoriya vneshnei politiki SSSR, chast pervaya, 1917–1945*. Moscow: Nauka, 1966.

Pope, Arthur Upham. *Maxim Litvinov*. New York: Fischer, 1943.

Post, Gaines, Jr. *The Civil-Military Fabric of Weimar Foreign Policy*. Princeton: Princeton University Press, 1973.

Potemkin, V. P., ed. *Istoriya diplomatii, 1919–1939*, vol. 3. Moscow: OGIZ, 1945.

Renouvin, Pierre. *Les crises du XXᵉ siecle, de 1929–1945*. Paris: Hachette, 1958.

Ripka, Hubert. *Munich, Before and After*. London: Gollancz, 1939.

Robbins, Keith. *Munich 1938*. London: Cassell, 1968.

Roberts, Allen. *The Turning Point: The Assassination of Louis Barthou and King Alexander I of Yugoslavia*. New York: St. Martin's, 1970.

Rosenbaum, Kurt. *Community of Fate: German-Soviet Relations, 1922–1928*. Syracuse: Syracuse University Press, 1965.

Rosser, Richard F. *An Introduction to Soviet Foreign Policy*. Englewood Cliffs, N.J.: Prentice-Hall, 1969.

Rossi, A. *Le pact germano-soviétique: L'histoire et le myth*. Paris: Cahiers des amis de la liberté, 1954.

Rupnik, Jacques. *Histoire du Parti Communiste Tchécoslovaque, des origins à la prise du pouvoir*. Paris: Presses de la Fondation nationale des sciences politiques, 1981.

[245]

Scott, William Evans. *Alliance against Hitler: The Origins of the Franco-Soviet Pact*. Durham: Duke University Press, 1962.

Šeba, Jan. *Rusko a Malá dohoda v politice světové* (Russia and the Little Entente in world politics). Prague: Orbis, 1936.

Shirer, William L. *The Rise and Fall of the Third Reich: A History of Nazi Germany*. New York: Simon & Schuster, 1960.

Slusser, Robert M., and Jan F. Triska. *A Calendar of Soviet Treaties, 1917–1957*. Stanford: Stanford University Press, 1959.

Taborsky, Edvard. *President Edvard Beneš between East and West, 1938–1948*. Stanford: Hoover Institution Press, 1981.

————. *President Edvard Beneš and the Crises of 1938 and 1948*. Vol. 5, *East Central Europe*. Pt. 2, pp. 203–14. Tempe: Arizona State University, 1978.

Tarulis, A. N. *Soviet Foreign Policy and the Baltic States, 1918–1940*. Notre Dame, Ind.: University of Notre Dame Press, 1959.

Taylor, A. J. P. *The Origins of the Second World War*. Greenwich: Fawcett, 1966.

Taylor, Telford. *Munich: The Price for Peace*. New York: Doubleday, 1979.

Thompson, Lawrence. *The Greatest Treason: The Untold Story of Munich*. New York: Morrow, 1968.

Towster, Julian. *Political Power in the USSR, 1917–1947: The Theory and Structure of Government in the Soviet State*. New York: Oxford University Press, 1948.

Trukhanovsky, V. G., ed. *Istoriya mezhdunarodnykh otnoshenii i vneshnei politiki SSSR, 1917–1939*. Vol. 1. Moscow: IMO, 1967.

Tucker, Robert C., and Stephen F. Cohen, eds. *The Great Purge Trial*. New York: Grosset & Dunlap, 1965.

Ulam, Adam B. *Expansion an Coexistence: The History of Soviet Foreign Policy 1917–1967*. New York: Praeger, 1968.

————. *Stalin, the Man and His Era*. New York: Viking, 1973.

Vondracek, Felix John. *The Foreign Policy of Czechoslovakia 1918–1935*. New York: Columbia University Press, 1935.

Walters, Francis Paul. *A History of the League of Nations*. London: Oxford University Press, 1952.

Wandycz, Piotr Stefan. *France and Her Eastern Allies, 1919–1925: French-Czechoslovak-Polish Relations from the Paris Conference to Locarno*. Minneapolis: University of Minnesota Press, 1962.

Weingartner, Thomas. *Stalin und die Aufstieg Hitlers: Die Deutschlandpolitik der Sovjetunion und der Kommunistischen Internationale, 1929–1934*. Berlin: Walter de Gruyter, 1970.

Werth, Alexander. *The Twilight of France, 1933–1940*. New York: Harper, 1942.

————. *France and Munich, before and after the Surrender*. London: H. Hamilton, 1939.

Young, Robert J. *In Command of France: French Foreign Policy and Military Planning, 1933–1940*. Cambridge: Harvard University Press, 1978.

Index

Library of Congress Cataloging in Publication Data

Hochman, Jiri
    The Soviet Union and the failure of collective security, 1934–1938.

    Bibliography; p.
    Includes index.
    1. Soviet Union—Foreign relations—1917–1945.   2. Security,
International.   3. World politics—1933–1945.   I. Title.
DK267.H596   1984   327.47   84–45149
ISBN 0–8014–1655–8